ADVANCE PRAISE FOR *I AM BECAUSE WE ARE*

"Chidiogo Akunyili-Parr has done something remarkable — she inhabits the multiple planes of person, family, and country as she explores not only what made one of the greatest women Nigeria has known but also how that sense of greatness can complicate love and life. Akunyili-Parr's care and honesty shine from each page, as her mother's power shone through the life she lived in service to Nigeria." — Uzodinma Iweala, CEO of the Africa Center and author of *Beasts of No Nation* and *Speak No Evil*

"*I Am Because We Are* gives us an intimate and uncompromising portrait of a remarkably brave woman who took on evil — and won. Akunyili-Parr's memoir encompasses not only the incredible life of her mother but also her times, including personal perspectives on some very difficult years for Nigeria." — Bruce Geddes, author of *Chasing the Black Eagle*

"As one who had the privilege of knowing Dora Akunyili closely when we were both in government, I felt chills like she was in the room telling me her story in that vivid, passionate, bold, endearingly loud, and assertive way she personified. It is truly uncanny to pull the feat that Chidiogo did with this book. She successfully entered into the full character of her mother and convinces the reader that Dora is the one speaking.

This emotional tour de force her daughter Chidiogo wrote has secured the eternal legacy of Dora like no other book can. In this book those who only knew the bravery and exploits of Professor Akunyili as Nigeria's Patriot-in-Chief will finally connect the dots to the conviction that was driving her in those years she straddled the country determined to defeat the scourge of fake drugs. In *I Am Because We Are* we see the intentional way the girl-child Dora was empowered by a doting father and her disciplinarian mother by the all-round mix of strong family pedigree, Christian values, and education to grow into the enigma we all came to love. Whether as a unique being in her own right, or a daughter, sibling, wife or mom, Chidiogo reveals so much more that made the shocking end of her two parents within a space of seven years too chilling and hard to endure.

This new author who writes like the ancients, however, leaves us with no right to dig ourselves into a destructive hole of despair in the way she beautifully weaves the tapestries of Dora and her husband Dr. Chike Akunyili's lives in this book that kept me on the edge of my seat, wanting to know what's on the next page. Get this book. No. Get two of this book so someone else gets the blessing of reading the story of a family that Nigeria and the world can never forget." — Oby Ezekwesili, former minister of education, Nigeria

I Am Because We Are

An African Mother's Fight for the Soul of a Nation

Chidiogo Akunyili-Parr

ANANSI

Published in Canada in 2022 and the USA in 2022 by House of Anansi Press Inc.
www.houseofanansi.com

House of Anansi Press is committed to protecting our natural environment. This book is made of material from well-managed FSC®-certified forests, recycled materials, and other controlled sources.

House of Anansi Press is a Global Certified Accessible™ (GCA by Benetech) publisher. The ebook version of this book meets stringent accessibility standards and is available to students and readers with print disabilities.

26 25 24 23 22   1 2 3 4 5

Library and Archives Canada Cataloguing in Publication

Title: I am because we are : an African mother's fight for the soul of a nation /
Chidiogo Akunyili-Parr.
Names: Akunyili-Parr, Chidiogo, author.
Identifiers: Canadiana (print) 2021027929X | Canadiana (ebook) 20210279346 |
ISBN 9781487009632 (softcover) | ISBN 9781487009649 (EPUB)
Subjects: LCSH: Akunyili, Dora N. | LCSH: Akunyili, Dora N—Family. | LCSH:
Women cabinet officers—Nigeria—Biography. | LCSH: Cabinet officers—
Nigeria—Biography. | LCSH: Nigeria—Politics and government—1993-2007.
| LCSH: Nigeria—Politics and government—2007- | LCSH: Nigeria—Social
conditions—1960- | LCGFT: Biographies.
Classification: LCC DT515.83.A38 A78 2022 | DDC 966.905092—dc23

Cover design: Alysia Shewchuk
Text design and typesetting: Lucia Kim

House of Anansi Press respectfully acknowledges that the land on which we operate is the Traditional Territory of many Nations, including the Anishinabeg, the Wendat, and the Haudenosaunee. It is also the Treaty Lands of the Mississaugas of the Credit.

With the participation of the Government of Canada
Avec la participation du gouvernement du Canada | Canadä

We acknowledge for their financial support of our publishing program the Canada Council for the Arts, the Ontario Arts Council, and the Government of Canada.

Printed and bound in Canada

To Ugogbe, with Love

"Dora Akunyili was like an elephant. Describing her or telling about her is like asking several blind men to describe an elephant. The descriptions one will hear will be as varied as the number of blind men describing it from how it feels to their touch. Depending on where the man is standing and what he is touching, the elephant can be soft, hard, spiky, scaly, bristly, rough, smooth, fat, slim, floppy, flabby, long, short, wet, dry, et cetera.

No one can really say they know Dora and can comprehensively describe her or talk about her. She was an enigma. She had varied sides to her. She was very good and very bad. She was very kind and could be unkind. She could be generously generous and some would say she was very stingy. She was very humble and some would say she was arrogant and brash. Some would say she was ruthless, some say adorable. Strict disciplinarian, ordered, organized, focused, ambitious, determined, go-getter, achiever. No one can exhaust all the epithets that can describe Dora. Is she indescribable?"

— IYOM JOSEPHINE ANENIH, FORMER
MINISTER OF WOMEN AFFAIRS OF NIGERIA

"Dora Akunyili once thrust a rosary into my hand.

'Keep it with you at all times to protect you, because success brings envy,' she said, and added, as though to brook no argument, 'It was blessed in Rome.'

A slate-coloured rosary with a shiny crucifix. I have kept it since, part comforting superstition and part tribute to a woman who was one of the best public servants Nigeria has ever had.

As the director general of NAFDAC, the food and drug regulating agency, she fought the importers of fake medicines and the makers of unsafe foods, unnerving business interests that had long been complacent in their corruption. They went after her, and she survived assassination attempts; a bullet once narrowly missed her head, striking her ichafu. She was radical because she had integrity in a system that was unfamiliar with integrity. A businessman once told me that Dora Akunyili was the only public official he respected. 'She smiles with you but she will insist that you do the right thing,' he said.

She was kind and vigorous, and when she spoke, she widened eyes as though to better convey the force of her conviction.

Nigeria lost one of its best when she died."

— CHIMAMANDA NGOZI ADICHIE, AUTHOR

Prologue: Chidiogo

"Ugogbe — mirror."

A FRIEND ONCE SUGGESTED that I would only be able to tell my mother's story once I had the experience of being a mother. It turned out that she was half-right. It took me losing a pregnancy to connect fully to the story of my mother, Dora Akunyili.

After my husband and I learned that our nine-week-old baby showed signs of incompatibility with life, I reached out to my father. "*Ndo*, sorry," he comforted me. "Even Mummy too experience loss with pregnancy ya," he said, speaking in a stylized Engiligbo. It was the first I had ever heard of this, and even more shocking was learning that such a loss had happened not once, not twice, but three times, with the third occurring right before she had me. Worried I had somehow missed such an important story, I inquired with all five of my siblings, none of whom knew. In sharing details of bleedings and operations, my father shared as well the tears that accompanied each experience. Yet, for all those years, she kept it to herself. Perhaps it was true to her personality — her ability to move through difficulty with learned ease, sweeping pain away

like dust under a dark stairwell — or maybe it was because of
the social stigma surrounding miscarriages, which compels
women to mourn in silence.

In the weeks that followed, as my husband and I navigated
the path of letting go, I experienced such dense pain marked
by a mix of sadness, rage, and complete dejection, which, at its
lowest point, called for a completely different texture of strength:
a softness that required me to fully acknowledge pain's powerful
embrace. I had to learn to recognize and reject anger as my
mask, as even the slightest things got me into a fit of violent
wrath, trusting that, with time, all would be well, and that it
was okay not to feel like my usual self — in control, unflinching.

In control was how I had seen my mother approach even
the most challenging situations. It was one of her greatest
teachings. Now I was searching for the right fit for my skin.

I wondered about my mother's pain — that which she
carried and that which she buried. The ache of leaving home
at such an early age; of living through a devastating civil war,
followed by the loss of those she loved the most. This all
happened to a girl still in her teenage years. And just when
life seemed to offer her a break, a different pain awaited her.
By then she had learned to transform her disappointment into
unshakable strength, which served her in battle against forces
contributing to senseless human suffering across her beloved
homeland, Nigeria.

What happens to pain over time when it's consigned to
silence?

As I wrote my mother's story as if in her own voice, weaving its complex textures into a narrative, I found that her
strength was far more apparent than her pain. On the journey

of piecing together her truth, I discovered that strength and pain are mirrors of one another, for strength grows to protect from pain, and pain builds strength.

My mother's legendary brand of strength did not allow for her to linger on that which was not as she desired; rather, she fought for that which was within her control. To this, she gave everything, trusting in her own capacity and the guidance that fuelled her fire. In her last public words, she said, "A society grows great when old men plant trees whose shade they know they shall never sit in." Therein was her truth: the belief and trust that she mattered, that we all matter, and that our actions have the potential to reverberate through time and space. As she saw it, it was in the best interest of our shared destinies to act in selfless dedication to truth and to one another.

This commitment to supporting each other, leveraging the power of unity, was shaped by her own experiences of how far people can go when they do just this, and it was reinforced by her strong Catholic faith and the Bible's teachings of the virtues of love and charity, especially for those most in need. This belief is captured by the humanist African philosophy of Ubuntu, which is also a personal guiding philosophy of mine. Ubuntu, which has its roots in the Zulu language, and its branches across various African communities, is an ideology of the universal brotherhood and sisterhood of all human-kind, upholding and celebrating our co-dependent human community: "I am because we are."

It was her focus on compassion that allowed her to trans-form her pain into support for so many others in their times of need — an unspoken conviction that another's healing was her own. I experienced this interconnectedness and transference

for myself: recovering from my loss, and simultaneously grieving the loss of my mother as if for the first time, I connected
even more deeply to the invitation to tell my mother's story.

While the world saw Dora Akunyili, known by many as
the Amazon, at the peak of her strength — a warrior with a
gap-toothed smile whose light-skinned oval face was crowned
with a colourful head-tie that doubled as armour against inces-
sant attacks against her values — I saw the complexity that
was hidden from sight. This is the story of her multiplicity:
the story of my mother.

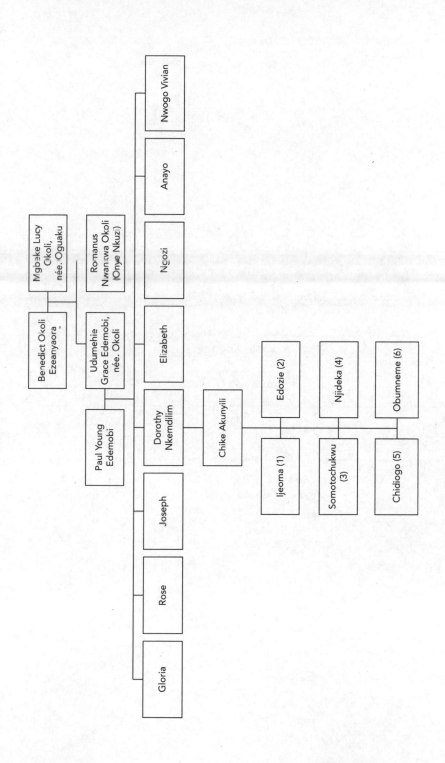

Kaduna

Jaban Kogo

Abuja

Makurdi

Nsukka

Lagos

Awka · Enugu

Agulu · Isuofia

Neni · Nanka

Umulolo
(Okigwe)

Part I

Dora

1954–1972

One

"A name is both a prayer and a story."

I WAS SIX, MY thick, tight coils in neat plaits, my bright face accentuated by my fair complexion, and my mind mature enough to understand that something major was happening.

In the late 1950s and early '60s, in the face of Nigeria's transitions, Papa would explain to me the history of colonization and that hitherto the country hadn't been free. With this, he often reminded me of the transient nature of things — one moment we were a part of Great Britain and with the stroke of a pen we were not. He underscored his message with his experiences and the drastic changes in his own life, having gone from riches to penury after his father's death and then again to riches in Makurdi as a business tycoon. He always returned to the emphatic reminder that no one knew tomorrow and as such nothing was to be taken for granted.

He loved to talk about change as captured by history and the passage of time. He spoke of Igbos and the great traditions that had shaped the people, like the very language itself. In the Igbo culture of southeastern Nigeria, he said, the power of words has always mattered, for words form stories, and stories shape mindset and reality.

When I was born in 1954, a kola nut was broken in honour of my birth, and *isee* — "and so it is" — was chorused along with prayers for a long and prosperous life. To support these prayers to take root, I was given the name Dorothy Nkemdilim Edemobi. *Dorothy* means "gift of God," and *Nkemdilim*, "let what is mine be unto me"; in other words, "may my destiny be fulfilled." Edemobi is short for *edeimobi*, meaning "I rest my soul." My name in full was the prayer for the "gift of God whose destiny will be fulfilled so that I may rest my soul" — a heavy name for a newborn girl.

Papa was a great storyteller and he loved to share details of my birth. "One look in your eyes," he said, "and I knew you were special."

Some children are drawn to a toy or a blanket; I was attached to my father. I loved to be around him, and I always sought out his presence and drank it in fully.

The affection was mutual. I was the fourth born of eight, but Papa lavished me with his attention. He insisted it was because I was very intelligent; I suspected that it was because I loved listening to his stories the most.

He liked to sit outside on the back porch of our home in Makurdi on the south bank of the Benue River, watching the day slowly turn to night, swatting away mosquitoes as we both listened to the sound of birds overhead saying good night to the day that was. It was his quiet time, and everyone knew not to disturb him, including me. I would sit curled against his chair, my legs sprawled out on a mat, taking in the lush green that surrounded the compound. I was happy to wait in silence until he felt ready to break it. In this setting I would listen to him share tales from times past, bringing people and places to life with each word, drawing me into unknown worlds.

One of my favourite stories was that of how Papa met Mama. I had heard the story so often I felt like I too had been there.

It was 1939. Afịa Ezi was a colourful festival that attracted dozens of young girls and their suitors from Isuofia and surrounding villages in Anambra State. As it coincided with the full moon, Afịa Ezi merged into Egwu ọnwa — "the dance of the moon."

In the light of day, the main attraction of the festival was the young women dancing in intricately choreographed sequences across the market square, naked breasts soaking up and reflecting the sun, colourfully clad bottoms gyrating to the music and attracting the attention of potential suitors.

Udumehie Grace Okoli was one of the women. All would agree that she was beautiful, with her coveted light skin, oval face, and pointed nose. My father, Paul Young Edemobi, followed her every move with his eyes, noting her confidence, her modesty, her beauty, and the grace of her movements. A young man from neighbouring Nanka, he didn't have much to offer in terms of a dowry, but he didn't let that stop him from dreaming.

He had seen Grace a few times in Afudo, a common market frequented by residents of Nanka and Isuofia alike. And he had gone every market day since his first sighting, hoping to catch another glimpse of her. There was something almost ethereal in her movements, like a Mami Wata. When he found out her name was Grace, he was even more besotted.

The day after Afịa Ezi, he called at the Obi of Mr. Benedict
Okoli Ezeanyaora, a medium-sized round hut with freshly
plastered mud and newly harvested thatch adorning the roof
and hanging over to provide shade.

It was Mgbeke Lucy Okoli — Grace's mother, whom everyone called Nne, meaning "mother," in recognition of the birth
of her first son and her role as the matriarch — who met
him at the entrance of the Obi. She was stooped low, a dull-
coloured wrapper held by a double knot tied under her armpit,
humming as she deftly shelled melon seeds over a large basket.
A sharp woman, she recognized their guest as one of the men
from the festival and as the son of the late Ogbueatụghịegwu,
the fearless warrior from Nanka. She invited him to take a seat
while she sought out her husband.

Benedict and Nne had just two children: Romanus, whom
Nne called by his middle name, Obidigwe, and Udumehie
Grace, whom both Nne and Benedict called Udum for short.

Paul Young was able to convince Grace's parents of his interest and worthiness. Grace's father gave his blessings in words
that stayed with Papa through the years: "I am sorry for the
misfortune that befell you when your father died. I am happy
that you haven't allowed it to hold you back. You are just starting your life, and the world is changing so quickly. I am sure
that the future is bright for a man with your determination."

Benedict liked a man with vision. He too had had to learn
to fend for himself from a young age as one of thirty children. He recognized in Paul Young's eyes the same fire, and
he valued the articulated dreams of the impressionable man
before him and, even more so, his meticulously argued plans
for success beyond the borders of Igboland.

Grace would have many suitors, of this Benedict was sure, but this young man was truly his father's son. He also understood that though he might be poor in material wealth, Paul Young had the wealth of his name. A name in Igboland is worth more than gold, and the Edemobi name was one of the best of them.

Benedict too trusted in the power of words. Grace's first name, Udumehie, foretold that she would raise her mother's status high among her people and that Nne's popularity in the land would shine through her daughter, Grace. It was written and had been said aloud many times, with each utterance of her name. He trusted that this young man before him held the key.

OVER THE NEXT DAYS and weeks, Papa called at the Okolis' Obi, spending as much time as possible getting to know Grace. He shared his dreams of a new beginning with her. Grace too was intrigued by the prospects of adventures to come. The thought of going so far away from home made her slightly uneasy, but her excitement was much greater. For hours they would imagine what it would feel like to be aboard the boat of steel — ugbo igwe — as trains were called, and journey by its coal-powered engines to their new life far away from everything they had ever known. There was no limit to their imaginations, and they dreamed of the unknown.

Soon, Mama's humble bride price of a goat and ten tubers of yam were paid. The payment itself was made possible by the generosity of friends of Papa's father because it is said that nwa agu anaghi ata afifia — "the cub of a lion does not eat grass."

Papa always emphasized his gratitude, recalling his pact with God in the wake of his benefactors' generosity that he too would always support those in need. When he would tell me this part of the story, his eyes and tone always signalled for me to note the significance of this commitment.

Soon it was time for the young couple to pack their bags as Mr. and Mrs. Paul Young Edemobi and make their way to a new life in Makurdi.

Moving there was a risk, like jumping into a lake without knowing its depth or the animals that make their home in the shadows.

Though a mere four-hour train ride north of Anambra, Makurdi was a strange new land. The local languages of Tiv, Idoma, and Igede were gibberish to their Igbo-attuned ears, and the people were rumoured to eat unimaginable delicacies, such as snakes and dogs.

Makurdi however proved to be a strategic choice due to the abundance of land and the increasing demand from the rest of Nigeria for its similarly abundant resources, especially timber. Construction was booming in those early years of the 1940s; Nigeria had a thirst for timber and Papa had a nose for opportunities.

Mama took care of things at home and Papa launched his own company, Paul Young and Co. From milling and selling wood, he began to take on small construction projects, building homes and then offices. Very soon, he had made a name for himself and his company as an honest and reliable contractor.

Papa's big break came when the local government hired Paul Young and Co. to build a school. He reinvested the profits to build a hotel. "People need a place to sleep," he always said. The Niger City Hotel was an easy success, catering to the influx of visitors and investors to the city. Their luck was just beginning, as in those years they had my sisters Gloria and Rose and brother Joseph. My mother was pregnant with me when they launched Premier Hotel, which in its first weeks attracted the who's who from Makurdi and beyond.

Despite all of his success, Papa didn't take any of it lightly. "Dora," he would say to me, "*E jiro ututu ama njo ahia*" — You can't judge that a market would be bad in the morning. Success is measured over the course of one's lifetime and marked by the lives touched.

Two

*"A child who is carried on the back will not know
how far the journey is."*

I WAS SURPRISED TO HEAR my mother's usually soft voice
raised. It was coming from her and Papa's room, its doors
slightly ajar.

Mama was uncharacteristically agitated. "She does not play
with the other children! She is always reading!"

"Please take it easy," I heard Papa respond; he otherwise
seemed to be listening intently to Mama as her voice rose
and fell.

"I can't, my husband," she retorted in Igbo. "She is nine yet
doesn't help in the house, and you are always saying to leave
her alone. '*Rapụ* Dora, *rapụ* Dora.'" Mama's voice took on
a mocking tone, mimicking Papa. "There is no replacement
for the grit that the village life will offer her. *Obodo ga-eme
ka anya chapụ ya*—the village will ripen her! So that like the
breadfruit, when she comes of age, she will have substance.

"Dorati'm needs to learn from the hardships of the village
to get her head out of the white clouds of her books. And who
better than Nne and Onye Nkuzi?" referring to her mother,

Nne, and her brother, Romanus, whom everyone called Onye Nkuzi, meaning "teacher," in acknowledgement and in honour of his chosen profession.

As if sensing my presence, Mama bellowed "Dora" in the direction of where she knew I would be, tucked away in my favourite alcove surrounded by my books. I scurried away to a reasonable distance so they wouldn't suspect I'd been eavesdropping.

"Yes, Ma," I answered, slowly making my way back to their doorway.

I was already confused by what I'd overheard, but I was immediately concerned once I came into the room and they asked me to shut the door behind me. I looked first to my father, only to see him avert his gaze.

It was Mama who spoke first. "Dorati'm, *gee m ntị*, listen to me," she said, drawing me closer to her and squatting slightly to make eye contact. "Your father and I have decided that you should go and live in Isuofia with your grandmother Nne."

I looked from one to the other, questions rushing through my nine-year-old mind, not quite sure which one of them to prioritize.

"Who else will come with me?" I asked, searching both their faces for the answer.

"*Sọ gị*" came Mama's response.

Only me! I stared blankly, willing them to explain themselves.

"*Kedụ ịhe m mere*, what did I do?" I asked, close to tears.

It was Papa who spoke this time. "Nothing, my dear daughter," he said, his eyes holding mine, his hands cupping my face. "We are doing this for your own good. You are not challenged enough here. I want you to be strong in a way I cannot teach you from here. I know there is more in you, and the village holds the key." He paused to see if I understood. "You might not understand now, but someday you will," he said, pulling me even closer still.

He watched me, as tears filled my eyes and overflowed. "Trust me," he repeated, and through my tears, I nodded.

My father prided himself on his strength of character. He loved sharing his own story so that I might remember the importance of grit. I would need it to make my own way through life without the disadvantage of blunted instincts, which he saw as the fruits of a cushioned upbringing.

"While I don't share your mother's frustration with your penchant for books, I understand the need for a tough skin and a connection to your roots. Igbos believe that a child needs to know the depths of their roots to seize the courage needed to bloom to the fullness of potential." He spoke in Igbo, his wisdom wanting to find my attention.

"I also want you to deepen your education, and what better way to further sharpen your mind than under the care of a school headmaster, your uncle? And schools in the villages are even better than the best here. Do you know why?"

I shook my head.

"It is because of all the Christian missionaries in the villages."

I knew better than to argue with my parents and it was clear this was not up for debate. So I did the only thing I could: wipe my face of tears, thank them, and go to my room. I spent the rest of the evening replaying the conversation, trying to make sense of what had just transpired.

No matter how much I thought it through, nothing could change their decision: I was to live in the village with my grandmother Nne, a widow since her husband, Benedict, had passed on, and I was to learn from my uncle Onye Nkuzi.

Three

"What an elder sees sitting at the base of a tree,
a child must climb the tree to see."

OF THE LITTLE I knew, village life was going to be very different. I wanted things to stay the same. For all of my parents' explanations, I still didn't fully understand why I had to go! Perhaps it was something I had done or something one of my siblings said. Maybe someone had told lies about me; could it be jealousy? Or maybe I had offended someone without even knowing it. No scenario was spared the imaginative questionings of my mind.

When answers failed, I resigned myself to what was to come. To best prepare myself for the journey ahead, I tried to picture my mother's village of Isuofia. Images of earthen huts that match the surrounding rich red and brown loam filled my mind, as did the weathered face of my grandmother. She always had a half smile on her face, especially when she teased me, like the time she'd remarked on how skinny I was.

It struck me that this was the extent of the information I had on Nne. On the few occasions I had seen her, like on Christmas or Easter breaks to the Southeast, Isuofia was always a brief stopover; such trips were mainly spent in Papa's village in Nanka.

My mind wandered to my more vivid memories of various Christmas and New Yam Festival vacations in Nanka. The many hours spent playing with my sisters and cousins in our family compound. The shapes in the endless forests of tall trees filled with strange fruits. The sticky nectar of udala, whose flesh chewed together with its skin turned to chewing gum; the taste of ukwa — African breadfruit, whose roasted seeds made for a delicious crunchy snack, my favourite. When cooked fresh with palm oil and spices, it was transformed into a pot of joy. And the nutty taste of fried aku, thousands of which flocked to the fire after the rains, their wet wings making them easy to catch.

My mind skimmed from thoughts of trees and their bounty, delicious insects, to the earthy scent of wet soil after rain; the feeling of my bare feet sinking into its dusty softness in the dry season; my senses conjuring the musky smell of the villagers; the feel of the sun drawing sweat from my skin; the constant sound of chickens as they roamed, small pieces of cloth tied to their feathers to identify the owners, and of small chicks clucking behind mother hens. I was always impressed by the transformation of the hen into a fierce warrior at the sight of a hawk overhead, wings and chest puffed in furious defence of her chicks.

One trip to the village stood out above all others, from the year prior, when I was not quite eight. It was just Papa and me on the long and tiring journey, which took just under ten hours by road. As we arrived at the outskirts of the village, I could hear drums from the distance, accompanied by their bride, the oja flute. I wondered if it was in our honour. The young man who had left the village as Paul Young was now returning as PY, a legendary figure as far as village stories went. Even the very fact that we arrived in a car was novel enough, without factoring in the importance of the man riding in it.

The energy in Nanka was infectious. A welcome party of ndị otimkpu met us and slowly walked alongside our car, which had slowed to a crawl. Clad in striped red and white wool hats paired with various colours of wrappers wound around shuffling waists, they sang, "Paul Young, *nwoke dị mma, osisi na-amị ego o, iyom yom*" — a song written in Papa's honour, praising his goodness as a tree that bears money. A smiling youth signalled for us to follow him to a wrought iron gate that opened up to a large compound belonging to the Igwe — the traditional ruler of Nanka.

After navigating a bustling compound, and a dark hallway of acquaintances paying their respect to Papa and patting my shoulders in reciprocated greeting, we arrived in the reception hall of the Igwe.

Papa, in his leisurely yet purposeful style, walked towards the Igwe and respectfully greeted him with the traditional handshake of titled men: striking his hands against the cere-monial fan of the Igwe — three backhands and a forehand sweep. Papa then motioned for me to come closer. "This is my fourth child," he said, and then added with pride, "She got pass mark in all her exams last term."

I observed Igwe's smile looking from Papa to me, as if to see which pieces of the famed Paul Young lingered in his daughter. And I watched intently as Igwe broke kola nut in welcome, whispering prayers for long life, prosperity, and fertility for all gathered, especially for us as their guests.

"He who brings kola brings life," Igwe said in Igbo (for everyone knows that the kola nut does not hear English), to which everyone in the room affirmed *"Isee!"* — and so it is.

Though tired, I found a new strength in following all the strange customs, which were a little recognizable to me from evenings spent observing Papa welcome and entertain certain guests at home. We went from the Igwe's palace to visit various friends of the family, but not before Igwe slipped a five-shilling note in my hand and murmured, "Keep being a good girl, you hear — *i nugo*." I thanked him politely and scurried away, happy for the pocket money; I could buy roasted corn from the woman at the main road leading up to our compound and have ample change for other treats.

Later that evening, the entire village was alight with a fever-like spirit. The oja continued to be played in a gentle accompaniment to the rhythm of the drums and the songs of clustered singers.

All paths led to the home of Paul Young Edemobi.

The sky that night was littered with stars, the bright half moon lighting the path for anxious feet walking in a stream of excited chatter. The rhythm of the music aiding the quickening steps of villagers as they neared and entered into the already brimming Obi.

I observed it all from the corner, in the shadow of flickering lanterns in the Obi. Watching my father standing before the gathering crowd, I tried to picture him as a child growing up in this very compound, alone without a father and mother.

To pass the time and feed my curiosity, I enjoyed listening to the excited mutterings of the thickening crowd, which made the space look and feel like a Sunday church gathering.

"They say it is a matchless fire" came excited whispers.

"It kindles on its own when you touch the wall."

"*Ọ dị egwu oo.*"

"See PY *oo*. Do you know that he was sharing wrapper with the women's group! Wrapper! You know how expensive wrapper is, and yet he can share it like that!"

The listener added, as if to outshine the knowledge of their companion, "It's not even just wrapper; he also shared rice, and onions on top of it."

"*Hei!*" they both exclaimed, clapping their hands rhythmically to signal their awe.

Another conversation was happening close by, between a mother and her son. From the look on the boy's face, he had heard his mother's lecture before.

"If you do very well and you pass *well well*, we will send you to Paul Young and he will pay your school fees. PY will pay only for the intelligent students, you hear! You have to pass, because we cannot pay for your schooling if not *ị nugo!*"

The son listened diligently, nodding his head.

In the midst of the crowd, PY stood tall in his trademark immaculate white linen shirt over white shorts. He looked every inch the highly successful contractor. Cries of his title name, Igwekanị — "king larger than the lands" — could be heard among the chatter, to which he responded, with a slight wave of his ceremonial fan, "*Nwa mmadu*," which translates as "true child," in confirmation of his appreciation. Although he smiled, he looked somewhat uncomfortable to hear his new hail name, although Igwekanị was certainly an upgrade from Agbiriogbu — "wiry rope" — which they had called him in his youth, thanks to his vine-like frame.

He motioned for me to come over to where he stood. Reaching for my hands, he signalled that it was time. The drums stopped. Silence like a fog stretched into the moonlit night. I felt my father inhale deeply, savouring the moment while the expectant crowd all seemed to hold their breath as one. Papa pushed the switch beside him, and a dim yellow light flooded the room.

Villagers shielded their eyes. Most allowed themselves only a gasp, lest they become the laughingstock of the village — the one who shouted "fire" upon seeing a light bulb illuminated for the first time — their pride outweighing their shock. Who could blame them, though? After all, *fire* and *light* share the same word in Igbo — *Ọkụ* — though only one commands the respect of fear; the other commands hope.

I loved witnessing the novelty of electricity for the villagers — something I had come to take for granted in Makurdi. Many had let me know that the choice had been clear as to the location of the first bulb in Nanka. The reason was simple, they said: Paul Young was the light of the people.

Papa looked down at my face, awash with enjoyment of the moment, and smiled. Looking up at the glow of the bulb and into Papa's eyes, I didn't know why, but I felt this moment mattered. I continued to watch the delightful glow of the bulb and whispered a prayer: "Let there be light."

Four

"It takes an entire village to raise a child."

THREE SHORT WEEKS after the conversation in my parents'
bedroom, and one year since my previous trip to the village,
it was time for my move to Isuofia. I wasn't ready. The entire
family, including all six of my siblings, had bid me goodbye.
Papa had explained to everyone how the experience would
greatly shape me. I was in the throes of a temper directed,
albeit quietly, at him and wished he would stop trying so hard
to convince them that this was a good thing. If it was so good,
then why was I to go alone? He and Mama escorted me to
the train station to bid me *ijeoma*, "safe journey," for the new
chapter of my life. Though I was terrified, I was able to dampen
my anger enough to say a heartfelt goodbye, which I was later
happy for.

During the train ride from Makurdi to Enugu, the past
already behind me, I tried to imagine the people whom I was
going to call family. I could see in my mind's eye Nne seated
on her usual stoop in front of her home, her wrinkled skin
shiny with Vaseline, her back supported by the red-hued walls,

which might have once been a shade of yellow, an old colourful wrapper tied across her chest. I couldn't recall any other faces beyond hers.

After a few hours' drive from my train stop in Enugu, I finally arrived in my maternal village of Isuofia. The driver had strict instructions to drop me at Nne's home. My heartbeat was slow and heavy as we pulled into the compound, which looked somewhat familiar to me. This time, there were no drums or fanfare.

And there she was, Nne, no longer a figment of my recollection but live and in front of me, her wrinkled skin dark and gleaming under the sun, her arms open to receive me in a brief hug and pat on my back.

Nne's son, my uncle Onye Nkuzi, was also there with his wife, who seemed aloof, and a dozen children who I understood were my cousins and extended family.

They all spoke in a quick flurry of an accented Igbo that I wasn't used to but for the few times Mama lost her temper. It sounded as if they were humming beneath their words. I took in the sounds along with the sight of red earth littered with clucking chickens and bleating goats tied up under various lush fruit trees.

It was odd to think that just that morning, I'd had breakfast with my family in Makurdi. Just a few hours ago, I was in a very different world in which I had been woken and dressed by a maid, who had also packed my bags for my trip.

Shortly before the sun set, my uncle and his family departed, and it was just me and Nne seated outside, surrounded by the sounds of crickets.

"Nkem" came the voice of Nne, calling me by my middle

name of Nkemdilim. "*Bịa oo nwa m* — come, my daughter."

She motioned for me to follow her into the small bungalow. We made our way up a short flight of stairs onto a small porch adorned by stone columns standing strong in front of windows with wooden shutters that flanked a wooden door of the same style. We walked through the door and down a short, narrow, cemented corridor. The sitting room was to the left of the corridor and on the right was a closed door that led to the only other room. Once the short tour was over, we turned back towards the main entrance. Nne pointed at what looked like a makeshift closet.

"Your mat is inside there, *ị nụgo*; you can sleep in the sitting room," said Nne in her matter-of-fact tone. "And that," she said, pointing to a dark corner beside the corridor, "is where we keep the clay pot for water, and the iron pot for cooking." I wondered where the actual kitchen was.

She spoke no word of English; each word of her Isuofia Igbo was emphasized by eyes that didn't miss a thing.

"Salt, fruits, and vegetables, we keep in the cold storage," she said, opening a little door in the wall to reveal a clay-lined cupboard. At this, she made her way outside again.

"The toilet," she said, pointing to a corrugated structure in the corner of the compound, "is over there. Make sure you close it after use to prevent flies from coming. You can take your bath behind the palm fronds." She gestured to the left of the toilet at a structure made of four heavy squares of intricately woven dried fronds to provide privacy.

And with that she repeated, "*Nnọọ*, welcome," and walked in the quiet shuffle of a woman in her later years back into the house and into her room, which seemed more like a small alcove with a large rosary hanging above the wooden door's frame.

I followed slowly and sought out my mat, a thin rectangle woven from the same dried palm fronds. Mosquitoes buzzed around and I wondered how I would protect my flesh from their thirst with nothing but a thin wrapper as defence. I steeled my mind with the reminder that hundreds of villagers were thriving and slept under the same conditions. There was no reason I couldn't too, I told myself. I hummed songs to try to distract myself to sleep.

It was easier said than done. I tossed uncomfortably all night, unable to find sleep, alert to the songs of the mosquitoes in my ears and the discomfort of lying on the cement floor. And just when I was beginning to drift, the cocks were crowing and Nne was shaking me awake.

It took me a few seconds to remember where I was; who was this old woman looming over me, telling me to get up?

"*Chi abogo*, the day has dawned," she said, oblivious to me still rubbing my eyes. "*Bia*, come let us pray," she added once I had risen, yawning and stretching.

Back home in Makurdi, we always prayed together as a family in the evenings, but less often in the mornings. I did not expect that prayers with Nne would last so long that my knees would start to hurt, or that after we said the entire rosary we would continue on to include the litany and a series of prayers to a long list of saints.

She finally made the sign of the cross to end our prayers. I vowed to be better prepared in the coming days, starting with finding a position that allowed me to relax like Nne, who leaned against her bed for support.

As soon as we had risen, she began listing the tasks she expected me to carry out. She spoke quickly.

"In the morning we clean both the home and our bodies. Start with sweeping the house. Push all the dirt outside, and once you are done, you sweep the compound with the dried palm fronds. Please make sure you sprinkle water on the soil to prevent too much dust. When you are done, pack the dirt in the bush, you hear?"

I nodded. Satisfied, Nne disappeared to sit quietly in the front of the house, rubbing her chewing stick in a cleaning motion against her teeth, leaving me alone in the backyard with broom in hand.

Every day from that first morning on, I was tasked with sweeping the compound—just one of so many chores, since my days were free with the school year in Isuofia not yet begun. Housework was divided between the home and the farm. Each day, even before the cock's crow, I had to go fetch water. This included a trek to the stream, which was about thirty minutes away. Upon return, and with the sun now risen, we always prayed together, after which I swept first the cement floor of the house and then the compound clean. The latter sometimes seemed like a fool's errand, pushing the red dust across the compound, imprinting in its wake the pretty patterns of the dried palm fronds, before the footsteps of man and of roaming chickens and ants returned the soil to its prior state.

Only then could I have breakfast, and afterwards we would depart for the farm. There was never a lack of work waiting for us there. Initially, I was tasked only with uprooting and cutting weeds with a blunt cutlass, but I soon took over tilling the soil after Nne complained of back pains. It was no wonder, given the countless hours she had spent bent over hoeing the soil into mounds and heaps.

In those weeks before school began, we farmed in the morning before the sun got too hot. In the afternoon, I had time to roam the village, allowing my curiosity to bloom, nurtured by endless novelties. Like the way everyone stopped and asked who I was, then questioned me for details about Makurdi. Or the many paths that connected homes, farms, and huts across the village.

In the early evening, after we had digested our lunch and the sun was less intense, we would return to the farm.

I enjoyed learning about the different plants and their various preferences for the ground in which they made their home. I wondered if yam tubers would grow if the soil was not piled into mounds to suit their needs, or if the cassava needed to be planted in perfectly straight lines.

Only when the sun started to sink over the distant hills did we make our way back to the house. The walk was not wasted, for it was Nne's designated time to teach me new prayers and hymns.

Once home, one last task awaited me — fetching firewood. This was my least favourite chore, as it involved a short walk past farmlands into the dark, mosquito-infested interior of the bush, the deeper parts of which were filled with an ample supply of dried branches, sticks, and twigs, as well as snakes and scorpions that made their home in the dense foliage.

Once I had enough wood gathered into a bundle tied around the middle, it was time for the walk home. Navigating dusk with firewood balanced on my head brought unique challenges, not least of all the fear that I couldn't easily twist away from an unexpected attack by an animal lurking in the shadows.

Back home, it was time to make a fire in the heart of the compound, surrounded by three low stools, one for each of us, with a spare for any guest that might stop by.

Nne cooked and I assisted in preparing the vegetables. The days we had chicken, which were too far between, were my favourite. I didn't mind at all having to kill the chicken, as Nne had shown me how: hold the wings together pressed against the ground, and cut its exposed neck from the front with a quick motion with the knife. The cut had to be deep and thorough or else the chicken would run around, head hanging loose, shrieking in pain and fear. She also showed me to soak the chicken in scalding hot water to soften the feathers before plucking. And once it had been stripped of life and feathers, it was time to cut its naked form into small pieces to be washed and prepared for cooking.

We often ate in silence, surrounded by the sounds of the fire crackling, of frogs and crickets, of the night, which replaced those of the day. My last act before finding my mat was to take a bath to wash off the day, a task that required filling a small bowl with water and retreating behind the coverage of palm fronds, cupping two hands together to pour water over me to wash off the white soap suds.

Very soon, I no longer felt lost or out of place in the village. I also knew how long it took to get through most of my chores, that I might have time to explore the village, or play with my age mates, or, better still, read a few chapters of my novels, which were otherwise gathering dust. I liked to go to the village square, where I was always certain to run into a distant relative or friend of Nne. It was the same square that drew dozens and hundreds of villagers on market days to exchange news and goods. It was here that a small crowd watched young boys play football in an adjacent field, and men and women gathered in small and separate groups to discuss the latest matters of interest. Nne always attracted a small crowd of women, and I would watch from a distance as she commanded their attention, pausing intermittently to listen to a question or a comment that would inspire more talk from her. As I was not allowed in those circles, I could only imagine what was transpiring.

In those months I wondered if I was succeeding in becoming the chiselled, stronger version of myself that my parents wanted.

Five

"If you are building a house and a nail breaks, do you stop building or do you change the nail?"

I HAD MANY DREAMS of Makurdi. Oftentimes I would be with my father watching the sunset in colours that were even more exceptional than I remembered. Or piled in the back of Papa's chauffeured black Mercedes with my sister Rose and brother Jo, dressed in our wine-red school uniforms with red-and-white checkered three-quarter-sleeve shirts.

As if to savour the lingering taste of the past, I developed a habit in those years of reflecting on my dreams upon waking up. I wondered if dreaming of my brothers and sisters meant that they might come visit. Perhaps I simply dreamed of Makurdi to help me feel closer to my family. It didn't stop me from seeking hidden meanings.

Before the school year in Isuofia began, I had a chance to visit my new school. Central School Isuofia Primary was about three miles from Nne's home, which I suppose had become my home as well.

The grounds were expansive. Unlike the multi-storey design of my former school, single-storey bungalows were arranged in a U shape around a sea of red earth that served as a playground and assembly point. The walls of the buildings had been painted a dull beige, but their dusty top coat matched the earth's red. The classrooms were spacious and filled with piles of dust-covered notebooks and textbooks that lined entire walls. The wooden two-person bench and desk sets felt intimate, with the promise of fostering friendships. It wasn't Makurdi, with its volleyball court, typewriter rooms, and well-equipped lab, but I knew that the ultimate experience would be dependent on the people I was to meet.

The first day of class I was up bright and early. But it was also my first time navigating my chores, getting ready, and walking to school, which was past the town square and beyond the market.

I arrived a few minutes after 8 a.m. to an already full general assembly of about seventy students, all dressed in matching blue and white pinafores, the booming voice of my uncle, Onye Nkuzi, projecting across the field.

The first rule I learned that day was that lateness was not tolerated, a message that was emphasized by the lashes of long, wiry canes administered by one of the teachers whose name I didn't even know yet. It didn't matter that my uncle was the headmaster — or maybe it did, but for all the wrong reasons. I was never late again.

Despite the shaky start, I grew to love school as a respite from the endless drudgery of chores at home. School was my happy place. I loved that my curiosity was invited, though sometimes not given the full access it desired.

I loved the carefree way we played during the hour-long break at midday. My favourite game was ọga, best described as a sort of rock, paper, scissors, but played with the feet. It consisted of four moves — open, close, leg raise left, and leg raise right — in a non-stop dance-like flow to the rhythm of clapping hands. Because ọga was played solely by girls, I made a lot of girlfriends very quickly.

Sometimes, we would continue with an unfinished game after school, and I would have to drag myself away for the rest of my day. It was that or face the wrath of Nne. I had an hour and a half after school before I was expected at the farm, and I was to spend it in Onye Nkuzi's compound, having lunch with my cousins. It was also the time to get as much of my homework done as possible before going home to change out of my uniform and into house clothes to join Nne at the farm.

Depending on the season, we were either planting or harvesting. In the rainy season, from March to the end of October, we planted maize, groundnut, cocoyam, and various vegetables, like okro and cassava; in the dry season, after the harvest, we planted onions, carrots, ụgụ, spinach, and eggplants.

The end of every day left me exhausted, but I would have to find the strength to attend to any remaining schoolwork before I could call it a night. A new day was always just around the corner — beginning at 5 a.m.

I found myself increasingly resigned to this life, with the understanding that I had been sent to the village to become the best version of myself, so the fastest way back home was to do just this.

My only moments of idleness were on rainy days, when chores were impossible, water not needed, and school closed. Nne and I would sit close to the house, under the protection of the corrugated roof, listening to the sound of rainfall, warmed by the smell of corn roasting on a smouldering fire.

Other quiet moments were to be found at the odd sunrise, sitting briefly on Nne's stoop to watch the hens cluck back and forth with a line of chicks trailing behind, breaking rank to fight for a minuscule grain of food that the hen would unearth. Nne also kept goats, and I would watch them in the corner chewing endlessly at the patches of grass, once in a while looking up to stare blankly back at me, like I was the curious specimen.

The rhythmic repetition of my days was sometimes disrupted by extraordinary events.

One day, I was with my friend Nnenna on our morning trek to the stream. We were walking in silence, as the morning was far too young for idle chatter. At some point I broke into song, a ballad about lost love in the time of war, which I had learned from listening to singers in the village square. Exaggerating the final emotional lament of the song, "*ewooo*," we watched the first rays of light colour the skies a pale, hazy orange.

We finally reached the end of the path, where the bush opened up to a slope that led down to the stream. We started to make our way down the loose earth with the ease of habit but with the caution the steep drop commanded. Nnenna followed behind me, matching the placement of my feet. The soil erosion common in the region was worse this time of the year, following an especially wet rainy season.

Once at the bottom, we both filled our buckets, careful not to disturb the water bed from its peaceful sleep. Then we unwrapped and rewrapped the piece of cloth that would cushion the now-heavy clay pot on our heads. The most difficult part of the journey was still to come.

I found that whenever I focused on the difficulty ahead, I would have trouble, like the time I was so concerned about the slipperiness of the path after the rains that I ended up breaking my pot in a minor fall. I had since adopted a successful strategy: to see the desired end before I even set off. This day was no different: I envisioned myself at the top of the eroded cliff, taxed but triumphant. I held this thought in my heart as I wound my way up in short zigzags, maintaining the momentum and balance needed to get both me and the pot of water to the top.

We had almost made it to the top, Nnenna walking ahead of me, when on a narrow bend with nothing but cliffside below, I felt the ground shift under my feet. The pot tumbled quickly off my head and into the gully. As I slipped, I heard Nnenna crying "*ewooo*" and "*Chineke* God." In that moment, a hand swung down to help me.

I grabbed at the hand with all the might of my ten-year-old body, using my feet to stabilize myself against the side of the cliff—four limbs working in unison to get me to safety.

Once safe, I collapsed, out of breath and stunned by what had just transpired, rejoicing at being alive and safe. Nnenna seemed to be in even more shock than me, her eyes still bright with fear and excitement.

Still holding my hands was an old woman, about the same age as my grandmother. In spite of her advanced age, her grip was firm, and her body strong.

"*Daalụ, Daalụ, Chukwu gọzie gi,*" I said again and again to her once I caught my breath, thanking and blessing her at the same time.

"*Chukwu daalụ*" was all she said. Thank God! Then, as if in an afterthought, she said, "You must be careful, because next time I will not be here." I nodded in understanding, not quite sure what else to say.

When I got home and shared my story with Nne, she listened patiently. Instead of her informing me, as I imagined, that my days of fetching water were over, she simply reminded me that this was a lesson to pay even more attention, especially when the road is treacherous. It would take more than a potentially mortal fall for Nne to soften in her approach.

Then I fell ill — an unwelcome event in any circumstance, but a potentially deadly one in the village. It was a little over a year since I had arrived in Isuofia, and a few months after my near-death fall. Every bone, every muscle in my body twitched and ached from a fever tearing through me. I wove in and out of consciousness, fighting to stay alive, my body consuming every ounce of energy in the process. Nne and Onye Nkuzi tried everything — calling upon healers, God, Mary, and the wisdom of medicinal plants, and forcing brown liquids down my throat that caused me to violently expel the contents of my stomach.

The battle against the sickness already felt lost as I lay in a pool of my own sweat, a broken body holding me hostage to this life. In my struggles, I felt like I was straddling death with a loose grip on the reins, the veil between this world and the shadows continuously thinning as I went in and out of consciousness.

On one occasion, I jerked awake from a dream only to find that I was no longer on the camp bed my father had sent from Makurdi a few months prior; instead, I was suspended in a pool of water. Sinking deeper into nothingness, I panicked and began clawing at the water.

I opened my mouth to scream and was surprised to hear

the sound of my own voice in the water as clear as a cock's crow. I called on God in desperate supplication.

"*Chineke*, Jesus, *biko*, help me, Mary!" I cried, feeling myself losing the struggle with the water. "*Nne* Jesus, mother of Jesus, *biko*, *nyelụ m aka*, please help me," I continued in Igbo mixed with English, lest the latter be a better bet for their comprehension.

My tears were running freely down my cheeks, mixing with the unusually thick texture of the water. Drained, I stopped fighting and surrendered to the voice that was inviting me to trust. Perhaps I was already in heaven?

I felt the force of the water move through me, gently yet powerfully, and intentionally pulling me deeper and deeper into its bright-blue depths. I closed my eyes and surrendered fully.

Moments later I was no longer suspended but on dry land. I sputtered awake, surprised to experience my lungs free of water and discomfort. I found myself at the foot of an aged Iroko tree in a place that I didn't recognize. I stood up slowly, leaning on the tree for support, testing the strength of my legs. I felt a strangely familiar presence, and I knew instinctively that I was in a special place.

The message came from the tree and from within my own body.

"It's not your time yet. You have been delivered into a new life."

I bowed my head in thanksgiving.

I woke up in the hospital in Adazi to the softness of blue hospital sheets and the bleakness of white walls. I smiled weakly and saw Nne's eyes alight with joy, her aged body shuffling in an ecstatic dance.

"*Į fụkwanụ Chukwu oo! Chukwu dike! Mariah dị asọ, ị dị able*— Mary full of grace! You are able!" Nne shrieked, half in prayer, half in disbelief.

Still unsure if I was indeed awake, I added a silent prayer of thanks and fell back asleep. It was a long, peaceful sleep that I always remembered in the many years of sleeplessness that plagued me through most of my adult life.

They said it was pneumonia — a disease that spelled death. Perhaps I had died, or perhaps I had been given a hint of the mysteries of life and death. Healed, I felt protected from the fear of death.

Life went back to its usual routines after I fully recovered from the ordeal, except our prayers increased in frequency and duration. In the past, I had always bemoaned the prayer times with Nne, but I started to enjoy the quiet moments, so much so that I continued in my own moments of silence to commune with the Almighty. I felt the most myself in the presence of God. It was in silence that I could feel everything without holding back, without filtering out the parts that I usually did not welcome, if nothing else, for lack of time.

For weeks after, even when I was feeling better, Nne insisted on doing all of my chores herself and working the farm alone, giving me a glimpse of how such an old woman had managed all these years without me.

Soon, I was back to fetching water, sweeping the compound, and warming whatever was left from the night before for breakfast, followed by a quick pre-school "rub and shine," a delicate process of running a wet cloth over the essential parts of the body that needed cleaning.

Often, on the most difficult days, when I wanted my old life back, I questioned my parents' decision and felt anger, especially towards my father. On particularly low days, I resented them, entertaining feelings of being unwanted. Wondering how I could prove myself ready to return home.

It took decades for me to have no hard feelings about the difficulties I suffered in the village. With time I realized that it had trained me to be strong and resilient, able to adapt to any situation, no matter how harsh. For what was rest when there was grass to cut; palm kernels to harvest and process into rich red oils; breadfruits to shell, wash, and sieve to extract soft ukwa seeds to sell at the market; goats and chickens to feed; and vegetable gardens to tend and harvest lest hungry pests make them their supper?

Six

"No matter how full the river, it still wants to grow."

NNE WAS BORN WHEN the passage of time wasn't recorded with numbers but with the unique events of the year. No one knew her age, not even her. She once shared that the day she was born, the sun went black. The lines on her face showed the effects of time, and her stories of times past were a window into another world, where cities didn't exist, and everyone lived together in villages, with no means of transport, not even bicycles, to travel from one village to another.

Nne was deeply convinced of the importance of continuity, which she saw as the key to the strength of the Igbos. Her views had relaxed since she was baptized, sometime in the 1930s. Before her decision to convert, the world around her had already made a choice, as tradition was replaced with the teachings of Jesus Christ. Age-grades — groups in the same age bracket who maintained social relationships based on the belief in the power of their interdependence — were replaced with Bible groups, and visits to shrines to secure the blessing of the gods were replaced by wall paintings of the lamb of God, altars, and Sunday Mass.

One quiet night sitting watching the fire, she shared her story. It reminded me of when Papa and I used to sit together, the setting sun as our fire.

"Christianity changed so much," she began. "Some were afraid of it because it was the end of what we had believed for so long to be true, and an invitation to believe instead in something that was not a natural part of us.

"As our people say, 'One who has been bitten by a snake is afraid of an earthworm.' We had been bitten before, and the white man in the past had brought much sorrow. Now they promised salvation. We liked the story of Jesu Christi, but you couldn't blame our people for struggling with the decision. But for me, the choice to convert happened as quickly as lightning.

"I was young then. The skin of my twins was still wrinkled and covered by blood and the white creamy film of their internal protection. Only one had fed and the other was wailing when the midwife heard the sound of approaching feet. I remember being surprised because I thought that the changes of the time meant that the village elders might allow the twins to live." She paused and I saw her internal struggle with how much to share with me.

"They took them from my breasts. Their only crime was that they were twins — an evil omen that had to be killed to safeguard the village and its people from harm." She paused again, before continuing in fast Igbo. "Can you imagine, eh Nkem, babies considered dangerous?"

I could not even presume to imagine the pain of these women and men who for a long time endured the death of their twins until fewer and fewer of these so-called abominations were born.

I felt her sadness deepen as she continued.

"All these years, my heart breaks to imagine how long they must have cried, abandoned in the forbidden forest, screaming in fear and hunger until they finally gave in to death by starvation or wild animal.

"It was then that the argument for preserving culture and tradition which I clung to stopped making sense."

I didn't say anything, for there was nothing to say. We continued to watch the fire in silence and in appreciation of the bond that had been formed.

One thing she didn't share was that while she rejected traditions, one still held sway for her.

I would have to experience this for myself. It was a normal night: I had made a fire, cooked dinner, and was cleaning up in the corner of the house when I noticed visitors arriving. Soon, there was a group of about five women seated around the fire, and I was serving them garden eggs and ose ọjị. I recognized three as Nne's friends; the two others I had never seen.

I didn't think it odd when Nne asked me to boil water and set up a mat close to the fire beside the trunk of the mango tree. I did find it strange when she asked me to clean myself and come join the group as they gathered around the mat, as if waiting for someone. I soon understood that that person was me.

I was offered a bitter drink, which I knew not to refuse, and told to lie down. Nne assured me that everything was going to be all right.

It was also Nne's voice that urged me to stay still as hands began to coax my legs apart. I obeyed out of respect, but once I saw the glint of metal held over the fire, I began to panic, writhing against hands that now held me pinned to the ground.

The touch of the blade was as painful as I feared. I couldn't stay still if I wanted to. "Why are they doing this?" cried my whole being in unison, mind, body, and spirit screaming against having a piece of myself removed. I mustered a superhuman strength to wrench away from the hands whose job was to prevent this from happening.

Half running, half crawling, tears dripping down my face and blood dripping between my legs, I made my way from the fire as fast as possible.

"*Rapụ ya*, leave her," Nne said to the figures moving after me. "*O zuola*," I heard Nne answer to the silent question from women who insisted on the importance of such a practice. "It is enough."

At her words, their figures stilled, but I didn't stop moving away into the dark night. With effort, hunched over from pain and shuffling to minimize the friction of my thighs, I made my way slowly inside and to my corner of the room.

The pain lasted a few weeks, and when Nne examined me, she gently lamented that the interrupted procedure was not as thorough as it could have been. Her critique however did not carry the usual weight of her convictions. Many years later, Nne shared with me that allowing me to go was her moment of redemption from upholding a tradition that inflicted pain and reminded her all too much of her own.

Nne knew that some wounds never heal. But she couldn't know that this scar would be a painful and important reminder of what happens when people impose their expectations and beliefs on others.

In years to come, when I would meet the edges of my own understanding, I knew that even if everyone else might say one thing, the key was to find my own truth — what felt right for me. I would soon find that what doesn't feel right, especially as pertains to our actions towards others, often isn't right.

Nothing about that night felt right for either one of us, and even though we never spoke of it then, we both felt that it changed something for us.

Seven

"What else is expected of a cigarette if not smoke?"

TIME IN THE VILLAGE has a way of slowing down and speeding up all at once, the cock's crows and hoots of pigeons blending into one another. So too the chatter and habits of village people.

Three years went by and I had become a village girl, no longer distinguishable from the other girls. I had long ago ditched my city clothes, which had become too small, too old, or too impractical, for two cotton wrappers I wore interchangeably under old T-shirts. I was now just a few inches short of my adult height of 170 centimetres (five feet, six inches). My fair skin was considerably darkened by daily extended exposure to the sun, and my hair was still unpermed and habitually woven into intricate plaits or threaded into mounds. My friend Adaobi had the most creativity with designs and her hands were gentle, which suited my very sensitive scalp.

While my identity morphed, that of my family remained relatively stable, an upper-class family living in the breadbasket of the country. I had just completed primary school with an ease that proved that hard work paid off. My secret plan to return home was on track!

With my grades, I gained admission into the prestigious Queen of the Rosary Secondary School, QRSS, a highly regarded missionary establishment for girls run by the Catholic Church. It was in Nsukka, which, although not Makurdi, was a comparable town in size and development, bringing me closer to my stubborn dream of living a life beyond the village.

Although only an hour's drive from Isuofia, Nsukka would be the farthest I had travelled since I arrived. I was the only one of my friends from school to go to QRSS; they were either going to closer schools or continuing on with life in the village. Nnenna, for example, was going to train with her auntie as a tailor.

Papa was kept abreast of every major development via courier sent through and received by my uncle Onye Nkuzi. Each of Papa's letters, without fail, began with the question: "Are you happy?" He always asked in English, our language of written communication.

I developed in those years a habit of reading the lines of his distinct writing again and again, each time discovering a nuance I had missed the first time. This practice helped me to feel the emotions of the letter, to feel his pride beyond the blue lines of his biro like a whisper carried in the wind telling me that everything, as he always predicted, was going to be all right.

At first, I couldn't wait to leave for Nsukka, but the closer it came to my departure, the more confused my feelings were. Change was both exciting and something I had learned to dread. "But," I reminded myself, "as tough as the move to

Isuofia had been, my time here has also become a part of my story." In realizing this, I had discovered the power of changing my perspective. "Everything is going to be okay," I echoed Papa's words as my own.

We spent my last days in Isuofia preparing the harvest of cassava tubers for drying, as it would be too much work for Nne to manage on her own. Although she tried to make light of it, Nne was sad that I was leaving. She showed her love with food.

I observed with excitement as, day after day, she came home with snacks that would tide me through the months to come, including my favourite of dried ụkwa — the roasted seeds of breadfruit with honey — sweet, hard, and crunchy and made even more delicious paired with fresh coconut meat. And there was groundnut, roasted for hours during the day in a pan of hot sand. Tiger nuts were rare in those days, as they had to be brought all the way from the North. But nonetheless, Nne came home from one of her trips with a clay pot filled with the small tubers.

Nne had never been one for excessive emotions, but not so in those final hours. We went together to Mass on the Saturday evening before my Sunday morning departure, asking for blessings for the journey before me. Private prayers with the priest lasted well into the night, every angel and saint called by name; no harm could come to me even if it tried.

"*Chineke, Chukwu nna* — God, the father in heaven, we beseech you to guide your daughter, Nkem," the priest prayed to the blue eyes of Jesus watching over us from a large portrait that hung over the prayer room, my eyes shut and hands clasped in connection to the spirits with whom we were communicating.

The next day I packed up the camp bed, rolled my mat away, and stowed both under Nne's bed. That single action felt like the end of an era. My uncle, his wife, and my friends Nnenna, Nwazu, and Adaobi were there to say goodbye.

Onye Nkuzi accompanied me on a journey marked by an unending change of modes of transportation until, finally, we arrived. Nsukka felt to me like a big city with sprawling markets and the impressive buildings of its famed university. After a short ride along untarred roads, we arrived at QRSS. Onye Nkuzi left me at the gate, as was the rule, but not without a short lecture about focusing on my studies and the importance of avoiding distractions and bad friends. I nodded in acknowledgement, though without really listening; I was distracted by my curiosity.

Soon, I thought, I would be one of the girls I could see beyond the gate in their blue and white uniforms. A new chapter had begun.

LIFE AT BOARDING SCHOOL was not for the faint-hearted. And this was not coming from the Dora who had left Makurdi, but from Nkem of Isuofia. I imagine it is most similar to being in the military. QRSS, with its almost decade-long experience of training unruly girls, had perfected its military-like efficiency. The strict hierarchy of the system was designed and upheld by the students themselves.

To be a first-year student at the bottom of the power chain meant so many different things, none of them good. Take, for example, waking up at 2 a.m. to shower; any later, and the senior girls would cut the line and shower before you.

Some days, the difficulties of taking a shower were even worse. When there was no water dripping from the rows of taps outside the bathroom, we had to walk around to the back of the building to reach the water closer to the source. On those days we would all have to line up, sometimes for hours, waiting to fetch a bucket full of water from the emergency water tank. As the clock creeped closer to 5 a.m., senior girls would wake up and that meant an even longer wait for us first-years. On such days, we would simply "rub and shine" — a useful routine I was already familiar with.

From cleaning the toilets to washing our uniforms, bedsheets, and sports clothes; sweeping and scrubbing the floors; sweeping dusty pathways to make room for fresh dirt; and cutting down stubborn weeds with a machete, all the upkeep of the school grounds was done by us students. The only exception was the cooking of meals, which was done by hired hands. The hardships might have been daunting for other students, but it sometimes felt like a break for me, for at least here, the tasks were shared among hundreds of us.

It was the constant alertness one needed against the demands on one's time by senior girls that tasked me the most. One could easily spend the day running one errand after another if caught in the wrong place and time by a group of older girls.

In early 1967, only a few months into my time in Nsukka, news of unrest started to circulate around school. There were so many versions of the story — some said that young Hausa men in the North were eating Igbos alive, others spoke of politicians and their egos causing trouble for Igbos — but every version painted a picture of Igbos as victims of oppression from other tribes. None of us thought that the rumours would affect us, for surely young girls had nothing to do with the politics of the country.

That was until war broke out. There was no assembly announcement, nothing. Instead, frantic teachers were soon joined by students running around to the classrooms, declaring to all that Biafra — the chosen name of the southeastern part of the country that we occupied — was intent on seceding from the rest of Nigeria and, to this end, was at war. Everyone was to find their way home. On a major artery for the Southeast, Nsukka was an important city and would be close to danger, very much in the eye of the storm. Not a minute was to be lost.

I had barely been half a year at QRSS when I found myself returning to Isuofia.

I hitched a ride with a stranger to a village close to Isuofia; from there, I walked the rest of the way. I arrived to meet a man waiting for me, who had come to bring me back to Nanka, where I understood the rest of my family was.

Though invited, Nne insisted on staying behind; at worst, she repeated again and again, she was content to die in her home. I grieved at the thought of leaving her behind on her own.

Nne's consoling words pierced through my tears: "I am not alone, I have God with me. And, Nkem, I know that it's not my time to die. I will be okay, everything will be okay. On top, I have *ndị be* Onye Nkuzi to take care of me." She looked directly into my eyes. "And you, my daughter, will be okay as well. You can withstand anything, even a war."

I nodded, embracing her prayer and blessing and saying a silent one for her in return.

My mind turned to my pending reunification with my parents and with all seven of my brothers and sisters. It would be the first time I met my youngest sister, born just a few months earlier. I had imagined many times over the years what it would feel like to be with my family again, but I never expected that it would be under such circumstances. No one could have.

Eight

"A boat cannot go forward if each rows their own way."

THE BIAFRA WAR BROKE OUT in July 1967. The part of Nigeria that is often designated simply as the East, and home mainly to Igbos, wanted to break from the rest of the country, which had once been home to all. This desire was born of anger, following the massacre of Igbos living in the North. The Nigerian government would hear nothing of Biafra's desire for secession, not least of all because Nigeria's oil wealth was buried in the same lands that wanted independence.

It was akin to Igbos wanting a divorce, while Nigeria believed in the sanctity of the marriage as ordained by Great Britain. Both sides felt equally passionate about their stance, and both were willing to fight. The months leading up to the final decision by the Igbos to secede were filled with all manner of speculation as to what exactly was at play.

At QRSS before the war broke out, I had been in charge of cleaning the teachers' lounge after class. The teachers didn't mind that I lingered to do my homework. Being there reminded me of my years in Makurdi listening to adults discuss politics.

"Should we remain with Nigeria?" was always the question that got all the teachers in passionate debate. Their response was unanimous in favour of Igbos embracing their sovereignty, with a new identity as an independent Biafra. However, it was clear to anyone paying attention that Nigeria had no intention of letting go.

One day, there was so much anger in the room in reaction to news of a killing spree in the North, which had targeted Igbos on the basis of their ethnicity. Voices were livid with indignation.

"*Alụ*, abomination," exclaimed one of the teachers after another had shared the account of thousands of dead bodies of tribespeople deposited at the doorsteps of Igboland.

"Over thirty thousand dead and yet you don't see the reason to break away!" said another teacher to the minority voices who preached prudence. "Men, women, and children killed for the crime of being Igbo, their bodies piled on trains to be sent back east."

"*Tufiakwa!*" came an impassioned exclamation from another, accompanied by a snap of the fingers following a counter-clockwise rotation of the hand over the head.

"Can you imagine, on top of it all, the feeling of having everything you've worked for — your home, your business, everything — looted and burned to nothing?"

"Why are they doing this?" another asked. It was Mr. Enezi, the geography teacher. "We Igbos," he continued, in answer to his own question, "we have lived in peace for decades, with everyone: Hausas, Yorubas, Ijaws, Efiks, you name it. All of us were living as brothers and sisters. And now this nonsense story about us wanting to control the rest of the country!" He spat the last words as if disgusted by its very utterance.

"And just like that, based on rumours and misplaced anger, there is a 'them' and an 'us.'" At this, everyone shook their head in disappointed resignation.

I listened intently to their conversation, making a mental note to ask why there was so much anger and violence against the Igbos.

It was Mr. Enezi who later explained to me that it had started on January 15, 1966, when a certain Major Chukwuma Nzeogwu, led the first ever military coup in Nigeria. The coup led to the deaths of Sir Ahmadu Bello, the sardauna of Sokoto and premier of Northern Nigeria, and of Sir Abubakar Tafawa Balewa, a beloved figure from the North who was also the prime minister of Nigeria.

By killing prominent religious and political leaders from the North, Mr. Enezi patiently explained, Nzeogwu and his co-conspirators stepped onto a landmine. The North accused Nzeogwu and his accomplices of staging what became known as an "Igbo coup" — an accusation that gained steam given that most of the officers killed during the coup were not Igbo, while most of the leaders of the coup were.

"Imagine," Mr. Enezi said, pausing to make sure that I was following, "if something bad happened here in our school. Everybody is affected negatively but for one group of people, say from one class. On top of it all, picture that this same group of people was the last to be seen at the scene of the crime. Whether they are guilty or not, who do you think people will blame? Perception is a powerful thing."

The idea that the attack was an "Igbo coup" went from private whispers to full-fledged stories of how the coup was a proven sinister plot by the greedy and ambitious Igbos to take control of Nigeria. This was even though some Yoruba top officials like Major Adewale Ademoyega also took part in the coup.

"Opinion swayed further against Igbos with the claim that Igbos, often flashy and flamboyant with their wealth, cared only about themselves and did not care about Nigeria or Nigerians. As far as these voices were concerned, Igbos were worse than the deposed government they were claiming to reform."

The conversations in the teachers' lounge got more tense in the following weeks with yet another coup, this time masterminded by Lieutenant Colonel Murtala Muhammed and other northern military officers in direct reaction to the "Igbo coup" and the killings of northern politicians and officers.

One coup was destabilizing enough, but two back to back left the country in a deep state of volatility and created fertile ground for further conflict. Between revenge killings and the inaction of the government, which was focused on keeping power by fuelling an anti-Igbo rhetoric, violence, like a destructive genie, was fully unleashed.

This complex play of violence, fear, xenophobia, and revenge in the form of coups and counter-coups was understood by Igbos as evidence that the rest of Nigeria was out to destroy the Igbo people.

"*Alụ emego anyị!*" — an abomination has fallen upon us — was a lamentation on many tongues.

"If they don't want us, why continue to supply an ungrateful country with all the riches of our soil, our crops, and oil from our lands?"

"Why stay in this land that has defiled us and itself?"

And with a cry of pain, and of defiance, a premature baby

with low chances of survival — not unlike an Ọgbanje — but with every intention of living was born. Her name was the Republic of Biafra, born on the thirtieth day of the fifth month in the year 1967. She was to be known also as the "land of the rising sun." She was loved by so many but threatened by many more. Her existence signalled for the rest of Nigeria a disrespect of her autonomy, while her birth meant for Igbos a new dawn as citizens of a country that upheld and respected its people — a country to call their own.

General Emeka Odumegwu Ojukwu, a thirty-three-year-old, Oxford-educated Igbo soldier with impeccable diction and astute powers of persuasion, was the leader who laid claim to Biafra. Igbos were happy to have him as father and guide, though he couldn't have imagined the hardships of caring for and protecting this fragile newborn.

My family was part of the estimated one million Igbos who emigrated in those months leading up to the secession and war, all coming from other parts of Nigeria back to the Southeast to escape death and persecution. Papa had been the last to leave Makurdi and join us all in Nanka. He left in June 1967, a month before the war broke out and a few short weeks after the rest of the family had arrived in Nanka. Weeks before his speedy departure, clients had stopped staying at his hotels, as going to an Igbo man's establishment seemed unwise in those volatile days. He still had full possession of his businesses only because he had pulled all the strings of his impressive network.

It had been his good friend Joseph Tarka, an indigene of Makurdi with strong ties to the government, who warned him that he couldn't stay on any longer. "You must leave Makurdi,"

Joseph had said, knowing that death was all around and would now come for my father.

While the news didn't come as a surprise to Papa, it was clear to all how hard it had been for him to say goodbye to his home and all that he had worked for.

And so it came about that my entire family, later joined by Papa, journeyed east along with thousands of other families on overcrowded trains that smelled of death, of fear, and of decay.

Nine

*"Don't think there are no crocodiles just because
the water is calm."*

ON MY JOURNEY from Isuofia to Nanka, I kept wondering how the moment of seeing my family again would feel. Would there be familiarity? Would it be uncomfortable? I had been informed that my father was still in Makurdi, and as disappointing as it was that he wouldn't be there, I was still excited to see everyone, most notably my baby sister Nwogo.

The moment I did arrive, I felt I wasn't welcome. It was an odd feeling because it was Mama who met me at the metal gate, surrounded by my brothers and sisters. My sister Gloria was carrying Nwogo.

I didn't know what caused the discomfort that prickled my skin, especially considering the excited smiles of my family, their warm greetings, and their brief but warm hugs.

Through the gap of bodies, I spied narrowed, disdain-filled eyes in the distance that quickly looked away, surprised to be caught in naked judgement. There was no love, no warmth, and no apology in them. I filed this observation away until I could speak with my mother or one of my siblings to understand whose eyes they were and why they took so much offence at my presence. I soon found out that they belonged to my uncle, whom everyone called Ben, pronounced Benu.

Benedict Obiekeli was the head of the Obiekeli family, who had been stewards of the Edemobi family land following the death of Papa's father. Papa had been too young to take care of the family Obi, too young to take care of anyone, even himself. The Obiekelis cared for the land until PY came of age.

Time has a unique ability to morph truth to suit the needs of its speaker.

After so many years of caring for the land, Ben believed that he and his family had as much a right to it as PY, who, according to him, had abandoned the land many years ago, well after he attained manhood and the capacity to care for it. Ben saw our coming as opportunistic and, further, was afraid that our family would lay claim to the Obi and turn away him and his family, unprepared, from what had become their home.

Now he made no secret of his displeasure at having the entire Edemobi family descend upon the compound. We could do little but wait for Papa's return and avoid Ben's wrath.

For many years, especially those days spent together in Nanka, Papa had shared a dream to build a house on his family's compound. It was to be a place to call home for him and his children after him. How could Papa have known that time was against him and that a home in Nanka would be needed decades sooner than he envisioned? That, in our moment of need, our hopeful sanctuary in the Edemobi family compound would not be?

Papa's arrival in Nanka was met with no fanfare this time, only with the reserved greetings of people whose minds were preoccupied with worries of the times. He couldn't have expected the coldness with which he was greeted once he arrived at the Edemobi family compound. By now, the animosity towards our family was in full display.

Ben met him at the gate, and we all followed in tow. Ben was wearing a wrapper tied low across his stomach, his chest and belly exposed, a walking stick in his right hand, which, given his lingering youth, seemed more for effect than need. He was surrounded by a few friends dressed in similar fashion. They did not come with kola nut, nor with joy or welcome in their eyes. Instead, there were questions.

It was Ben who spoke first. "Where are you going?" he asked scornfully. "This is not your home." Ben's voice was raised and drew attention. "What happened to your mansions?"

Papa's confused gaze met Mama's, who was motioning for him not to respond.

Visibly tired and saddened by the reception, PY heeded his wife's wisdom and apologized to Ben, for what, he wasn't quite sure, as he made his way towards Mama and us, his children, his eyes connecting with mine for the first time, managing a strained smile as he averted his gaze from his cousin.

In a quiet corner of the compound, Mama explained the situation to him, of the taunts from Ben since their arrival. How and why Ben was denying that PY had any claims to the land.

Nothing of our reunion was as I had so often imagined it. For the first two nights of his return, Papa barely acknowledged my presence. I saw and felt his preoccupation. I could only imagine the weight of his emotions — a refugee in his own ancestral compound, with a wife and eight children, and no place to call home.

In the coming days, several Nanka indigenes, having heard of the dispute, came to the compound to mediate. Back and forth they went with Ben, who argued that Papa had no claim to the home that he and his family occupied, which Ben said had been given to him in exchange for caring for it and the land all these years.

It was the first time I saw my father walk around without his usual energy; he was moody and listless. Soon, he stopped arguing in his defence and simply asked that Ben do this favour for him in his time of need. Ben was not interested.

When all reasoning and persuasion failed, and Ben still refused to support our family, some of the villagers suggested that they bring the dispute before the local deity.

"I am happy to go to the gods, I have nothing to hide," Papa announced to the gathering of elders in the village square.

"*Eh*, me too!" Ben insisted in response, conscious that any hesitation from his end might signal his own guilty conscience.

I watched from the edge of a small crowd drawn to the scandal.

"Then it's settled" came the firm voice of the oldest member of the delegation. "We will let the gods decide." He looked intently from one to the other to make sure that they understood the gravity of their decision; there could only be one truth, which meant that one of them was inviting the anger of the gods.

PY and Ben were to present themselves in two days.

On the designated day, not even Mama was allowed to go with them. But her eyes followed Papa in the form of a trusted male friend. She shared with us how Papa and Ben would make their way into a dark shrine filled with sacrificial objects. I allowed my imagination to fill the gaps, concocting images of skulls of various shapes and sizes; cowrie shells for divination; long feathers of colourful birds; live chickens in cages fashioned out of cobbled wooden stakes; and goats tied outside.

It was there that they made their case.

The general consensus was that Papa and Ben would wait ten days after their visit; should any form of malaise befall one of them, this would be proof of their guilt. And if nothing happened to either one, then the one who wanted no change in the status quo — in this case, Ben — was to have his wishes respected.

Ten days later, and both Ben and Papa were unharmed and healthy in every way. The gods had spoken: Papa was to leave his Obi and seek shelter elsewhere.

Everyone, for many years to come, would hear the story of the conflict between Ben and Papa. Over time, and even long after the war, Ben continued to insist that he did no wrong against PY. And over the years, the silence of the gods was a mystery to everyone, many of whom believed that Ben had abandoned his cousin in his time of need.

Ben, as the story goes, eventually passed away in his post-war base in the North. As is customary with the Igbos, his body was to make its way back to Nanka. It was accompanied by Ndị Igbo Union, who lived to tell the tale. The car carrying his body broke down three times. By the third engine breakdown, with his corpse smelling from decay, there was a consensus by union members that the land had rejected his body. And so it was that Benedict Obiekelu was buried instead in the bushes of Taraku in Ugwu Hausa.

His body has not reached its ancestral home to date. Many

believed and continue to believe that it was because of what was considered to be an abomination he committed against PY and against the gods.

In addition to his unfortunate lack of burial rights, the disputed land is known to be unlucky, with several misfortunes plaguing occupants, including blindness, failed marriages, and barrenness. Parts of the land continue to lie fallow, with no takers.

Ten

"A tree is known by its fruit."

SINCE THE STATUS QUO was to be maintained, our entire family was without a home. Papa concluded that as long as we had life, everything was okay. As always, I trusted him and took up his usual optimism as my own, believing in it even more when we received an invitation to stay with a friend of Papa in his home until we ironed out our next steps.

The subject of a temporary home resolved, we now had to face the realities of war. With the advance of Nigerian soldiers, preceded by stories of raids and destruction, a veil of fear and despair hung across Nanka and the surrounding villages. Things were getting worse by the day.

Access to food was weaponized by Nigeria. A blockade was issued against Biafra as a sure way to bring the new country to her knees. The crippling restriction meant that no one in Biafra was spared a first-hand experience of the war. Even the most basic commodities, especially salt, became luxuries, and hunger was an ever-present companion.

The hollow, pale look of constant hunger was ubiquitous. I

watched the skin of some of the children in the village gradu-
ally change from shades of brown to pale and translucent, their
hair turning light and curly due to the onset of kwashiorkor,
a starvation-induced illness.

Our family got by selling and trading suitcases of Mama's
George fabric and lace. Her love for bundles of colourful African wax print fabrics imported from Holland had been so
great that it earned her the nickname "Madame Hollandaise."
She saved as much money as possible, spending thriftily on
the occasional bowl of garri (made of dried cassava), bottles of
palm oil, sachets of kerosene, and small mounds of yam tubers.
Our main sustenance was from international aid. Mama used
to queue up every week to get a ration of food from Caritas,
a German religious organization named after the Latin word
for charity — the virtue of love and compassion. Papa would
usually give me part of his ration, saying he would rather die
than lose his Dora. I doubt that made me popular with my
brothers and sisters, but he was insistent.

In the midst of the struggle to make ends meet, and the
emotional stress of knowing that we as a new country were
at war, I found myself missing Isuofia. I looked to the endless
chores of what now felt like the good old days with my grandmother with the envy of a woman in labour missing the earlier
pangs of contraction. At least back in Isuofia, we ate to our
hearts' content and I didn't have to trek three hours to school.

But the fact that I was walking so far to go to school was
my own doing. I had insisted, to my father's glowing pride,
that I continue my studies at the only open school in the area,
all the way in Agulu, a few villages away. Now, five days out
of seven, I walked on an empty stomach for longer than the

combined time it took to fetch water, firewood, and walk to school in Isuofia. I persevered, though, as school felt like the training grounds for radical self-reliance.

Despite my weakened body and the long walks, it had not escaped my attention that being at war and living in a different country could mean that returning to a life in Makurdi, now in the separate country of Nigeria, was less and less of a possibility. With our entire family destitute, the village and greater Biafra were possibly our only home. But still I had to trust that getting the education I wanted would be my ticket to a better future.

Over time, the stories of advancing Nigerian federal troops became more urgent. Not wanting to wait until Nanka fell under the might of machine guns, we and many others fled farther inland, away from the borders of an encircled Biafra. No one really seemed to know where we were running to, simply that we were fleeing approaching danger, seen or heard. We walked and sometimes ran from one safe village to the next, with each falling in a spectacular domino.

With any fuel long dried up, we went by foot, as did everyone else, with the exception of a few lucky bicycle owners, who guarded their rides with extreme caution.

The roads were filled with people lugging their meagre belongings, sometimes along with domestic animals. We each had a bag, carefully packed with our remaining provisions, as well as some of Mama's trinkets and fabric to sell or exchange for food and shelter. Papa and Mama alternated carrying two-year-old Nwogo on their backs. We stopped more than most groups for Mama to feed her an akamu cornmeal mix, which needed nothing but hot water to turn the lumps of pap into a quick meal. We often relied on this too, supplemented by pieces of boiled yam we carried discreetly in our bags to be dipped into a tin of palm oil.

Among the stream of war refugees were several families, infants strapped on their mothers' backs and older ones hanging onto their parents' hands. Because of malnutrition, most notably from lack of proteins and salt, many of the children had developed swollen bellies from kwashiorkor. Afọ, which should be the evidence of good living, instead signalled the famine that ravaged Biafra. Many had taken to eating rats and lizards as well as cassava leaves, which had to be plucked early in the morning because if the sun shines on the leaves, the cyanide content increases, leading to even more death.

I watched it all with the eyes of a teenager, feeling pity for the children and knowing there was nothing I could do to help. We could only gasp at some extreme cases of the physical distortion of hunger, curbing our desire to share our too-small ration, as it would do little to help when hundreds were suffering. I felt a terrible sadness for the waste of human life and potential that was happening right in front of our eyes. I did the only thing I could: I prayed. I called on Mary, for she was compassionate and she had a son, to please help her children in our time of need. I called on Saint Nicholas, the patron saint of children, and on the archangels Michael and Gabriel to fight for the safety of all, especially the children.

On our long walks seeking safety and shelter, we, like many others, slept at the side of the road, in the clearings of harvested and abandoned farms, and on the floors of abandoned churches and schools. The sound of hungry children wailing for food, and the terror of bloodsucking mosquitoes, kept me up most nights. The worst days were during heavy rainfalls when no shelter could be found and we waited, drenched, for hours until the sun emerged. Dry or wet, rested or not, and always hungry, at sunrise we unfailingly continued on our journey, seeking refuge.

More than once we saw dead bodies along the way. As no one had the capacity to care for the living, let alone the dead, we all did the best we could, making a sign of the cross as we walked around unburied bodies out of respect for the dead. Some things remained sacred: no matter how hungry people got, no one ate dead human flesh, although there were tales of mothers who had to kill their babies and share their flesh to feed their starving children. It was also still inconceivable to kill and eat the vultures that fed on the dead bodies.

On the journey, once in a while, our paths crossed those of weary Biafran soldiers. They didn't bring the hope we desperately needed. Too many of them were little more than young boys, some armed only with farm tools, while others wore heavy guns with no sign of bullets hidden in their thin camouflage uniforms. I quickly concluded that basic weapons needed for the fight against the federal troops were lacking. As much as they tried to look brave, saluting us refugees in response to our excited greetings, it was clear that they too were struggling with hunger and despair.

Going into the war, being such a small and very young country, we knew that the chances of easy victory were against us, but we were the "land of the rising sun," and everyone knows that once the day is ready to break, no one can stop the sun. So we pushed against fear and hoped instead for our heart's desire. But really, *we*, as a term to capture the will and desire of all Biafrans, was somewhat misleading, because we, as a group that included not only Igbos but also other ethnic groups such as Efik, Ibibio, Ijaw, and Ogoni, didn't really choose to secede or to go to war. The choices were made *for* us, but it was indeed we who suffered and we who had to be strong.

Biafra was facing a truly indomitable foe.

The Nigerian federal government troops were backed by many years of experience as well as the support of Britain and the Soviet Union. British support was inspired by a desire to secure its crude oil interests against the threat of Biafra to its historical monopoly. The Soviets opposed any and all internal secession movements, so as to prevent their own people from witnessing the precedent of successful secession.

Biafra struggled to gain international and regional recognition as an independent state. Its few supporters — including France, Portugal, and Israel, each with its own agendas — provided some weaponry as well as financial and moral assistance for Biafra's war efforts, but none fully went to bat for Biafra. The aid and support, while instrumental, proved insufficient to curb the force of the federal troops. Moreover, the international aid was frequently the target of sabotage attacks and failed to sufficiently feed a starving Biafra.

In those years, I learned first-hand then the importance of hope. Each triumph of Biafra, no matter how small, was just enough to sustain even the weariest Biafran until the next victory. One such accomplishment that still stands out in the hearts and imagination of every Igbo man, woman, and child was the production of *Ogbunigwe* — "the one that kills in multitude."

Ogbunigwe was a warhead that killed hundreds with each detonation, vomiting shrapnel to a range of up to eight hundred metres. It was designed and manufactured in Biafra by Biafrans, a point of great pride for Igbos. It was created out of dire necessity in a time of scarce ammunition, and for many years, parents would use its existence to buttress the teaching to their children that necessity is the mother of all inventions.

The very invention of the Ogbunigwe seemed to taunt Nigeria to beware of the strength of the Igbo resolve and the certainty of their independence.

However impressive a weapon, the Ogbunigwe was no match for the military-grade weapons the United Kingdom supplied to the Nigerian military. Ultimately, scrap weapons, international aid, bush meat, and the hope of victory could only propel Biafra, its soldiers, and its people so far.

By 1969, Biafra was barely hanging on, the death toll having surpassed half a million soldiers and civilians combined. The wounds of a savage war were increasingly unbearable even for the most determined of Biafrans. But still the people believed and hoped for victory and a country to call their own.

Eleven

"When the roots of a tree begin to decay, it spreads death to the branches."

I TURNED FOURTEEN in the third year of the war in 1969, but had long before stopped being a child.

Our flight eventually led us to the village of Umulolo, near Okigwe. Umulolo felt more like a bustling town than a village, with a single road flanked by a mix of old bungalows and newer duplexes. The once busy market square had been abandoned, tables turned over and covered with dust.

With some of the money Mama had saved up, my parents opened and ran a small restaurant. Life for our entire family remained difficult, and going to school was no longer an option for me. It was time for us all to contribute to the family; I was expected to get a job.

We'd heard that the farm of a certain Mr. Nwokobia, two villages removed, was hiring. As there is safety in numbers, it was decided that my two elder sisters, Gloria and Rose, and I would go together. Excited, we set off in search of this job that promised wages for farmhands. It took a day and a half of walking from sunrise to sunset, with restless nights spent afraid of the unknown creatures that crawled in these forests, both man and beast.

Once at the farm at Ikpa Ora, we were swiftly hired to till and cultivate the land. I was no stranger to the hard work a farm required, but it was much different to work when I could not recall the last hearty meal I'd eaten.

For weeks, day in and day out, we hoed and planted under scorching heat and in extreme hunger. Our one meal per day was a piece of boiled cocoyam with red palm oil supplemented by the occasional increasingly skinny bush rat that came to feed on the farm. The hardships were exacerbated by the lack of payment. Not even the old men who had been hired as security against thieves had received their wages, let alone young girls like us.

We slept in a cemented room of an unfinished building. I wasn't sure of its intended purpose, but it was now filled with sleeping mats. The bushes surrounding the building served as our latrine.

Every day was the same, but for moments when a dim hum in the distance would alert us to approaching bomber planes. Shouts of "Take cover!" would reverberate across the farm, as we abandoned hoes and cutlasses for the cover of ukwa, udala, oroma, mango, and ube trees and thick bushes — anything dense enough to hide us, as well as protect the body from a spray of bullets should we be detected. Huddled in flat heaps, the air filled with the eerie silence of men, women, and children holding our breath until danger passed.

For three months, we received no payment. Rumours of the pending fall of Okigwe, coming from thousands of fleeing people, some of whom worked at the farm just to get a regular meal, made us anxious. As the news became more certain, we feared that Umulolo would be the next target. Knowing that our family could not leave without us, we headed home, sad and defeated to be returning without a shilling.

Home was now a two-day trek away, as the main roads had grown too perilous to travel. Back in Umulolo, everyone seemed to have aged, including my mother, whose agelessness had been a constant source of marvel for all. Those days in Umulolo would be one of the last times we were all together as a family.

In the coming weeks, things were quiet as we awaited whatever was to come. The only interruption was the news of Gloria's marriage to a man from Isuofia. We were all happy to hear that Isuofia was still unharmed by the war. Gloria was to make the two-day journey with a companion and friend of the family and our younger sister Ngozi, who would live with her in Isuofia.

Meanwhile, Papa and his new friends gathered nightly in the courtyard of the apartment complex we were staying in, whispering news of the advance of the Nigerian army and the exploits of the valiant Biafran soldiers. Their quiet voices and the slow pace of the day were only disturbed by the sporadic sound of the radio coming on with news of the war.

In those quieter days, Papa and I took many evening walks together. I always enjoyed watching him get ready with the same attention he paid to everything he did. His black leather shoes had lost their Makurdi shine from the dull red earth of the village, and his white clothes had long since turned brown and yellow from use. But he still looked every bit the distinguished man. As always, he would hold out his hand in readiness for mine and it would be hand in hand that we set off for our daily father-daughter time. In this space together, he imparted knowledge and wisdom to serve my own growth. I didn't mind that he repeated some lessons over and over.

"You see, Dora, *uwa enweghi isi* — this world is an empty one. Beware of placing your life worth on material things or on the approval of others, because one day you are on top and the next you find yourself at the bottom."

He always paused to emphasize this point. "You know what this means, *nwa m oma?*" he asked, referring to me as he often did as his "good daughter." "When you are at the top, treat those beneath the same way you would like to be treated when fortunes reverse."

As always, I nodded my understanding and saw the joy it brought him to know that his words had found their mark.

The war, as I saw it, was changing our very culture, and I wondered if things would ever go back to how they had been before. Before the war, we had lived in a fragile union of brotherhood and sisterhood. The experience with my uncle Ben and then at Mr. Nwokobia's farm were indicative of the moral corruption that was eating away at Nigeria and Biafra. In listening to Papa, I always concluded that while the world around us was changing, who we chose to be was within our control.

When it became apparent that Okigwe's fall was certain, we started to close up the family restaurant and plotted our return to Nanka, which had survived in spite of the threats. My parents, tired of running and wanting to be home, believed that if we were going to be killed in the war, it was better to die in our village than elsewhere.

Back in Nanka, we were taken in by a distant relative. By December 1969, our new compound was bustling. Gloria was visiting with Ngozi from Isuofia, bringing news of Nne and Ndi be Onye Nkuzi, all of whom had mercifully survived the war.

While we didn't have much as a family, this didn't deter Mama from putting on her bright-red lace wrapper and preparing a feast of roasted yam and stew — a concoction of aged onions and unripe tomatoes. Mama's disposition was sunny, and her smile distracted from her markedly changed appearance, softening her now-drawn skin and adding a spring to the cracked soles of her feet.

From our seat on a low bench, humming and preparing the meagre feast, we could see our youngest sister, Nwogo, whom I had also taken to calling by her middle name Vivian, whisper a question to our eldest brother, Jo. Her finger discreetly pointed to the figure of Ngozi.

"*Onye ka o bu?* Who is that girl?"

"*Ewoo*" came the response from Jo, whose back was already fully twisted into a hunchback that would plague him all his life. "Tha— tha— that girl is your sister!" he responded, his shock that Nwogo did not recognize her sister Ngozi causing him even more difficulty than usual with his stammer.

Nwogo, just one year old when the war broke out, had been too young to remember the earlier days in Nanka and too young to remember her own sister from the family's brief reunion in Umulolo.

At Jo's words, a sadness enveloped the otherwise cheery day as everyone felt anew the tragedy of a family torn apart by the war — of sisters who were strangers to one another.

Twelve

"An arrow can only be shot by pulling it backwards."

IN JANUARY 1970, after thirty months and an estimated two million dead, and just as quickly as it started, the war was over. After a valiant and stubborn battle, Biafra surrendered in a hastily delivered speech on Radio Biafra by the vice-president, Lieutenant Colonel Philip Effiong. He had assumed the position of president the week before, after the former president and leader Odumegwu Ojukwu had fled the country. Under immense pressure and in the face of inevitable loss, Effiong had no choice but to surrender.

Nigeria, once the oppressor, came to the service of a defeated Biafra, casting itself in the role of victor and saviour — there to restore order to a unified Federal Republic of Nigeria. Sitting head of state of Nigeria, General Yakubu Gowon, referred to the period as a "victory for common sense." The government's idea was to erase history. Guided by the phrase "no victor no vanquished," Biafran flags and money were confiscated and burned. The intention was clear: once again we were one nation, united in brotherhood and sisterhood. All was forgiven, all was to be forgotten.

I wish I could say that the end of the war signalled the end of hard times, and that the three-year-long ordeal had begun to fade into the realms of a nightmare from which the dreamer had awoken. I cannot.

Biafra's dance with freedom had been a glorious dream but disastrous for her people. The war left scars, physical and emotional, on every Igbo man, woman, and child. Many spirits were broken in those three years, though some were strengthened by a resolve to rebuild.

There was so much anger. So much disillusionment and, even worse, there was the loss of hope; dreams were considered foolish, even for children. For many, the end of the war was just the beginning of even greater hardship.

One example of this was that during the war, Nigeria changed its money. This meant that after the war, all money owned by Igbos in their Nigerian bank accounts, running into millions if not billions, had to be changed to the new money. There was, for many, at least still the real aspiration of recovering their savings from before the war. For Papa, this hope was a powerful driver. I was with Papa in the short weeks after the war when he was desperately seeking information on how to access his money. It was a friend of my father who came by with the best news yet. Nigeria was ready to return the savings of Igbos by allowing for a one-time exchange of the old Nigerian pound against the new naira.

The exact words were "All you have to do is complete a form with the balance of your bank account and bring it to the bank for conversion."

The next day, Papa visited a few more friends to confirm the exact process needed to access his savings. Once satisfied, he set off for Enugu, where he knew they would have the capacity for the size of his intended transaction and exchange.

He was joined by three other friends, who were making the visit on behalf of their extended families. Given the amount of illiteracy and the hassle of travelling to a city to visit a bank, many families relied on just one member to do this conversion on their behalf.

At the bank, they soon found that regardless of the amount of money they had in their accounts, no matter how many names and accounts individuals represented, each form translated to only one transaction. Each form, no matter how ample its balance or long its list of accounts and its owners, translated to a direct exchange of twenty pounds.

The result was that many families — mothers, grandfathers, aunties, uncles who transacted via their relatives — were left with only twenty pounds at the end of a war that had cost them everything.

While the now united Nigerian government had its own reasons for this decision, including a stated lack of funds and insufficient records of old balances, the meagre compensation was a dagger to what was left of the heart of the Igbo people. The disenfranchisement of Igbos didn't stop with their bank accounts. Many no longer had a job or a place to call home, their houses and businesses destroyed or confiscated during the war, acts legally justified under the claim they had been abandoned.

I thought that nothing could cripple Papa more than the war had, but he came home a broken man.

I couldn't fathom how so much human pain could ever be worth it. How could we ever justify such injustice committed against one another? War was one thing, but so much else was choice. Seeing Papa this way, I felt so much anger against the part of human nature that knowingly causes such suffering.

In those years, I shed the last remnants of a soft skin, no longer believing that the world was always fair. It was Papa who reminded me that as bad as everything might seem, we had our health and each other, and those were the only things that really mattered — more than money, reputation, victory, loss, and everything in between. Life was the most precious gift.

Thirteen

"An orphaned calf licks its own back."

THOUGH I WAS JUST SIXTEEN when the war ended, I felt like I had already lived many lives, from a life of riches to that of a village girl, and then a refugee in a war-torn country — each a brief taste, as if developing the sensitivity of my palate.

The first stop I made after the war was to visit Nne in Isuofia. They had been untouched by the war. I allowed myself to cry when Nne took me in her arms. I wept for so long that I realized I had not allowed myself to cry in all the long months prior. I felt fortunate to know that all members of my immediate family were spared from any physical harm. The same could not be said for so many millions more.

Postwar, as water started to find its level, I could finally contemplate enjoying the life of a young woman happy to be alive and able to return to school at QRSS. That was only made possible by the generosity of the Catholic Church, which accepted all students of former Biafra tuition-free, knowing that none of us had any money to pay for the continuation of our studies.

Nsukka, the home I had known for those brief months of peace as a secondary school student, was now a shell of itself. The once bustling university city had been heavily bombed by Nigerian soldiers during the war and had taken on the dull colour of defeat and death. Street lights hung gutted, their inner tendrils a disturbing echo of human bodies laid open against the once pristine pavement. Neighbours greeted each other in the light of day, trading stories of misfortunes, mentally tallying the number of friends lost, as information travelled back along with people.

At dusk, against the yellow half of a setting sun, neighbours retreated to the safety of their homes, leaving the town centre, under the soft glow of kerosene lanterns and candles, to reckless youth, of whom there was no shortage. They were young men, many of them former soldiers, disillusioned by war and filled with an unquenchable thirst for the unfulfilled rewards of their sacrifices. Many had since turned to vices that promised they would never again feel less than a victor or have to relive memories of battle.

No institution, public or private, had been spared by the war. QRSS was no different. I was shocked to see the extent of vandalism and destruction, dorm rooms stripped of their already meagre furnishings. The classrooms were in no better shape, with missing window panes and broken desks. Empty wooden window frames hung open at every corner, exposing classrooms filled with shattered glasses, blood, and dirt smeared across the walls. The entire school had no running water or functioning septic system, and dried feces lay in various corners of the cemented corridors, which had served as toilets after those filled up and overflowed.

In spite of it all, I was overjoyed to be back in school. I had lost two whole years of studies when the war had rendered my treks to Agulu impossible. I was content to pick up where I left off. I wasn't alone. We were all desperate for normalcy.

So much had changed after the war, a change that went deeper than images of visibly skinnier girls and decrepit classrooms.

Though my fellow classmates and I had spent only a few short weeks together before the war broke out, you would think we had known each other for years, given the way dozens of us girls screamed and hugged one another, filling the room with tears and shrieks of joy. The enthusiasm of those who had returned showed me the strength of bonds that can rise from loss and grief.

I spent a lot of time in prayer those days, as always calling on the Blessed Virgin to intercede on our behalf. I knew now more than ever that I needed the hand of God to fulfill His promise that "not only does He carry us in His hands, but He has engraved us on the palm of His hand" (Isaiah 49:14–16). I had to trust that I was held in the palm of His hands.

While I never lacked friends, I buried my head in my books and did not allow anyone to get too close. It suited me to have company without the risk of opening up, afraid of what might pour out of me if I let it.

Fourteen

"One arrow can knock down an elephant."

QRSS AND ITS STUDENTS were not alone in the desire for normalcy; everyone was trying to make life postwar work — including Papa and the rest of the family.

At the end of the war, Mama disclosed to us that she had diabetes. She had been diagnosed in the late 1960s before her last pregnancy with our sister Nwogo, but she hadn't wanted to worry us, especially when the war broke out and so much of life was alarming.

It explained all the times when she said she wasn't feeling very well, which I dismissed as tiredness. Or why she was so particular about her diet during the war. All the times she said no to the endless starches — yam and garri, grains of dried cassava, which when mixed with water takes on a doughy consistency perfect for stews and soups and for filling the belly.

I trusted and I believed in the hand of God, but I also knew that heaven was helpful to those who help themselves and now we had to prioritize Mama's health, which meant ensuring that she had access to insulin. It was especially hard to come by in those days.

For Papa, the end of the war was an even greater test than the first time he set out without any money in his pocket, for then he didn't have a family to feed nor fully know the taste of comfort that made poverty even more bitter.

He had lost so much: his homes, not only in the village but also in Makurdi, which had been occupied by others who had no intention of returning it to its rightful owner; his hotels; his fleet of lorries; and his bank balance. Everything was as if it had never been.

Somehow, Papa stayed positive.

After the war, it was Papa's friend Nelson Onuzulike who secured us an apartment in Enugu, one of the biggest cities in the Southeast. I once asked Papa why Uncle Nelson was being so kind to us, already fully cognizant that everything seemed to come at a price. I will never forget his response. "Have you forgotten what I taught you, Nkem? Always treat others the way you want them to treat you. Nelson and I share this philosophy. We both know that we have to take care of each other, especially when the other is in need. Never forget this."

Enugu, a dusty city made even dirtier by all the cars driving on its unpaved roads, was a fresh canvas for Papa and for our entire family. Papa heard there was a need for strong, capable hands to farm the fertile land after the ravage of war. Enugu was to be the new land of opportunities, central to the redevelopment of the region. It was the miracle of a new beginning we all needed.

Papa soon acquired a small farm in the famed Milliken

Hills on the then-virgin outskirts of the city. As part of the rebuilding efforts, the land was going for almost free. No stranger to building from the ground up, Papa hoed and tilled and reaped the fruits of a first harvest. He loved sharing his joy of watching the mounds of earth transform into tall stalks of maize plants and the green leaves of ụgụ, which always fetched a good price in the market.

Mama, Rose, Jo, Anayo, and Nwogo, all of whom were living in Enugu, were there to celebrate the harvest. Once again, the Edemobi family was hopeful for the future.

And once again, hope was crushed.

Some said it was his gallbladder, others that it was *juju* — the evil eye — others still that it was from a heart broken by the war.

I was nineteen when Papa died in April 1972. He was fifty-nine.

I felt Papa's passing before I heard the news. I didn't want to believe it, but I knew better than to ignore what my spirit was telling me. I was no longer a stranger to my premonitions. The war had provided ample opportunity to experiment with the truth of their predictions. So when my school mother, a certain Josephine Akunyili, came to my dorm room, a solemn look on her face, I savoured the last seconds until her words would upend my world. *"Papa gị anwụgo!"*

At her words, I felt a wall around my chest closing in, shutting out the last whims of a girl. Not wanting to get lost in my own pain, I focused on worrying about Mama and how she was handling it, and thinking of my siblings, including my youngest sister, Nwogo, who soon wouldn't even remember her own father. My heart broke for my loss and theirs, and for all our unborn children, none of whom would have a chance to meet their grandfather.

I had to wait until the morning to board the first bus to Enugu from Nsukka. I was sadder than I knew possible, but my eyes were as dry as a bucket drawing from an empty well.

Fifteen

*"No matter the grief, nothing the eye can see
will make it bleed."*

CHANGE AND I HAD become well acquainted over the years, but this was the most difficult of its visits to date. It felt like no matter how confused life got, or how tough things were, Papa had always been my anchor.

And now he was gone. He was only fifty-nine, far too young to have breathed his last breath. He'd still had a dream of rebuilding and had trusted the ingredients of its success: his own capacity, hard work, trust in God's grace, and an honest dedication to his craft. I too had trusted that he would achieve his dreams and more.

I think his death caused me to withdraw into my own world, while refocusing on how to make him proud of me, even in death. I vowed to never again leave something for tomorrow that could be done today. I never wanted to run out of time like my father did.

I found comfort in praying, communicating with the heavens the way Nne had taught me to. I prayed for Papa's soul that it might find its way to heaven, and I prayed to God the father,

God the son, the Holy Spirit, and Mary the mother of God, and all the angels watching over him and over us.

The weeks following his death were dedicated to planning the funeral — an event often grander than a wedding. As is customary with Igbos, he was to be buried in his hometown in Nanka.

Mama cried easily in these months, but she was especially emotional when Papa's friends, without prompting, started to donate money towards the funeral costs and to support Mama and our family. Mama spent almost every kobo of the money she received, insisting that Papa have a burial fit for a king. All of Nanka came to honour the life of a great man. Even we hadn't fully realized how beloved Papa was. So many people he had supported were there that day, arriving from their homes in the East, in the North, and all around.

Navigating the thick crowd in my white lace funeral ensemble, I felt older than my years. There I was, somewhere between a young woman and a girl, hair bound up in black thread, my eyes red and swollen from the tears I only allowed myself to shed in the privacy of my own company.

Everybody around me seemed to be breaking down, and so, between the desire to always go against the current and to be strong for my family, I saved my emotions for another time. In public, greeting the many sad faces and expressions of well-wishers, my eyes remained dry.

It had become a habit of mine during the war to worry about my siblings like an eldest sibling might. When the family returned to Nanka to seek refuge, I had become the one they all turned to for help, especially since I knew my way around the village and its ways. This dependence on me tilted the natural order of age-defined leadership in my favour. I quickly ascended to become the general in charge of the home, second only to my mother, and I stayed there, even after the war. This dynamic meant that, after the death of Papa, my siblings, and even Mama continued to look to me for direction.

In those years, various members of our family were still finding their postwar identity. My elder brother, Joseph — scorned for his disabilities, both a stutter and an extreme hunchback, and frustrated that they didn't reflect the man he wanted to be — had become an alcoholic. Jo surrounded himself with dubious company with whom he could drink the cruelty of the world away.

My eldest sister, Gloria, married to the man from Isuofia, continued to take care of our younger sister Ngozi, and was expecting her first child. My older sister Rose was to be married very soon, and Elizabeth, whom we all called Eliza, the fourth of the six Edemobi girls and just a few years younger than me, was completing her teacher training in Uwani.

Anayo, the younger of the boys, was in boarding school and was mostly supported by the patronage of wealthy relatives who had come in support of the family, including the Adimorahs as well as the Ezeilo family.

And lastly there was Nwogo, the youngest girl and baby of the house, who lived with Mama. After our father's death, Mama sold the farm and began trading food and provisions, which she bought in bulk and sold to neighbours.

Mama didn't like that I worried about her, but it was like asking a cock not to crow. I worried especially as I noted a steady decline in her health. She insisted, as she always had, that she was fine and that God was her strength. But I saw that bearing so much of the weight of her grief and worry for the well-being of her entire family was exhausting the last of her will.

I desperately wanted to keep the promise I made to my father as his frozen body was lowered into the ground: that no matter what, I would take care of them all.

Part II

1972–1994

Sixteen

"Those who are born on top of the anthill take
a short time to grow tall."

EVEN AFTER PAPA'S DEATH, the Edemobi family name continued to earn me and the rest of the family the goodwill of others.

One notable family who came to our aid was the Ezeilos.

Professor J.O.C. Ezeilo was a man of medium build, with an expressive face and slender body. His glasses always perched atop his small eyes, emphasizing his receding hairline. Mrs. Ezeilo was a small, birdlike woman with a warm smile. Both natives of Ifite Nanka, Mrs. Ezeilo was also the principal of QRSS and her husband served as the vice-chancellor of University of Nigeria Nsukka. They had become close with Papa and Mama over the years. After the war, even before Papa died, they had taken me under their wing, treating me as one of their own; their care was rooted in the love and respect they had for my father and the privilege of both their positions as heads of key educational institutions.

The Ezeilos' comparative wealth, their interest in me, and their mentorship meant that while I was living in the boarding quarters of QRSS, I had access to their family home at the vice-chancellor's lodge. The atmosphere in their home reminded me of Makurdi, as it attracted dozens of visitors over the course of every week, allowing me a glimpse of the sophisticated life I had left behind. But this access, however welcome, highlighted even more all that we had lost as a family.

It was in those years that I perfected my adaptability. I could fit in with anyone—rich, poor, old, quiet, boisterous; whatever the circumstance required, I could morph effortlessly to fit. All worlds felt familiar to me, be it in the village or the city, with the young or old, or with seasoned diplomats and intellectuals, or teachers, farmers, and traders. I knew them all intimately.

I valued how human interactions allowed for this gift to flourish, and did not take the relationship with the Ezeilos for granted. They were generous with their time; I greatly enjoyed conversations with both the professor and his wife, which filled the gaps of knowledge that books could not give me. These conversations were particularly special as they reminded me once again of those with my father.

I spent my time in class, studying, doing chores, in the dorm room, or at the Ezeilos. Twice every three months, during midterm break and at the end of term, I went home to visit Mama and my brothers and sisters still in Enugu.

Towards the end of 1973, I sat for the West African School Certificate (WASC) regional exam along with students of different ages who were all still trying to catch up following the disruptions of the war. I felt confident going in, as I had worked hard, staying up late and waking up early to study. Whenever I had felt tired, I would think of the vow I had made to my father and found new strength to keep going.

Still, I waited for the results with some trepidation. When the announcements were posted on the school board, dozens of girls, myself among them, all strained for a glimpse of our names. There it was: Dora Edemobi, aggregate seven. The best score possible. I later found out that it was one of the best results in the country that year.

In fact, my result was apparently so outstanding that it almost got me into trouble. That year, as we would find out, there had been an unusually high incidence of "expo" — questions leaked in advance of the exam. The government was cracking down, and they were starting with those with suspiciously high grades.

Early on a Monday morning after school assembly, Mrs. Ezeilo had been surprised to be informed of the presence of two policemen in her office, asking for me by name. Even more shocking was the revelation that they wanted to interrogate me, as they told Mrs. Ezeilo they suspected me of expo.

At this, Mrs. Ezeilo burst into a fit of laughter. Seeing the bewilderment in the policemen's eyes, she excused herself, imploring their patience. A few moments later, she returned with my results from the previous years, each showing my near-perfect scores with a wide margin over the next pupil.

It was clear to the policemen that they were mistaken and that I had earned my distinction. She had been all too happy to share with me the details of their visit, a story she told many times over.

My result attracted the federal government of Nigeria undergraduate scholarship. The scholarship would cover my full tuition as well as provide a living stipend for the entirety of my university studies. I was relieved and elated. Securing the scholarship was the centrepiece of my plan to succeed and support my family. It was also the only feasible way I could have continued to shoulder the financial burdens of my studies. It was somewhat surreal to not only get something I had been dreaming of for years but, even more so, to finally feel my luck change.

And with this, happy and grateful to God, I transitioned from secondary school to university.

Seventeen

*"If you wish to move mountains tomorrow,
you must start by lifting stones today."*

UNIVERSITY OF NIGERIA NSUKKA (UNN) was founded in 1955 as the first indigenous and first autonomous university in Nigeria, boasting an expansive campus of green fields and neatly lined buildings framed by tall trees filled with the sound of birds.

UNN was a clear choice for me for two reasons: despite being greatly impacted by the war, it remained one of the best universities in the country, famed for academic excellence; furthermore, I wanted to stay in the region to be close to my family.

Once at UNN, I finally began to feel a semblance of control over my own life — a new beginning where the sky was the limit. I lived on campus in a dorm room I shared with three other women, one of whom, Ijeoma, would become a close friend.

My exam results meant that I could have my pick of any discipline. I made the choice to study pharmacy. It aligned with my passion to study the properties of the local plants we

95

had used as medicine in the village — I had always marvelled at the ease with which Nne and her friends worked with plants to heal whoever was ailing — and with the dream I had of someday becoming a renowned professor.

Convincing the faculty, led by Professor Ezeilo, of my choice of pharmacology over medicine would not be easy. Medicine was the more impressive choice and as such the expected path for me.

I knew that true to the Igbo proverb *Ewere ọtụtụ chọọ ewu ojii tupụ abalị aru* — "It is best to look for the black goat in the light of day" — the sooner I addressed my choice with Professor Ezeilo, the better.

I made my way to the vice-chancellor's office, taking my time to greet lecturers and students I passed on the way, our conversation a fluent mix of English and Igbo. I knocked lightly on Professor Ezeilo's door, knowing how he hated to be disturbed.

"Come in," he barked, softening once he saw that it was me. Even professors had their favourites. He knew me well enough to notice right away that I was deeply distraught.

Going over pleasantries with the deftness of a skilled diplomat, I dove right into the matter. "I have decided not to go for medicine."

There was an uncomfortable pause, during which I knew he was weighing all options.

"Why? It should be a natural step." I could tell he was being gentle with me, which he had been doing since Papa died.

"Daddy," I said, calling him by a name of reverence and familial intimacy, "in all those years living in the village, one of the things I enjoyed most was learning about all the plants that I had never seen before.

"Imagine learning all their uses! For example, in the first months I was in the village and I always had rashes, Nne used a concoction of coconut and aloe vera to cure me, which worked better than the expensive ointments Mama had sent over from Makurdi. And this is just one example. There are so many other plants Nne and other women in the village use whose properties have not been understood, or even recognized. Pharmacy feels for me to be the future. And it lies in how we can study and expand the knowledge and uses of our indigenous plants."

Impassioned, I continued: "How many people in Nanka can afford medicine from the hospital? Yet how many need health care? Pharmacy is going to be more important than medicine, especially when it comes to exploiting the benefits of local remedies that are more accessible to a larger group of people. I want to work on preserving this heritage, but even more importantly, I want to dedicate myself to researching and better utilizing these natural gifts."

Professor Ezeilo was already nodding his head, perhaps seeing the wisdom of my words and knowing that passion was the greatest instigator of success.

I had his blessing.

Eighteen

*"Who knows how water entered into
the stalk of the pumpkin?"*

UPON BEGINNING MY STUDIES, I was shocked by just how arrogant and condescending the student doctors could be towards everybody else. Pharmacists, it seemed, bore the brunt of their disdain, for we were seen as wannabe doctors who didn't make the cut.

In my lowest moments, I questioned my choice to study pharmacy, knowing how easily I could have been on the other end of the arrogance with the almighty medical students, even if only to get a break from their snide, thinly veiled taunts.

Working in the dispensary of the teaching hospital of UNN, I had ample opportunity to observe and interact with these doctors. The power of healing that had once been reserved for the gods and their messengers was now theirs. You'd think they owned the very earth on which they walked. But I swallowed my pride and applied myself to the study of pharmacy.

My roommate Ijeoma, who was studying to be a veterinary doctor, and I had become even closer. But try as she

may, she could not persuade me to join her on evenings out
with other students, who enjoyed gathering at the back of the
dorm to listen and dance to Fela Kuti. His Afrobeat music was
reigning along with the hi-life sounds of Orlando Julius. I had
nothing against the music, although I did prefer the gospel
singers whose songs could be heard blaring from the stalls
that bordered the campus where local traders sold anything
and everything that a student might need.

Some said I was boring, especially after I rebuffed the
advances of Titus from Asaba, whom many regarded to be
a very eligible young man. He was a trader and brought me
crates of Fanta whenever he came to visit, which made him
even more popular among my friends. I was never too sure
why I rejected his advances. Part of it might have been the
voices of the nuns at QRSS reminding me to beware of men
leading me astray. But I think the truth is that I was still grieving Papa's death and afraid of any frivolity. This meant that
instead of thoughts of Titus bringing me joy, they caused me
concern. I was in the middle of my first-year exams when I
concluded that I didn't see a future for us and that his attention
was just a distraction. He was sad when I told him to stop
coming by, and he knew me well enough to know that I was
serious. I never saw him again.

I WAS STANDING in my usual place behind the counter of
the dispensary at the teaching hospital, my eyes not missing anything, observing the comings and goings of students,
professors, and patients.

I was in a good mood that day, and it helped that I was

looking good. I had just been at the salon over the weekend to get the roots of my permed dark-brown hair relaxed and set in rollers. Soft curls framed my face.

I didn't wear any makeup in those years, preferring the natural glow of my caramel skin, which shone with youth and health. My wide smile reflected my state of mind. I had learned to fully embrace and love the gap in my teeth between my left lateral incisor and canine. While I took care with my appearance, I liked to keep things simple, with minimal jewellery and long, high-waisted skirts that flattered my athletic figure.

He pierced through the blur of my thoughts. A tall and very dark man, skin the colour of coal, dressed in the signature white coat of doctors, but too young to be a doctor. A medical student, I concluded. He had the wide smile of someone aware of his own charm.

"*Nne Kedụ*, good morning," he greeted, without the usual condescension of a medical student.

I smiled in response. "May I help you?" I wondered why I suddenly felt so nervous.

"Please, I am not well. I need Lariam. I think I have malaria."

Doctors, I had noticed, loved to self-diagnose. I nodded and asked him about his symptoms, listening intently before fetching the requested medicine.

"I am sure you know how to take these," I said, "but please just be sure to try to get some rest so that your body can heal."

He took the pills from me but he stayed where he was.

"Please may I talk to you?" He asked, his eyes darting from me to my colleague counting pills in the background, motioning to the open doorway and the privacy of a busy hallway. With the signature spring to my step, I got up and followed him, curious and intrigued.

"You are the opposite of what people told me about pharmacists working here."

For such a strong aura, his voice carried the tremor of hesitation. He later told me that he had been reluctant to come to the pharmacy, given the reputation of the department pharmacists as "pompous, full of themselves, very cocky, and insolent, handling drugs as if they are handling your destiny." Funny how pharmacists thought the exact same of doctors.

"I wondered," he added, "how do I subject myself to the insult of these pharmacists!"

I laughed and he immediately softened, a vulnerability seeping into his eyes that felt like a window to the man behind the white coat.

Regaining his composure, he asked, "Who are you? What's your name?" He beheld me as one would a precious and unrecognized discovery.

I laughed again, this time at his charm, appreciating the attention and aware of my growing curiosity about this dark doctor.

"I'm Dorothy," I answered, rewarding his smile with one of my own.

"Dora, Nne" came his response, *Nne* in this case meaning "Ms." "Well done *o*, keep it up," he said as he turned to walk away and meet the rest of his afternoon.

"You asked me my name, but you didn't tell me yours," I chastised him, causing him to stop in his tracks.

"Chike, Chike Akunyili" was his response. We stood smiling, both knowing that something had changed in those few short minutes.

I found my voice first. "Are you by any chance related to Josephine Akunyili?" I asked. I observed his happy surprise.

"How do you know my sister?"

"Your sister! Senior JoJo was my school mother in QRSS," I answered, pleasantly surprised at the coincidence.

"Small world," he said before he began to walk away. He hesitated, turned around, and said, "I hope it continues to stay small." I hid a laugh as he walked away, but not before I caught his own smile.

He came by often after that day. There was always something to talk about: the school body; the Nigeria of our dreams; the state of the country under the military leadership of Olusegun Obasanjo, who had just taken over from Yakubu Gowon; and the plight of the people. He was deeply knowledgeable and I was happy to have the intellectual stimulation beyond the dry interactions of prescription and gossip, the latter of which I abhorred.

He often shared stories of his experiences as a soldier in the Biafra war. Chike had been just a boy carrying a heavy AK-47 and in constant search of the enemy. He told me stories of days spent walking, swollen ankles encased in heavy military boots, unable to slow down because of the threat from Nigerian soldiers. He got emotional when he spoke of the challenges of being alone with his thoughts in the bush after his entire squad had died or scattered in the aftermath of an attack, with the situation further exacerbated by no real means of communication — there was only so much that fires and smoke signals could communicate. And with so many villages burning, no one could be sure if smoke rising in the distance was a cry for help or a sign that it was already too late.

It broke his heart, he said, to watch as Biafra burned. He, like many young men, had signed up to defend their fragile newborn nation. Nothing could have equipped him for what was to come. During the war, he had seen too many deaths. Wailing children still strapped to the backs of their dead mothers, both unclaimed, left to rot in bushes. He witnessed the unchecked male rapaciousness of both Biafran and Nigerian soldiers driven by power as much as by their own lust. Hunger, we agreed, was the worst enemy. The people had eaten the lizards, the snakes, and the rats, until nothing crawled by anymore. It was as though the Earth too was mourning and had nothing left to give.

"Some even ate their own children!" When he said this, my mind went back to the rumours I had heard. I still couldn't imagine what a decision like that would cost someone.

Chike often shared long into the night, about times when he had to walk away from families starving to death, swollen stomachs, bloodied and sometimes maimed people looking at him imploringly with sunken eyes. The desperate mothers begging for him to take their children with him. There was never anything he could do to help them.

Even sleep could not stop the images and the sounds of men, women, and children calling to God — *Chi ike*, "great God" — imploring the Almighty to hear their pain. It felt, he said, like they were calling directly to him by name, Chike. He had never felt more powerless, knowing there was nothing he could do but steel his heart against pity, lest he himself be lost in the pain. He prayed that God would be more successful.

The war tested him in every way, and it would be many years before he would once again know the warmth of having a lighter heart — according to him, this happened when he met me.

The many times Chike had come by my hostel were evidence enough of his interest. And we had so much in common, including our shared faith, as he too was a God-fearing Catholic and had even served as a Mass servant for a large part of his childhood.

We were both single and interested in one another. The next step was for us to get married; otherwise, there would be no reason to continue to see one another.

Nineteen

"A person who arrives at a feast when the cooked meat is being pulled out of the pot does not know what was endured by others to catch and cook it."

CHIKE'S FATHER ALWAYS THOUGHT he had been the one who introduced us to one another.

It was a Friday and I was looking forward to my regular weekend trip to Enugu. In addition to visiting my mother and siblings, I was also keen to make another stop. Since I had found out that my QRSS school mother was also Chike's sister, I saw it as a welcome sign to reconnect with her. I was excited at the thought of stopping by Chike's family home in Coal Camp, imagining that seeing where he came from would allow me some insight into his life.

I rang the bell of the Akunyili family flat, barely containing my eagerness to see the look on JoJo's face upon seeing me. JoJo had graduated a year ahead of me, so it had been a few years since we had seen one another. I would mention knowing Chike, our friendship, and the happy coincidence of him being connected to her, but I wasn't sure I would share that we were interested in one another. That felt more like news for Chike to break.

An older man answered. From the look of him, he was Chike and JoJo's father. He smiled, clearly delighted by the visit, though his eyes were questioning.

"Papa, good afternoon, sir," I said in respectful greeting. "I am looking for JoJo."

At this, his smile widened, revealing beautiful white teeth. "*Nnọọ*, welcome, come in," he said, ushering me inside. He insisted that I stay for a Fanta and wait for JoJo, who was not home, all the while observing me keenly.

"*Onye ebee ka ị sị na ị bụ?*" he asked. Where a person came from said so much about who they were.

"*Abụ m onye Nanka*" came my confident answer. Nanka people were known to be industrious, and I was proud of my stock.

"*Kedụ afa gị*," he asked, wanting to know my name.

"Dora Edemobi," I answered.

"*Gịnị?*" he all but shouted in response. "What? You mean you are related to Paul Young?"

"He was my father," I answered. I was no stranger to such interactions, as my father's reputation had remained well after his death.

"*Ewooo, nwa m*, my daughter, my condolences." It would seem he had heard of PY's untimely death. "*Onwụ ajọka*, death is ugly," he added, almost to himself.

Although JoJo was not home, leaving was no longer an option and I spent the afternoon with Julius Okoye Akunyili. I learned that he was a trader who sold textiles in Ogbete market and that his wife, who usually would have been home, had gone to visit a relative. He was a very expressive man, and he made no secret of the joy he felt that he had been home to greet me. Saturdays, he said, were usually his busiest day at the market, but he had been feeling slightly unwell and had decided to rest his ageing body that day. That it was the very same day I chose to come by was not lost to him. He was the kind of man who avoided whistling at night and carried a rosary in his front pocket. He saw everything that transpired to lead me to their home as auspicious.

With the sun making its way west, he bid me farewell but not before asking me to come back the following weekend. Not one to refuse the request of an elder, I agreed.

True to my words, I came back to the Akunyili family home. This time, Chike was also there. It was to be an introduction!

I had to struggle the greater part of the evening not to burst out laughing at the situation I found myself in. I held back giggles and exchanged stolen glances and smiles with Chike, seated across from me in the now familiar sitting room.

More than once, I caught Chike's mischievous eyes. We seemed to have established an unspoken agreement not to let Papa in on the fact that we had already met. He seemed all too happy with himself that he was the one to introduce us to one another.

So we sat and smiled, listening to him encourage us to get to know each other and emphasizing that we had everything it took to start a family together — the compatibility of education, the pedigree of family, and the gift of youth.

I knew that it was not my place to speak, and Chike seemed to be nodding enough for both of us, clearly happy with his father's choice.

At the end of Papa's lengthy speech, as much an attempt at persuasion as a celebration of his own matchmaking skills, he said, "If you give me the go ahead, I'll organize everything!"

At this juncture, he discreetly left the two of us together, claiming he needed to send the lurking house help on an errand.

Never one to mince words, I looked directly into Chike's eyes and said, "He has a good point, it is a good match."

I knew the glimmer in his eyes signalled his full agreement. I could tell that Chike was happy that he didn't have to convince me. And I was happy with a man who knew what he wanted. Fifteen minutes later and we had the answer Papa wanted to hear.

We were to be married.

It was agreed that the Akunyili family would come calling for my hand in two weeks, just enough time to get together the customary gifts that would comprise my bride price.

In the meantime, I had to inform my mother.

I made my way from Coal Camp to number four Ani Street. I turned into the muddy lanes of our street aboard an okada motorcycle, which was doing its best to avoid water-filled potholes. As I greeted the gatemen of her apartment complex, my mother stepped out onto the cemented veranda overlooking the street, surprised to see me back so soon.

"*Nwa m nnọọ,* welcome," Mama called out with a wave and a quiet smile. She returned to the parlour to wrap up a conversation with a friend, who Mama would share later had come to seek counsel on marital issues she was having with a wayward husband.

"*Mama Kedụ!*" I asked as I hugged her, greeting her guest as well, before sitting down on one of the low couches with matching satin fabric. A picture of the Virgin Mary was the sole artwork in the room. Once the niceties of our reunion were done with and the guest had departed, it was my time to announce the news.

"Mama, there is a man who wants to marry me. His name is Chike Akunyili. He is a doctor and a God-fearing Catholic from Agulu," I said, giving her all the information I knew she would want to know.

My mother rejoiced at the news. While she was very grateful for my support over the years, which extended to my younger siblings Anayo and Nwogo, she had always been concerned about who would take care of me. In addition, marriage was seen as such an important part of the coming of age of a woman, overshadowing any other success.

In the days to come, Mama had the chance to meet Chike. Not only was he a doctor, but Chike was also a man of faith who knew the value of hard work. Her joy was complete. Now, she said, she could rest in peace to see me settled.

When I took Chike to meet Nne and Onye Nkuzi in Isuofia, Nne, not one to mince words, said to Chike, "You are a lucky man; Nkem will be a great woman."

Chike took this in stride, smiled, and added, "I will do everything in my power to ensure this."

I too felt lucky, as I had absolutely no hesitations about getting married to Chike: he was God-fearing, charming, handsome, successful, smart, funny, and the only one I had ever felt strongly about. Before I met him, I hadn't really made time to be a young woman, nor had life allowed me much of an opportunity. This felt different. It was beautiful to fall in love.

Just weeks after our meeting, our two families had met and were discussing my bride price. I was twenty-two and Chike twenty-seven when in 1976, just five months after we met, we were married.

Our traditional wedding was a small affair in Nanka. Agulu kinsmen gathered with offerings of yams, goats, chickens, and bags of rice worthy of an educated woman from a good family. I wore gold and red, colours that highlighted my light skin, with bright-orange coral beads draped across the heavy lace. My love for weddings was born on this day. I couldn't remember ever being happier — my heart was light and I had so much trust in the future. Anything was possible.

The traditional wedding was followed by a church wedding, one of the greatest ever seen in Enugu. Professor Ezeilo was the chairman of the wedding. Through a combination of influences, everybody who was anybody in Enugu was there, even the attorney general, Justice Adimorah, an old friend of the Edemobi family, made excuses just to be present on the day.

I wore a lace ballgown, long and white, with a delicate long veil that made me feel angelic. Chike was resplendent in a light-coloured suit with striped tie adorning a formal shirt with decorative pleats. His hair was combed out in a rounded afro, his face framed by trimmed sideburns. We both smiled constantly. I sometimes caught the critical glance of some of Chike's siblings, but I dismissed this; nothing could take away from the joy of the day. We were married by a dear friend of Chike from his time volunteering at the seminary, Father Akpunonu.

My name changed from Dorothy Nkemdilim Edemobi — "Gift of God whose destiny will be fulfilled that I may rest my soul" — to Dorothy Nkemdilim Akunyili, "Gift of God whose destiny will be fulfilled that my wealth overflows."

Twenty

"If a child hungers for a palm nut, it does not
upset his stomach."

I FELT LIKE THE HAPPIEST woman in the world. I walked around with a smile carving a permanent indention in my heart. I liked the sound of my new name, Mrs. Akunyili, as much as its meaning, which mirrored my current state of mind — my wealth truly did overflow.

I felt so deeply blessed for this man that I now called husband. Chike reminded me of my own father and the gentleman he had been. I felt lucky to have found these traits again, and in the person of my husband. A man who loved me so fully and admired me so openly, who insisted on opening and closing doors for me, who stood up to offer me his seat. A man with whom I danced into the early hours of the morning. He was everything I prayed for, and together we dreamed of the life we wanted to build together.

My prayers were all thanking God every day for the way my life was revealing itself, thanking His son and His mother Mary and the Holy Spirit. I was nothing if not thorough.

We had big dreams to open a hospital together, where I

would work as the lead pharmacist and he as the head surgeon. We would have children who would all become doctors and go on to be powerful and influential, impacting the fabric of the country. We dreamed of a home that was filled with people, food, and laughter. It was the beginning of a new chapter of dreams that overwhelmed me with how big they were, born from a place I had ignored and now bursting forth.

Soon after Chike's graduation, a few months before mine, he was posted to Kaduna, in the far north. In the village of Jaban Kogo, he was to serve his mandatory youth service, a government program that aimed to foster a culture of servant leadership and intercultural dialogue. He would be there for almost an entire year.

He couldn't have been gone for more than a few weeks and I already missed him. The last man I had missed was my father.

I missed Chike's jokes, his company, the many moments spent together, feelings that were even more intensified because I was carrying his child. I was aglow with love, for life, for Chike, and for our unborn child. This was especially so after the pain of losing an earlier pregnancy in the first weeks following our wedding. Chike had reprimanded me for crying, reminding me how normal it was for a woman to miscarry. I felt irritated that he would ask me to dismiss my feelings in service of rationality, but I also knew that he had a point. So I wiped my tears and intensified my prayers, making sure this time to ask God to protect future pregnancies.

I was in my first trimester when Chike had to leave for Jaban Kogo. It was difficult to go through the weeks that followed with Chike not being home, but luckily for me, I didn't have any morning sickness, and the pregnancy was relatively easy.

In my fifth month, I decided to make a trip north to surprise him, not least because it was a very important day for him, marking the opening of a clinic for which he had fundraised. I journeyed for nine hours by rail and by road, with nothing to do but watch the landscape change from lush green to arid brown. I thought about the last time I was on a train, from Makurdi to Enugu. I tried to picture the girl who sat alone by the windows, searching her face for my likeness.

Soon, the faces of people coming on board the train changed, as lean, tall men in caftans replaced short, stocky ones. I observed women dressed in several layers of fabrics and scarves, which covered everything but their faces — they reminded me of the Virgin Mary. In witnessing the physical manifestations of our differences, I couldn't help but think of the bloodshed of the last years and a country still trying to heal.

In the centre of Jaban Kogo, a small crowd was already gathering, braving the evening sun and the heat. I had arrived earlier in the day and bided my time until I could blend with the group of people heading towards the day's festivities. I beamed each time I overheard the whispers of strangers commenting on this Igbo boy, a doctor who had come and galvanized the town in a way no one had before.

Once at the town centre, my surprise trip north was rewarded when Chike's eyes met mine and lit up with bewilderment. He burst into a wide smile; his expression seemed to say, "I am surprised, but then again, I am not!"

I watched the day unfold alive with pride to see my husband being carried shoulder-high. Chike too fed off the adulation, clearly happy that his wife could be there to see him in his glory. From that day forth, and for many years to come, I would sing and dance, teasing him with a newfound name — Doctor Jaban Kogo, Doctor Jaban Kogo.

Twenty-One

"A tree cannot stand without roots."

THREE WEEKS BEFORE OUR first child was due, I was at home resting in our new flat in Enugu. It wasn't much, but it was one of the perks of Chike's new role as the house officer at the university teaching hospital. I had just received the result of my final exam; I made second class upper, short of everyone's expectation of first class. I felt no disappointment, for I had given it my best. Between being heavily pregnant all through-out the last year and taking the exams at the same time, I knew I was pushing things even by my standards.

Lost in thought, I heard a rustle of keys in the front door, and my heart skipped, as I was sure it was Chike. Never one to hide my joy and excitement, I jumped up and ran to the door to leap into his arms, forgetting that unlike the last time we embraced, my swollen stomach stood between us.

I went into labour that same evening, and Chike would tell the story for many years to come that I was so excited to see him that my water broke, or as he put it, "She started draining liquor."

He was by my side when our first-born child came into the world on September 15, 1978. We named her Ijeoma — meaning "safe journey" — for ours was a beautiful journey and we wished the same for our daughter, a prayer we bestowed in her name.

Mama insisted on coming to stay with us for a few months after the birth, as part of a customary practice of Ọmụgwọ, a form of postpartum care and intergenerational knowledge transfer where mothers visit their daughters at the birth of their child, especially the first born, to ease them into their new role.

Between graduation, my first internships at the University of Nigeria Teaching Hospital (UNTH), and motherhood, life became a crash course in juggling.

I don't know how I would have done it all without the support of my mother. First, her presence meant that I could rest. She was with me every step of the way, showing me everything from how to breastfeed — even though I insisted on switching to Nan milk, which was marketed as being better than breast milk — to how to wrap and pin cotton napkins, which I soaked in a basin to be washed at the end of every day to be ready for yet another day of use. I already knew how to strap the baby on my back following years of practice with Nwogo, my youngest sister. Mama encouraged me to let Ijeoma cry so she could learn independence, to not worry about her when she had a fever, or when she would have light falls and hit her head, promising me that her falls were part of her learning journey.

A few months after Ijeoma was born, just when life was finally beginning to resume normality — even Mama's diabetes and health were stable — we found out that Nwogo was also diabetic.

Nwogo was in junior secondary school and sickly. I had initially dismissed it as a result of the struggles of a new school and being away from home. But this became more unlikely when she started to lose a lot of weight and complain of abdominal pains. I insisted that she visit the university hospital for tests.

"Sister Do Do," she teased cheekily, "you worry too much. Remember I am not your child." She knew that this always made me rethink my actions. And her sweet disposition meant that I would forgive her teasing very easily. Nwogo was thirteen years younger than me; at not quite twelve years old, she sometimes did feel more like my daughter than my sister.

I was glad I had insisted when the tests came back with the news of her condition. Mama was devastated by the news, understanding perhaps more than anyone else what this diagnosis signalled for her daughter's quality of life, with the endless dependency on insulin. I found myself consoling both my mother and my sister, assuring them that, no matter what happened, everything was going to be okay.

In truth, I was less confident.

In a country with an unreliable power supply, made even worse by the series of coups that had crippled our already stretched infrastructure, I was alarmed for the well-being of my sister. My alarm was even greater knowing just how hard it was to ensure that the medicines we were selling in UNTH were not counterfeit. Lawlessness in the country felt like it was attempting to break its own record on a daily basis, and the counterfeit drug market had become a lucrative niche. How could I ensure that the drugs for Nwogo were not fake when even within the hospital we had no way of knowing for sure?

I could not allow myself to dwell on the worst, so I held my fears hostage. I focused on a plan to ensure that Nwogo had the support she needed to fight the disease and intensified my prayers. We decided that she should come live with Chike and me, so that I could better care for her, and she me, helping with Ijeoma.

Half a year later, I found out that I was once again pregnant.

"Chike has to keep his hands to himself," Mama teased, as we discussed what this would mean for her, for me, for school, for Nwogo.

The entire year of that pregnancy was spent serving as a youth corps pharmacist. While many of my friends were sent to different parts of the country to serve, I stayed in Enugu to serve at UNTH, where Chike was working. It was nice to see so much of each other away from home and a newborn. It felt sometimes like old times, and I welcomed these moments when life seemed a lot simpler.

Our one prayer in those months was for a boy. While I welcomed the blessing of a child of any sex, I already had a girl, and I knew that a boy was important for Chike, who after all was a typical Igbo man. I too was a product of a culture that valued and prized a male heir above all else, and a boy would give me peace of mind.

Our son Dozie was born March 25, 1980. He was thin but strong, with wide eyes that shone against his dark skin. I had completed my youth service just in time and had two months to stay home with him before I took on a full-time position as hospital pharmacist at UNTH.

Mama ignored my objections and came once again to do Ọmụgwọ for me.

"You need me, Nkem, and it is my greatest joy as your mother to be able to support you." I continued to resist until she said, "Dora," uncharacteristically calling me by my baptismal name, "let me do this for you."

She was right: I did need her. Though the experience of a first child greatly helped to prepare me, nothing compared to having my mother so close at hand.

Twenty-Two

"No matter how big a child is, she cannot deny that she
was once carried on the back of a woman."

EACH OF OUR CHILDREN has a story to their name, and I sometimes wonder which came first: their name or their personality.

Ijeoma's name was a prayer for her safe journey through
life. And over the years, as she grew in height and years, she
always amazed me by how she was a way-finder for herself
and all her siblings.

At the birth of Dozie, I had my first son. A boy to carry
on the Akunyili name. He was a skinny, blank-eyed boy with
drool running down his chin well into his later years. He was
dark like his father and named by my father-in-law, who died
shortly after his birth. The birth of a boy in Igbo culture signals
the continuity of a lineage — a moment of great celebration.
This was especially so for Papa Julius: it was the birth of the
first son of his first son. So it was that Papa Julius, in his joy
at being alive to witness the continuity of the Akunyili name,
exclaimed, "*Chukwu edozigo m ndụ.*" — "God has restored my
life" — which was shortened to Nnaedozie and then to Edozie,
which simply means "has restored."

As far as I was concerned, he was perfect and all was well with the world.

I was pregnant again just a few months later. Mama hadn't even left since the last Ọmụgwọ, and she was still teasing me about Chike and his excessive love for *our* wife, her term of endearment for me in relation to Chike.

As much as she tried to hide it, I saw Mama's health declining every day.

I REMEMBER THE AIR feeling dryer than usual that year. And like the harmattan, which turns everything from vibrant, lush green to a dusty brown, brittle landscape, it was clear that with each day, the life force was draining from my mother. But unlike the harmattan, it seemed that it could easily be her last season.

She was constantly lethargic and disoriented, and experienced several bouts of nausea that caused further weight loss. That she was visibly in pain and weakened was a critical sign, because her emotional resilience had always shone through in the strength of her body. She was almost never sick, and even when she was, she brushed it off, successfully hiding any pain she felt, perhaps even from herself. There was no hiding now, and my heart ached to see her in so much discomfort.

She didn't share my state of mind. Whenever I fussed or when she caught me praying for her recovery, she said, "Nkem, *o zugo*, it is enough. I am ready."

I wasn't ready.

I didn't want to imagine a world without my mother. I didn't want to once again feel the emptiness of loneliness and of grief, like an empty stomach with no prospect of food. I could not give into this void, reminding myself that it wasn't about me: all that mattered was Mama and relieving her discomfort.

She died in our home, on her bed. I was by her bedside when she took her last breath.

I wasn't yet thirty, and life as I knew it had been shaped by so much loss. And with each, there was a familiar pain. I recognized the sadness in my heart as one might an old friend, and we sat together, in silence, once again reminding one another to keep our strength.

With her death, I vowed once again, on the souls of Papa and my mother, that I would do all I could to take care of the younger ones, especially Nwogo and my younger brother Anayo, who was away in the States on a government scholarship — which was graciously facilitated by Chike's senior sister Mrs. Bosah. I knew I had to be more, to do more — good was not enough. Mulling this over, I made the decision to get a Ph.D.

But first, there was the task of birthing my third child.

I was not due for another two weeks and Chike was at work when my water broke. As Chike tells the story, in the middle of his lecture at the university, he saw a familiar yellow Toyota drive by. He wondered for a moment if it was me, but he dismissed it, as I was home that day resting. He went back to teaching the small group of medical students until his friend and colleague Dr. Osefo rushed in and announced to Chike and everyone else in the lecture hall that I was in labour.

Chike rushed out and headed directly to the delivery ward in the next building, but by the time he arrived, I had delivered. Unable to contain his joy, the words of thanksgiving came to his lips, or as he would later say, "I ejaculated the name": *Somtochukwu* – "join me in praising God." A name of thanks, marking a moment of gratitude. We all called her Somto, meaning "join me in praise."

Somto was born October 6, 1981, my third child and second daughter. She came into the world screaming, either to go back where she came from or as a precursor to a voice that could sing as clear as a bird. Unlike her older siblings, who had their father's colouring, a midnight shade of black, Somto had my fair skin, and with heartbreak and joy I saw in her my mother. I hadn't expected the overwhelming exhilaration I felt to hold her and to know that my mother's spirit had returned in her grandchild.

Twenty-Three

"Listen to the ground and hear the footsteps of the ants."

SOON AFTER THE BIRTH of Somto, I was enrolled in my Ph.D. program at UNN, which meant that mid-1982, I once again had to relocate to Nsukka to take a position as the graduate assistant at the Faculty of Pharmaceutical Sciences. I often had to leave my three children behind in the care of our maid, Antonia, who was a godsend, caring for the children as her own, and of Nwogo. (Chike was not predisposed to caring for the children.) With my entire family in Enugu, I had to make a trip, at least once a week, from Nsukka.

The first weeks were understandably hard; soon, I began to feel like I was sleepwalking between my different identities of scientist, wife, mother, and sister, in that order. The best and most difficult parts of life were during my Ph.D. program.

I was researching the development of a snake antivenom from a native plant, *Schumanniophyton magnificum*; locals called it *agu'uakanmanu*. The plant has short, thin stems and wide leaves and is found only in the bushes of Cross River State in the South South. For many years, locals had brewed a concoction of its leaves or fruit to apply to bites as an elixir for a speedy recovery. The origin of the plant's use as an antivenom is said to trace back to a time when the natives of Cross River noticed something peculiar while watching two snakes fight in the bush. The snakes would pause between deadly strikes to chew the leaves of the *agu'uakanmanu*. And so the locals themselves began to chew the leaves and fruit as an antidote. Over the years, its fame grew and it became a local remedy, and a lure for a curious academic like me.

I was hopeful that my chosen Ph.D. topic would unlock some local wisdom and benefit the many victims of snake bites, which could be lethal. I found a great deal of satisfaction in the dedication of hours spent tabling various samples of plants, snakes, and their venom against the test results of lab rats.

On two or three occasions I had to go to Cross River, some 250 kilometres from Nsukka, for fresh samples. Chike always insisted on coming with me on the five-hour drive to Calabar, the state's capital. The children, so often left to their own devices, would stay home with Nwogo and Antonia.

The first time we went, we weren't sure where to find the plant, but I had heard it could be found in the lone forestry reserve in the state. We must have made quite the picture, with Chike, tall, athletic, wearing a shirt tucked neatly into well-ironed trousers, and me in a dress and low-heeled sandals, accompanied by a local guide in T-shirt and shorts into the bush, all with one objective. The plant was just small enough that it could easily be missed, but we sought out its unmistakable leaves and small brown fruit, and as is always the case with stubborn persistence, we found it.

As part of my Ph.D. program, I was also teaching. Between

teaching, my lab, a husband, and children, the oldest of whom was not quite five, I was exhausted. And as if that wasn't enough, I was once again pregnant, with our fourth.

I was also still a sister. I felt it was important to help support Anayo, who had been all by himself for years in the United States. During his calls, he always seemed like he was putting on a mask. I had an inexplicable ability to see through lies, and something didn't feel right with him. My intuition was proven right when I flew to the States to visit him. (In those days Nigerian Airways and the strength of the naira made such a trip more feasible for a student like myself on a government stipend.) The Anayo I met was worse off than I even imagined. He was so poor that I cried the moment I walked into the place that was his home. It was hotter than an oven, and cockroaches as fat as rats ran between the corners of the one bedroom with a dirty single mattress on the floor and an old sofa in the corner. His government scholarship provided only a minimal stipend. Coupled with the meagre funds I was able to send him, Anayo was mostly left to care for himself, without any family to fall back on. Was this the better life America promised? Wouldn't he have been better off back home in Nigeria? I felt disappointed in myself but also reinvigorated to move up the social ladder so that I might provide him support in the manner that my heart desired.

I stayed on his couch, cleaning and tidying the place as best I could, though it did not seem to make too much of a difference. It was a temporary fix. I vowed that I would go beyond the edges of my perceived best to ensure that he didn't continue to live in this way.

After I bade him goodbye and made my way back home, I

began to push myself harder. Nights got shorter, and sleep less of a necessity. The exhaustion was made much worse by the constant travel between Enugu and Nsukka, the overwhelmingly negative part of my Ph.D. experience.

Initially, not having a car, on most days I had to walk to the end of the street to catch an infrequent, unscheduled bus to the main market, which served as the transportation hub for Enugu and surrounding towns. Before me were always dozens of buses, bare-chested bus conductors shouting at the top of their lungs along narrow streets to win the attention of clients, each promising a departure in the coming minutes, if not seconds, which was rarely the case.

Once in the bus, the discomfort didn't end. Every inch would be filled, our sweaty flesh pressed against each other, the heat made worse by the exhaust fumes floating in from the open windows. In Nsukka, I had to get on yet another bus to the university. In the rainy season, this two-hour ordeal could last up to three or more hours, with cars stuck in the mud creating nightmarish traffic situations.

Eventually, there was some respite, as with Chike's invaluable support, I was able to buy a white Peugeot 504, which Chike brought down to Enugu from Kaduna. Against all hope, this did not make things drastically better, as I lost several hours in traffic, and unlike the days of public transport, I could do nothing other than drive, often at a snail's pace.

There was only so much of this repeated torture I could take, and at some point, I reached my limit and broached the subject with my husband.

"Chike, *ike agwugo m*, I'm tired. I don't think I can do this much longer."

"*Kedụ?* What's wrong?" he asked, concern written all over his face.

I simply shook my head.

"This is about Nsukka, isn't it? I have been telling you that you have to slow down!"

"I know, I know," I said. "I really thought I could handle it, but at this point, I feel that my research is suffering. There is only one of me."

We could both agree that something needed to change; the question was what. After much back and forth, we concluded that I would live temporarily in Nsukka. For various reasons, some based more on feeling than rational thinking, we decided that I would take the children with me, accompanied by Nwogo and Antonia.

As I was now heavily pregnant, the move was slated for after the birth and my recovery. Njideka, or Nji as we all called her, was born January 24, 1983, our fourth child and third girl. By nature, she simply observed, her curious eyes taking in every detail.

While I had been pregnant with her, pushing my limits, no one had been more worried than my mother-in-law, who was concerned for both me and her grandchild. And now Njideka had come into the world with no signs of the stress I'd been under, besides a crooked, overlapping toe. In recognition of the hardship that I had to endure, and perhaps as a slight rebuke, it was my mother-in-law who named her Njideka, meaning "the one I have is greater." A reminder to be satisfied and not fly too close to the sun — for ambition, she said in Igbo, "could scald a woman."

In the coming weeks, with Njideka just a few weeks old,

all four of the children, Nwogo, Antonia, and I moved into a small flat in Nsukka.

None of the changes were easy. In truth, it was harder than I would have cared to admit, but there was no other choice. However, the most difficult parts of juggling so much were made sweet by the joy of the children.

When I arrived home late in the evening, we would huddle together in my room, which I shared with Nwogo. Njideka would be swaddled in the middle of the bed, flanked by the rest of the children, and together we would share tickles and laughs. Our favourite game was when I blew into their belly buttons, which always caused shrieks of joy. There was something really special in those months of all being together. I allowed myself in those moments to be just one of the children.

Once in a while, I took my oldest, Ijeoma, with me to the lab, as I knew that her curious mind enjoyed the plethora of stimulation, not least of all rats in cages and vials of snake venom beside ethanol-filled jars of preserved snake carcasses.

Soon, my trips back to Enugu became more infrequent, which meant that Chike went many weeks on his own. I spent many years afterwards wondering if I had made the wrong decision. After all, who leaves their husband alone and goes to another city? How could I have known that this would be the straw that broke the camel's back, which I didn't even know was overburdened?

The first time I found out was during a visit to Enugu.

At about the same time I left to temporarily live in Nsukka, we had moved out of our flat in Ochumba Close to rent a slightly nicer one in Achara Layout. One day we were visiting Chike in this new flat, which was still unfamiliar to me, when the telephone rang. I responded automatically to the piercing ring, answering, "Akunyilis' residence," coiling my fingers into the spiral phone cord.

"Is this Dora?" The women spoke in a whisper, as if she had a secret to tell and didn't want anyone else hearing.

Something prickled under my skin — and I knew what the strange woman would say before she even spoke. The voice on the other end of the line detailed the life she spent with my husband. She was no good Samaritan in telling me; her voice was filled with gloating malice as she informed me of all the ways I couldn't give my husband what she could.

After I hung up, all I could do was stare out the top-floor window of our flat. I was glad the children were all playing downstairs in the yard, and that Njideka, still just a baby, was taking a nap. Antonia had gone to the market. I was alone.

I started to cry. The type of crying that overtakes one's body. I crumpled on the floor in tears and lay there, wracked by the magnitude of the pain that coursed through my veins and threatened to split me apart. I surrendered to the invasion, heaving, hyperventilating, praying, crying; I allowed myself to feel it all.

Wary of jumping to rash conclusions based on one person's words, I started asking questions of my own. There is no pride in asking your husband's maid, friendly nurses at the hospital, and gatemen what they knew of his comings and goings. Some shared freely; others looked away demurely, telling me all I needed to know. The call was the first of several, as anonymous calls began to come in when word got out that I was asking questions.

I confronted Chike, but I was unsure what I hoped to

achieve with this. He didn't deny any of it, nor did he fully acknowledge the truth. The diplomacy I had always admired in him was now working against the reality at hand.

I sought the help of Father Muoneke, our trusted family friend, who had known me since I was a girl in Makurdi. Not only was he a priest but he knew both Chike and me. His advice to me was that I should forgive. I tried, but it didn't take away the pain. I wore the heartbreak like a second skin. It was raw, a wound that never seemed to heal, whose scabs once picked revealed the pus of a spreading infection.

It's a terrible thing when the source of your light becomes the source of your darkness as well. The worst was I didn't really have anyone to talk to. My hectic schedule and focus on success meant that I had made little time for friendships; with the few people I was close to, even my own sisters, the thought of airing my shame was too overwhelming.

I found some release in sharing my hurt with my best friend, Ijeoma.

"How could he?" I asked again and again. "How could he? Was this my fault? Could I have done more to keep my husband?"

To which Ijeoma reminded me again and again: "Dora, *gee m nti*, listen to me." (She always began like this.) "You have always said that marriage is forever, so no matter what, we just have to forgive and move on."

"But I thought he was different," I muttered, my voice defeated. "I thought he wouldn't disappoint me."

"You did not marry Jesus, okay? Dora, *i nuru ihe m kwuru*, do you hear what I'm saying? You married a human being, okay?"

"Yes, I know, but he was almost like Jesus!"

At this, we both burst out in laughter, which soon faded into silence. I resigned myself to letting it go. It didn't help matters that I was pregnant yet again, with my fifth child.

In my womb was the evidence of the light that had been, and the shadows that lurked in tandem. I feared for the connection between me and the baby, and despaired even more wondering how much of my sadness I was sharing with my unborn child.

Twenty-Four

*"The ocean never swallows a person with whose leg
it does not come in contact."*

IN THE COURSE of a daughter's development as a fetus, she
will develop her entire reproductive capacity for her entire
lifetime — her ovaries filled with millions of eggs. One of the
eggs, once mature, may someday be fertilized and conceive
another girl. That girl in turn will develop her entire reproductive capacity while still in the womb. That is the depth of
the connection that is between mother and daughter across
hundreds of generations.

I was in great emotional turmoil as the fetus grew in my
womb, soaking in my pain along with the vital life force of
my body.

As she grew in my belly, my emotional pain manifested
in physical sickness. My diagnosis was pancreatitis, a condition caused by gallstones that led to severe pain in my upper
abdomen and constant bouts of nausea. Pregnancy was hard
enough in the best of circumstances, but coupled with a sick-
ened body, the entire situation *ajoka* — it was ugly. The doctors
feared for my life and the baby's, and strongly counselled

against any future pregnancies. This child was to be the last, assuming either or both of us survived.

"Poor child," I thought, "to be born out of so much sadness and carried by a severely weakened body." I nurtured a long-time dream of a second son, and I hoped it would be a boy, willing the fetus to sprout small, round testicles.

My body grew weaker with each passing day and under the weight of my pregnancy. Chike worried incessantly about me and wished only that my life would be spared. The child I was carrying was dispensable; although it would be missed, life would rebalance. It wouldn't be the first time we would lose a life, and four children were already plenty. My life, however, he saw as irreplaceable. So the prayers would be for mother and not for child, as no one truly expected that we would both make it through the ordeal.

Imagine, then, the surprise that came when they cut me open and she came through alive and strong. Her name would bear the mark of celebration: *Chineke melụ anyị ọgọ* — "God was merciful to us." Though traditionally a name given to a boy, it seemed apt for her birth and was shortened to Chid-iogo — "God is gracious." A child is a blessing regardless of its sex, so we gave her the middle name of Blessing.

The year was 1985, the month, September. The same day she was born, she was taken away from my deathly sick and weak body to the home of my dear friend and my daughter Ijeoma's godmother, Mrs. Bene Nwachukwu. It would be Bene who raised Chidiogo in my place for the first months of her life. It was the first of many times that we would be separated, testing the bonds between mother and daughter.

With my life and that of my daughter spared, my hope and

trust that everything would be okay was fortified. Even in the height of my sickness, though feverish and weaving in and out of consciousness, I did not lose hope. I made an agreement with God: should He spare my life, I would reclaim for myself the blessing of being fully alive.

Five months after the birth of my fourth daughter, who I called ChiChi, I finally recovered from the illness that nearly claimed my life. And in keeping my pact with God, I no longer allowed myself to dwell on my pain, which I felt was limiting me and, even worse, causing me to be sick. Every day, I pasted a smile on my face. Though cracked, I was far from broken. Without fully healing, I moved on.

The first step was to properly meet my brand-new baby. My friend Ijeoma picked me up from the hospital, and we went directly to Bene's house. ChiChi was sleeping when I arrived. I was happy to simply observe her. I smiled to note that she had lost her lighter skin colour, which is how I remembered her at birth. She was now a darker shade closer to her father's complexion. She had been so tiny then, but now she looked stronger, with skin that folded around her neck and thighs. She was truly *Oyirinnaya* — a carbon copy of Chike. I lowered my body to the floor to better observe her. As I watched her breathe, for the first time since just after her birth I shed a tear. It felt like a catch-all tear and I didn't even try to make sense of it. All that mattered was that I was there, healthy, with my child, and with trust in my heart that everything was going to be okay. It was still with tears in my eyes that I picked her up, her sleeping face resting on me. "Chidiogo," I said slowly, in thanksgiving to God. And with that I got up, holding her with one arm and supporting my still weak body with the other.

With each step as I walked towards the front door and the waiting car, I felt my resolve and knew that I was beginning a new chapter — one where my focus would be on building the best life for my children so that they might not know the hardships I had endured. "Perhaps," I thought wistfully, "it is why I have lived through so much, that they might be spared."

MY RELATIONSHIP WITH CHIKE continued to be tense, but I knew that I had to let my anger and disappointment go. The truth was that there was not much I could do, except find the strength not to dwell on my sadness. We were held by the sanctity and bond of marriage; our contract was "in sickness and in health, till death do us part." I was alive, as was he, so we stayed together, and I focused my energy on the myriad things that required my attention.

Life would soon have gone back to usual but for the added complication of quarrels with my extended family. It is no exaggeration to say that some of Chike's eight siblings quite simply despised me. Their disdain towards me had started slowly, then built over the years. The impetus, according to everything I understood, was that they felt that Chike was too attached to me. This planted the seeds of jealousy, which were not improved by their perception of me as a person. My crimes were multiple but could be summarized as follows: I thought too much of myself and had bewitched their brother, who because of me had no time for them.

"Who does she think she is?" If I had a kobo for every time I heard one of his sisters hiss insulting words . . . They called me names, wouldn't sit in the same space with me, wouldn't eat anything I cooked, wouldn't look me in the eyes. The only words they shared with me were barked. I could do nothing right in their eyes, and I was judged with every step, every word, and sometimes even for my silence.

"The Witch" was what they called me — and in front of me. This name had its origins in a story from an unnamed someone who had seen me go to the village herbalist, a custodian of knowledge about the use of plants for medicinal and healing purposes. No one was interested in my explanation for my visit to these guardians of local wisdom and the connection to my Ph.D. research.

Spurred on by the drama of their accusation, other stories emerged of how I had buried the tendrils of a python at the roots of the avocado tree in the family Obi, and of how during our family's weekly visit to the village, I turned into my snake form at night, slithering around haunting the dreams of sleeping members of the extended family.

I hoped that the situation would be alleviated when Chike purchased a piece of land near the family house and built a house separate from Papa's in which we all lived. Alas, this only brought some minor respite.

And so they did everything to break me, for deep down they wanted me to truly be part of their family, which meant to inherit their shared trauma as my own. Their behaviour had to have been learned from others who had called them names or blamed and shunned them.

Chike spent many hours for years trying to maintain a delicate peace to please both me and his siblings. Never quite putting them in their place, never fully standing up for me, he took on a neutral position. It would take him a lifetime to learn that he couldn't always please everyone, if ever the lesson was learned.

Faced with the challenges of our union and the malice of his family, I built steel around my heart against the ceaseless onslaught of pain. And I slowly and intentionally started to carve for myself a life that did not dwell on disappointments. I remained optimistic about the things I could change in ways that would expose and magnify the mysteries of God's will.

As motivation, I reminded myself of the story of Job from the Bible. Surely this was my test, and I was committed to staying faithful to my belief that "this too shall pass."

Twenty-Five

"A little rain each day will fill the rivers to overflowing."

DURING THOSE PAINFUL YEARS, outcast by Chike's family, and healing from the pain of betrayal, my sister Nwogo had become my rock. Being so much younger than me, and living under my care for so long, she had become even more like a daughter to me.

In many ways she was the one who cared for me, as the last years of living together had been an important solace for me. In my most difficult moments, I had someone, family, with whom I could spend lighter evenings, ignoring the pain that lurked around every corner.

We were very similar; it was hard to pinpoint exactly how, but I would say it was our spirit. We both had an essence that meant that you couldn't miss us in a room, but Nwogo's potent charisma was in the pure satisfaction of being in her presence. Her generous heart added to the feeling that just being around her was a gift within which was the promise of joy. Over the years we had become inseparable, bound by blood, the likeness of our personalities, and this mutual care role we played for one another.

As the last child — the baby of the family — she was loved by all, but I cherished her. I called her Nwogo *nwa mma*, meaning "Nwogo, beautiful child," in acknowledgement and praise of her exquisite beauty, inside and out.

Over the years, helping her manage her diabetes, I had continued to stay positive, as I could not allow myself to dwell on the worst. "*Chetekwa*," I told her, "remember that *onye kwe, Chi ya ekwe* — if you say yes, your personal Chi (Spirit) also says yes. So, no matter what the challenge may be, the final word is with you and your God. You must believe that everything will be okay."

My words seemed to calm her. I would add for extra measure: "Three times I have almost died, three times I have fought death, and now I know that one's own personal conviction is just as powerful a medicine as any drug. You must have faith."

So Nwogo said yes to living, and yes to the insulin I procured for her from the university pharmacy. The years had been good to her and her health stayed stable. We now were able to laugh at memories of how squeamish she had been in the first weeks about injecting herself.

Soon, however, between power outages and increasing incidents of fake insulin, we had to come to terms with the truth that Nigeria was no place for Nwogo to thrive in the long term. The fake-drugs epidemic in those years was getting worse. A study conducted in Nigeria in the late 1980s by former deputy director general of the World Health Organization showed that 54 percent of drugs in every major pharmacy shop were fake.

Before long, me and the rest of my siblings were discussing sending Nwogo abroad. Our brother Anayo already living in the United States made America a natural first choice.

Our disappointment was acute when Nwogo, for no apparent reason, was denied a visa. Not an unusual experience for millions of Nigerians over the years, but with this rejection her ticket to life was also denied.

Undeterred, I redoubled my efforts to care for my sister, and together with the support of the rest of the Edemobi family, we managed her diabetes all through Nwogo's primary school years into secondary school and university. We celebrated the news of her acceptance to the University of Nigeria Nsukka. It was still no small feat for our family with Nwogo as the third one, after Anayo and me, to achieve this milestone. Perhaps with an education she could chart a different path for herself.

In 1987, in her second year studying agricultural science and education, our joy turned to anxious messages and phone calls — Nwogo had fallen very sick. It all started with her getting malaria. While malaria was not usually a cause for alarm, akin to having the flu, something you take pills for and sleep off, it was not so this time. Nwogo was gravely ill, and her fever worsened with time.

"I have finished two bags of IV on her and still no change to her temperature," declared Chike, who was treating her from our shared home in Enugu, "and the quinine is not working, *o ka mma*, it is better that we admit her to the hospital."

Nwogo was admitted at Royal Hospital in Enugu, where Chike also worked as a surgeon. I was with Nwogo in her hospital ward when a doctor I didn't recognize delivered a shot of insulin for her diabetic condition. No one expected that an hour after she received the injection, her fever would take a turn for the worse. Soon, Nwogo was frantically scratching her buttocks, prompting me to look closer. What I saw alarmed me to the point of panic. Nwogo's buttocks were swollen to twice their normal size, the light-brown colour a black, purple, and red riot.

I urgently called for the doctor, trying to think what could explain this. The only thing that made sense was that Nwogo was having a severe allergic reaction to the injection. This was odd, given that it was far from her first time taking insulin. Could it be that the injection was fake?

The doctor confirmed my suspicions. "We just received this batch!" was all he could say as he stood defeated, unsure what to do. They resorted to pumping liquids into her in an attempt to flush out the fake insulin, whose content they didn't even know. It was like fighting in the dark against an unknown attacker. I was tasked with icing the swelling.

Between the infection spreading across her buttocks, the fake medicine masquerading as insulin still flowing through her body, the malaria, and her diabetic condition still untreated, Nwogo deteriorated very quickly.

Early the next morning, before the nurses came to check on her, she died in my arms. She was twenty-one years old.

I allowed myself to cry without holding back. I had lost what felt like my own child — my first daughter. And the worst part was how avoidable her death was. At the age of thirty-three, I was once again grieving.

The doctors said her death was due to complications. I knew that they would report it as such, if only to maintain their reputation. My frustration was deep. Her death had been preventable. Nwogo *nwa mma* did not have to die. She still had her whole life waiting to be lived — she was only just beginning. In the midst of my grief, I resigned myself to mourning her, knowing that any battle with the hospital or any other responsible party would only be a way to avoid dealing with the tragedy.

Nwogo's death confirmed for me that life is uncertain and indeed can be too short. My father had had it all, then lost everything. The war cost us and millions of others almost everything — the lucky ones, like us, got to keep our lives. And just when we were finding our footing postwar, we lost Papa. And just when I found love, a love that I hoped would heal my pain, it hurt me. And then there was Mama, and now my beloved sister.

"*Ọnwụ dị njọ*, death is ugly," and loss is painful. Loss had marked so much of my life, and the hardest part was the realization that I had to accept it.

Twenty-Six

"Even as the archer loves the arrow that flies, so too he loves
the bow that remains constant in his hands."

LESS THAN A YEAR later, I followed the guidance of my
intuition and applied for a post-doctoral to King's College,
London, with Dr. Houghton as my doctoral adviser.

While I was excited for the opportunity to explore a new
environment that could support my scientific curiosity, pursuing this doctorate would mean leaving my five children behind.
Ijeoma was ten years old, Dozie was eight, Somto seven, Njideka
five, and Chidiogo three. Unlike my first move from Enugu to
Nsukka in the early 1980s, this time I would have to go alone.

What if something happened to them? I knew I could never
forgive myself. But I was not willing to start letting fear dictate
my path. It did not hurt to apply, and I could take the rest
of the process one step at a time. I had faith that I would be
guided on the right path, and while this didn't stop me from
worrying about the children, I concluded that nothing bad
would happen. I would make sure that Ijeoma, who was very
responsible and mature for her age, would have money to take
care of herself and her siblings.

As I always did with decisions that felt too big to make on my own, I laid this one at the feet of God, saying, "God, you have brought this opportunity my way, you have led me this far. You know the fears of my heart; you also know the joy I feel at this prospect. Please guide me, and bless the journey ahead."

Six weeks later an envelope marked with the insignia of the University of London, the umbrella institute of King's College, arrived in the mail. I had been accepted to the doctorate with the Pharmacognosy Research Laboratories in the Department of Pharmacy. Even better, my acceptance was on a full scholarship provided by the Association of Commonwealth Fellowship, which covered tuition as well as living expenses. As I always did with decisions that felt too big to make on my own, I laid this one at the feet of God, saying, "God, you have brought this opportunity my way, you have led me this far. You know the fears of my heart; you also know the joy I feel at this prospect. Please guide me, and bless the journey ahead."

The opportunity was an invitation to explore the broader benefits of local plants, not just for their antivenom properties but also for treatment of general diseases. For instance, plants with antimicrobial benefits, like the *Kigelia pinnata*, also known as the sausage tree, was used locally to treat dysentery by grinding up the bark with palm wine over a period of two to three days, the resulting paste to be consumed with more palm wine. I trusted the excitement I was feeling and had begun to see it as a sign of God's guidance, urging me on. So I packed my bags full of plant extracts and bid farewell to my husband and children.

I found an affordable one-bedroom flat in Wandsworth

Borough, a little less than an hour's commute from the university. It was basic, clean, and suited my needs. I was truly grateful for the research grant and monthly stipend, which I divided into four parts: one for my personal expenses, including food and housing; the second for savings; the third I sent to be shared between my siblings, depending on who needed help in the period; and the fourth part I sent to the children.

Overall, I found London to be cold and unfamiliar. I experienced so many firsts. Some I knew to expect, like winter, but nothing can really prepare one for the world becoming a deep freezer — unfit for human habitation.

There was the first time I went underground to find a train that snaked across the entire city. *Ọ dị egwu!* It was truly impressive. There was the first time I tasted wine, which I didn't much care for. Or the experience of the sun rising and setting at ever-changing times of the day. Of bushy-tailed rats that ran freely around the city — squirrels, they were called.

My favourite of my new experiences was the ease of buying foodstuffs. It was a far cry from my trips to the local market in Nsukka or Enugu, where I bargained at length with market vendors, who started referring to me as the "big madam" who haggled like a village woman. In the U.K., the only required interactions in the supermarket were "good day" and "thank you" and a muttered response from disinterested cashiers.

To save as much money as possible, I became creative. I made friends with a butcher who let me have the unwanted parts of animals he slaughtered, including the head, hooves, intestines, and skin, which he gave me either for free or at a giveaway price. These I cooked and stewed into various delicacies such as isi ewu — a delicious concoction of palm oil, herbs, spices, and chunks of goat head — as well as pepper soup, a light spicy broth with chunks of meat. I marvelled at my luck to enjoy otherwise expensive meals for almost free, as I chewed through eyeballs, juice squirting. That sound was distinct from that of chewing thick tongue; also different from the grind of eating my favourite part: pointy ears of cartilage, or towel-like tripe.

Another expense to cut was personal purchases. Given the novelty of being abroad in a new country, most people my age, men and women alike, would be lured by the urge to buy the plethora of niceties and cheap trinkets in brightly lit stores. I was no different, but I didn't give in to temptation. I curbed all personal indulgences, including eating out in restaurants and all forms of entertainment, and I maintained a simple wardrobe: a selection of colourful blouses and three skirts, which I wore interchangeably along with stockings to ward off the cold.

My sacrifices paid off, as my savings increased. However, sending money to my children proved to be trickier than I expected. Every other month I sent them money via Western Union and trusted friends with strict instructions that it be hand-delivered only to my first daughter, Ijeoma, and under no circumstances was Chike to know of it. Chike didn't believe in giving the children money, but he also didn't believe in providing them with anything other than food, the simpler the better, and the most basic of necessities. It was one of the ways the stark difference in our upbringing was beginning to show. I had known wealth and luxury, even if just for a short time, while he grew up in the blue-collar community of Coal Camp, formed to cater to the coal boom, and he had learned to shun excess. He also deeply believed in scarcity as a teacher of values in children.

The arrangement soon backfired.

I had sent money to Ijeoma, which was to last her and her siblings for about three months. Just a week later we were on a call and I asked her whether she had received the money and if everything was in order. Her silence told me everything. I always had a sense when people were withholding something from me, and it was even clearer if that person was my daughter.

Having calls was greatly frustrating due to the limitations in those years of transatlantic communication. Not only were long-distance phone calls expensive, but our phone line was frequently disconnected, causing me to rely on calling our neighbours, the Achikes. Moreover, during these calls, I could feel my children's unease about not having the privacy to share what was truly going on for them.

Crowded around the phone would be our five children and Chike, all waiting for it to ring. Chike's child-rearing tactics meant that his relationship with the children was akin to a strict warden and his solemn keep. Between being under the watchful eye of their father and in the living room of another's small apartment, the children kept most conversations to basic pleasantries.

I asked my older sister Rose, whom we all called Mama Ifeoma since the birth of her first-born, Ifeoma, to check in on the children and relate to me the real situation at home. She came back with the unsurprising news that Ijeoma had confirmed that the money had gone missing. But what was truly disturbing was the story behind the loss.

Ijeoma, knowing just how much I abhorred carelessness, knew to hide the money in a safe place, but somehow Chike had found out about it. My guess was that between her making repeated trips to her hiding place to retrieve the money as needed and the oddity of the children not asking their father for any money, Chike got suspicious.

Not only did he confiscate the money, but he failed to raise the issue with me. He chose instead to punish Ijeoma for it. I was disappointed but understood this to be Chike's brand of anger, silent yet effective. He was doubly angry: at me, for what he perceived to be a conspiracy that excluded him, and at Ijeoma, who he insisted should have told him that I sent money.

Over the years, in an effort to discipline five children under the age of ten, Chike relied heavily on the same tactics his parents used — the power of fear. Fear had a shape and a name: koboko, a long springy cane designed for maximum discipline and sold across town, especially close to schools. There was one for every child, differentiated to match each child in size and tolerance to its wiry electric bite.

My husband and I differed on our chosen approach. I didn't believe in hitting or flogging children, though I didn't hold back from verbally expressing my anger or displeasure. Chike, however, believed a cane to be the most effective communicator and was very generous with his floggings and sometimes his own strength. To hear his car pull into the compound was to witness a show of the children crawling, running, or scampering away like prey at the sight of an eagle overhead, slipping into various hiding corners, hoping not to be seen or heard.

After the incident between Chike and Ijeoma, I stopped sending money to the children, leaving them to their own devices, hoping that the two housekeepers I had hired, Mary and Vicki, after Antonia unfortunately had to leave, would ensure that they were cared for.

CHIKE CAME TO VISIT me in the autumn of 1988. My prayer all these months apart had been for a forgiving heart, and I had spent much time working on healing my hurt, knowing that this was the only way forward. I had no interest in spending the rest of my life soaked in the bitterness of the past. I even found that I was excited to see him after so long. Maybe time did heal all wounds, though the emotional scars might remain.

He was at his most charming, making jokes, reminding me of earlier years.

I took him to visit my world. Together, we toured the university and visited my London friends, such as Obasi Ezeilo, a relative of the Ezeilos, and Peter Houghton, who had gone beyond his role as my doctorate adviser to become a friend and mentor. He and his wife, Joanne, had become like family, which was such a gift being so far away from mine.

I took him to the supermarket so that he too might experience this marvel of goods bought without haggling. We were of one heart about the cold. Like me, Chike could not understand how people lived like this, and we made many jokes about our varying degrees of misery in being in the cold and wet.

I hadn't planned on getting pregnant, but when I realized I was, I felt joy. In spite of the doctor's warning that another pregnancy would be far too dangerous, I was eager for another boy and had a strong intuition that this was the one. Something inside me feared the duration of life, and wanted my only son, Dozie, to always have the support of a brother. So much pressure awaited him as the first son of his father, Chike, who was also the first son.

Long before this conception, I'd had a recurring dream of giving birth to a boy child in a strange hospital in what seemed to be a foreign country. A year later, lying alone in the same brownstone hospital of my dreams, I heard the doctor, a quiet Indian woman, announce the words "It's a boy." I wept. My miracle baby was now flesh. God of perfect timing had shown His faithfulness!

In my joy I named him Obumneme — a name that is at once both a question and a celebration, translated as "Is it by my might?" His full name answers the very question it poses: Obumneme? O buro m na-eme, oo Chukwu na-eme — meaning "Is it by my might? No, it is not by my might, it is God's doing."

He was a blessing in every sense of the word. I was happy I could honour the support of Peter Houghton and his wife, Joanne, by inviting them to be godparents to Obum. His middle name of Peter-Damien was after both Dr. Houghton and Father Akpunonu, the priest who married Chike and me.

When my post-doc was completed, pending the submission of my final papers, I came home to Nigeria with my baby boy in my arms and with a job offer to serve as a senior lecturer at UNN.

Twenty-Seven

"Ụwa bụ ndọlị — life is a hustle."

I WAS HOPING THAT MY return home would be accompanied by my large trunk, filled with all manner of toys and trinkets to share with the children as well as neighbours, family, and friends. There was to have been something for everyone: soaps, VHS tapes of the latest films, deodorants, keychains, socks, and various sizes of clothes and shoes. I lost count of the number of times I promised a lingering visitor that my trunk was delayed and that there would be something for them at a later date. It never did arrive.

The children had been visibly disappointed, but this was overshadowed by the excitement of our reunion. They didn't leave my bed on most nights as stories poured out of them like water through cracks in a dam.

Ijeoma had grown so tall and reminded me so much of myself in the role of the unofficial mother, caring for the rest of her siblings. She was the first to share details of how awful Mary and Vicki had been, forcing them to literally eat shit as punishment whenever their actions displeased them. Those whom I had hired to care for the children had done the exact opposite, forcing them to do all the house chores under threat of various creative punishments and insulting them at every opportunity lest they report them to their father. I fired them the same night I got home.

Dozie spoke the most, happy to add details to stories of their ordeals, his penchant for theatrics evident by how he mimicked the voices of various actors in his stories, including his father, causing us to roar with laughter at each imitation. Somto was so sweet and doted on me, asking always to refill my glass of orange juice, which she squeezed fresh in the kitchen whenever my glass was empty. Njideka mostly listened, interrupting a few times to add to Dozie's story. She too had grown so much since the last time I had seen her. They all had, and I felt like I was experiencing life with them on fast-forward. Chidiogo didn't speak much, observing me from the corner as if a stranger, curious about the familiarity I shared with the rest of the children. Obumneme, whom they all called "London boy," often lay asleep in his cream-coloured pram. In between listening, I shared stories of London. They were particularly fascinated about there being a place where the TV never stopped playing cartoons, all day, every day.

The job of senior lecturer in the Department of Pharmacology and Toxicology with the Faculty of Pharmaceutical Sciences at UNN, based out of Enugu, allowed us for the first time in almost a decade to be all together as family. I was thirty-six years old, with six children. My maternal instinct was in bloom, and it was revealing itself in a desire to provide for my family, to give them a life better than the one I had lived.

Nigeria's economy was in a state of unchecked inflation

under the military dictatorship of General Ibrahim Babangida, which meant that the cost of basic goods was always on the rise. In addition, I was still supporting some members of my extended family, including Anayo, as well as providing for my children. Although Chike was earning a steady salary as part of his government job as a medical doctor, it wasn't enough. All of this meant that I needed to supplement my earnings.

My first foray into entrepreneurship was a tailoring business in partnership with a young man named Lawrence from the Republic of Benin. When that didn't work out, I went into business manufacturing plastic, as I'd been told there was easy money to be made in plastic and shrink wrap manufacturing. Chike and I launched Chidora Plastic — a portmanteau of Dora and Chike, which we ran out of our backyard. This was also doomed to fail, due to pilfering by workers who threw bundles of finished plastic across the fence. I refused to give up. If anything, each failure showed me my commitment to doing everything I could to give my children the best life possible.

Next was a business growing catfish out of a fish pond in our family home in Agulu. However, when harvest weekend came, the net came up empty — the fish had been stolen. I kept going.

I started a resale business with a simple model: buy clothes, mainly men's suits on trips abroad, mostly facilitated by friends, and sell them back home in Enugu to university staff. To maintain a professional distance, I sold them via a clerk, Mr. Enezi, an admin officer who took a small profit from each sale. This time, business was very good and I started to import suits from other parts of the country to meet demand. I could not have known that Mr. Enezi would die while still in possession of a large inventory of suits and fabric. It was his widow who informed me that there was nothing left, as his relatives had already shared what was left of his belongings.

Armed with the lessons of several failed enterprises, I decided that the best way forward was to capitalize on what was working, notably being a popular lecturer at the university. The idea was to marry my passion for pharmacology with that for teaching by writing a book for students and practitioners. My hope was that the book would serve to increase awareness about the adverse effects of taking various incompatible drugs together.

After months of research, in 1991, I authored *Handbook of Drug Interactions*, which became a key reference manual. Unfortunately, it hardly made me any money because of the prevalent culture of photocopying long excerpts of the book for use, and because of an unfortunate incident with my supervisor at the Faculty of Pharmaceutical Sciences. I had been his star student over the years and he agreed to review the book; unbeknownst to me, he expected that his support meant that his name would appear as the main author of the book and mine as co-author. This, he said, was the standard practice. I respectfully refused on the grounds it was unjust. My defiance was not received kindly and my supervisor did his best to limit the success of the book.

So, in spite of my best efforts, I made little extra money over the years. Between my limited income and my husband's thriftiness, the children were left without much in terms of luxuries. Meat, usually chicken, one piece per person, was consumed only on Sundays after Mass, alongside jollof rice, and distributed according to age, with Chike getting the lion's share and Chidiogo getting the smallest piece until Obum was old enough to take over this position. We celebrated all six children's birthdays with one party once a year, and only in the years when I had the time to organize and budget for the cake and presents. The treat for the children was a local rock candy called nzu, which had a powdery texture and a sweet aftertaste; snacks were either cabin biscuits or kuli kuli, a northern delicacy that found popularity in the Southeast of ground roasted peanuts packed into a hard, dry paste.

Between little financial comfort, work, six children to care for, personal challenges, and the constant effort to restore trust with Chike, I was at my limits. My sleep started to suffer, so much so that I needed sleeping aids to allow my mind and my body to rest. Now more than ever, I needed someone I could lean on.

Twenty-Eight

"If the hen stops clucking, what will she use to train her children?"

MY BROTHER ANAYO, whom I fondly called Anny, had continued living in the United States for well over a decade, graduating and then securing a role as a teaching assistant at a university. While we had stayed in touch over the years, it wasn't the same as being together. With all my challenges, I needed family, and Anny and I had always been the most like-minded.

"Anny, please come back. I am here all alone," I pleaded.

Anny already knew of my struggles, as well as my desire to join forces, though I had not asked so bluntly before and with intentional exaggeration.

"Please, you must come back. I am here all alone. I will die here alone," I added, my voice in a low, broken, childlike pitch. I was truly desperate.

He mumbled his understanding into the phone and promised to do his best. I didn't stop asking until Anny came back, first on a sabbatical in 1992 and permanently by 1994. He moved into a flat in a newly constructed high-rise in New

Haven close to our home on Umuezebi Street, and in no time he became my right hand and confidant.

I started to flourish under the friendship and partnership with my brother. In addition, following strong support from Chike, who was dedicated to their academic excellence, my children were one by one leaving the nest, allowing me to dedicate more time to myself and work. By 1992, the first of the children, Ijeoma and Dozie, left for boarding school in Lagos, a full day's drive from Enugu. The two girls Somto and Njideka were only a year away.

There was a steadiness now to life. My weekdays were spent at the university and my weekends in the village. Every day, I woke up after a valium-induced sleep to say my morning rosary followed by a daily shower, in spite of one from the night before. I favoured in those days a Western-style suit that usually consisted of a knee- or ankle-length skirt and matching suit jacket and camisole. Breakfast of bread and tea would already be laid out on the dining table, along with signs of the children having already eaten. They would have departed earlier with Chike, who dropped them at school before he made his way to work. I never had a big appetite in the morning and drank Lipton tea with condensed milk, no sugar. I skipped the bread for a small serving of fried eggs and plantains when available. Chioma, the young girl who had come to live with and work for us in the months prior, was still learning how best to meet our needs, but she was a fast learner and I enjoyed the ease of not having to worry about everyone.

I came home at about 4 p.m. each day laden with stacks of unmarked papers. Chike would often come home much later from the hospital. The children who came home earlier would eat leftover soup cooked in large batches over the weekend and warmed up easily for lunch, after which they would be at Mrs. Ojukwu's for their daily after-school lessons.

Our family over the years had established a now entrenched tradition of spending weekends in the village. Friday evenings consisted of piling the children into either Chike's yellow Toyota or my grey Peugeot 505, which had replaced my white 504.

Some weekends were pleasant and others were difficult, especially when Chike's siblings were visiting. I tried my best to shield our children from the worst of their abuse, which luckily was mostly targeted at me. I didn't want them witnessing the insults, but the air was sometimes so thick with tension, and they quickly caught on that there was animosity between me and their uncles and aunties.

Nevertheless, I loved the freedom that life in the village provided the children. With fewer cars, ample farmland in the areas around the compound, and families who knew one another and kept an eye on each other's comings and goings, here the children were free to roam.

The village was also home to their yellow Raleigh bicycle, which I bought for them all to share for one of the yearly birthday celebrations. It was a great investment, as each of the children learned to ride on the bicycle when even I didn't know how to. I watched with pride as they would fall off and get back on again until they were making circles around the compound and then venturing farther away to the narrow paths that ran through the village.

Between their adventures visiting eroded valleys and discovering exotic animals — like the python they saw curled up in a corner, or crocodiles that made their home in Agulu Lake, or the dozens of baby tortoises that emerged after the first rains — they took little interest in my doings. They did notice, however, when more and more visitors started coming to our home. On more than one occasion, I heard their joy at the increased frequency of receiving small bills from departing guests to buy soft drinks and sweets. They were always happy when I was the one who witnessed the exchange, as it meant that they could keep the money for themselves; the same couldn't be said for their father.

In the months prior, I had become more involved in the Agulu women's union, a group of local married women with whom I spent many hours over weekends, plotting ways to better our community. I had quickly earned their trust as a member they could rely on to help devise strategies for local bazaars and fundraisers.

We were gathered at our usual Saturday afternoon post-Mass meeting at the dusty yet impressively spacious structure of Madonna Catholic Church. This meeting was different, for I had added my name to the agenda to speak. To mark the occasion, I dressed in my favourite white lace blouse with puffy sleeves, and tied around my now ample waist was the blue wax print Agulu women's union wrapper adorned with the face of the Virgin Mary and the words "Madonna Catholic Church *Ndị nne*."

After opening prayers and a review of the key news of the last week, it was my turn.

"*Ndị Nne maama*" — Mothers! I greeted them, to which they chorused in response, "*I sokwa!*" — as are you.

"How many times have you worried about your children's

health and well-being?" Encouraged by their attentive silence, I went on. "How many times have they fallen sick and nothing you do is working against their fever? How many times have you needed to take them to the hospital only to realize that it would take hours simply to get there?"

Sighs and tongue clicks of agreement could be heard bouncing off the hollow walls of the church, and several women nodded in recognition of the challenges of accessing health care for themselves and their families.

"And yet in spite of the urgent need, there are no health facilities to serve the thousands of villagers who call Agulu home. No hospital, no clinic, nothing! Where does that leave you?" I paused to allow this question to sink in. "We all know how hard it can be to take your sick baby all the way to Awka teaching hospital, or even Adazi hospital, for treatment!" Awka, the site of one of the closest hospitals, was about twenty kilometres away.

"First you have to carry them on your back to go to the main road because they are too weak from the fever. But this will be just the beginning, because then you have to wait, sometimes for up to an hour, for an okada to take you to the junction at Nwagu, only to start waiting again for a bus to get to the hospital in Awka.

"How many more of our children must die? How many more must suffer untreated because the hospital is too far and too expensive." I paused again to emphasize my point. "And yet," I continued on, my voice rising with each word, "this is not a small village! We have people in Agulu! We have wealthy citizens, we have us, *Ndị nne*, we have medical professionals, myself and my husband included, and together we can build a hospital for the people of Agulu. Together, we can make sure that no one from this village or from neighbouring villages will have to suffer to get medical care!"

The applause was loud. I had their full attention, and with it, I laid out my proposal that we refurbish an abandoned, dilapidated building that was supposed to have been a hospital but, never having been completed, had become a shell of its promise.

The support was unanimous. I felt in that moment something that I had never felt, not even in moments of academic excellence and recognition. I was connecting to people and they to me, and it felt so natural to stand there before them all, sharing my passion and truth.

To capitalize on the momentum, I quickly put together a committee to oversee various arms of the task ahead. There was the group whose focus would be to work closely with the parish priest to raise funds from average citizens via church donations; a group responsible for organizing a Saturday fundraising event; another group to galvanize the sons and daughters of the village to clear the current site; and another still to act as a delegation to meet with the state government as well as the paramount leader of the village, the Igwe of Agulu.

I took on the task of raising as much money as possible, relying on innovative approaches to fundraising. I went directly to the men, many of whom held the purse strings in their families but were not as likely to participate in church fundraisers, and from whom we wanted much more than the small change dropped into offering boxes.

Getting the men interested and engaged enough to donate generously required some thought. For one, I knew I couldn't just ask for the money. I needed more delicacy, especially as I was still relatively new to the village, with no track record to assure them of the safety of their money.

I decided the best approach was to appeal to their egos, and chose the busiest town hall meeting to do just this. I came with a full delegation of the women's group, believing in the African proverb "If you want to go fast, go alone, and if you want to go far, go together."

Upon arrival, I greeted the Igwe and other senior members of the village council assembled in a dusty building that served as the town hall and events centre for the village. The hall was especially full, as it was Easter weekend, and many members of the village were home for the first of two yearly pilgrimages, the other being Christmas.

The heat was unbearable that afternoon, made worse by a hall that seemed built to keep out air. The two dusty fans hanging precariously on loose wires blew stale hot air around the dark interior. The loud hum of the backup generator was audible through the open windows, but it was necessary to provide electricity to keep the fans going during one of the frequent power outages.

Dewy Agulu men and women were seated in various age groups around the room, some on the few wooden benches in the hall, and others on their own personal stools. They cooled themselves with pamphlets and open palms, wiping sweat with rumpled or carefully folded handkerchiefs, all of them soaked.

When it was my turn to speak, it was already an hour and a half into the meeting and eyes were beginning to droop from the heavy air coupled with the drudgery of listening to the monotonous voice of the announcer and long speeches from various villagers.

"*Ndị be anyị kwenụ!*" I greeted them in typical Igbo hail fashion, and just like that, the people's own shouted response of "*Yaa!*" woke them up from their lull. In speaking with the women, I had gone for their hearts; here, I went straight for their pride and kept it short and to the point. "*Ndị be anyị,* we need you, Agulu needs you!"

To best illustrate the urgent health care needs, instead of speaking hypothetically, I had invited two of the women to share their personal stories of loss due to lack of medical facility. Once the women were done, and satisfied with the impact of their words, I once again took the stage.

"No support is too small. And each contribution will be acknowledged publicly, including by engraving the names of benefactors on equipment and wards. Your name will live on as one who said yes when Agulu called!"

Moved and eager to contribute, especially in a public manner, the men came on board, each standing up to pledge monetary support.

In the eight months that followed, with countless Chapmans (a drink I made from a mélange of freshly cut cucumbers and orange slices mixed with Sprite, Fanta, and Ribena, a blackcurrant concentrate) served on a bed of ice to a steady stream of guests, all funds needed had been raised and the hospital was completed.

The ribbon-cutting ceremony was a grand affair, with tents that had been set up around the hospital. I was dressed in a golden head-tie, green wrapper, and golden lace blouse, while Chike wore a dark-grey suit. All six children were with us, the youngest now four years old. For all the girls I had made matching green satin dresses, and for the boys I got suspenders to wear atop crisp white shirts and pants. I felt so much pride to see an idea become a reality, and even more so, I was inspired by just how fulfilling the journey had been.

Through this process, I went from the little-known wife of Dr. Akunyili to the widely respected Dr. (Mrs.) Akunyili, otherwise known by my hail name of Ugogbe mmuta — which means "a mirror that reflects the virtue of good deeds to be learned and emulated," or more simply put, "mirror of wisdom" — a name and honour that was given to me by the women's group.

The months and the years to follow would see an even greater increase in traffic of visitors calling at our home, for me as well as my husband. All greeted me now as Ugogbe, "the mirror."

My contribution to the building and furnishing of Agulu's first hospital filled me with a new sense of satisfaction. I felt like dry grass after the harmattan, hungry for water. I knew that I wanted this to be a permanent part of my life.

I had a plan.

On a research trip to the United Kingdom, I stopped over in Lagos at the home of a well-connected family friend, Dr. Innocent Obodoakor, to talk to him about the possibility of a state government position. His home was sandwiched between houses in a crowded street on Lagos mainland. We were seated in a bright room lit by two rows of fluorescent light. There were cold drinks on the low table, but I always stayed away from sugar and chose water, which I sipped while I waited for Innocent to finish his call.

When I heard the name Okwadike, my ears perked up, sensing a sign. Here I was, wanting to share my desire to serve the state, at the very moment Inno was in conversation with the governor of the state.

I waited for him to finish the call, and without hesitation, I asked, "You know the governor like that?"

He nodded and smiled. "Yes, he is my good friend. Why?"

I smiled in return. "Because I want to be a commissioner," I said, without quite knowing how the thought came out so fully formed.

Innocent did not seem surprised. "Okay," he said confidently. "I will support you. When you return, bring your CV. I will take you to him."

He later drove me to the airport as we finalized details of our planned meeting with the governor, to take place in a few weeks during Innocent's next visit east.

It was all I thought about throughout the trip and upon my return. The excitement at the thought of what was to come was greatly marred by the news that my first son, Dozie, who was a boarding house student in King's College, all the way in Lagos, was sick. He had seemed even skinnier than usual on his last visit, and on more than one occasion he had sent word of high fevers. I feared it was multiple cases of malaria and continued to send malaria treatments. But malaria did not cause one to become unconscious.

Even though I had just come back, Chike and I returned to Lagos as soon as we got news that Dozie was suspected to have meningitis. He was still unconscious when we arrived. Later that evening, we were by his bedside when he awoke. He looked from me to his father, trying to make sense of where he was and what was happening. His first words, looking at me with an expectant half smile: "Have they made you commissioner yet?"

Laughing, I confirmed that it was still a work-in-progress.

Dozie in time recovered, but unfortunately I was not made commissioner. This was in spite of various attempts by champions including Innocent and a certain Chief Ogbuefi.

My disappointment was sweetened in 1994 when the state governor, under the newly appointed administration, requested that every village name one candidate to represent them in the local government, and I was unanimously nominated.

And this was how I became a member of the Caretaker Committee of Anaocha's local government.

Part III

1994–2008

Twenty-Nine

"A good tree cannot produce bad fruit, nor can a bad tree produce good fruit."

NIGERIA HAS A THREE-TIERED government structure: the federal government; state government, totalling thirty-six states and a federal capital of Abuja; and 768 local government areas. The government in each state delegates power to local governments, whose core functions include primary and adult education, public health, town planning, roads and transport, and waste disposal.

In my role in the local government, which I assumed in the beginning of 1994, life was about to take on a different tempo. I was made director in charge of agriculture. My main responsibility was to ensure that seedlings, pesticides, fertilizers, and all other inputs required for agriculture production would be distributed to farmers in the villages.

This appointment meant that I had to step down from my role as a senior lecturer at the university. To go from being a lecturer to a director at the local government filled me with apprehension. What if I did not live up to the people's expectations of me? What if the environment was not conducive for me to be effective?

Chike was very supportive, reminding me that I had already proven myself. It was amusing to see him encourage me the same way we did the children by calling to my sense of pride and competition. "Do the other directors have two heads?" he'd ask. "You have what it takes and then some."

Try as he may, the voice of my fear was loud in those days, and I leaned on my faith to quiet it. I intensified my prayers, saying the rosary sometimes two times daily, reciting the thirty days novena to the Blessed Virgin, and booking several Masses. My prayer was simple: that I might be a tool for the betterment of the lives of the people.

Luckily, I didn't have to care for all six of the children anymore. By 1993, four of our children had left home, so it was only me, Chike, and the two youngest, Chidiogo and Obum.

Soon, it was time to report for duty. I prayed all throughout the drive from Enugu to the local government office in Neni. Anaocha, which oversaw Agulu and a few other towns in the region, was one of the twenty-nine local governments in Anambra and also one of the largest. My office consisted of a dull white square room, the paint peeling in corners and showing signs of water damage. Overhead was a slow-moving fan, and in the middle sat a heavy wooden desk with a swivel chair, which was to be the heart of my activities for the next weeks and months. Behind the desk and chair was a line of cabinets, into which were jammed files that spilled out into piles around the room.

It didn't take me long to determine that my job description was on paper alone. Far from being expected to distribute the agricultural supplies, I was to become complicit in aiding an immoral practice of hoarding supplies for personal gain. Staff and appointed officials abused and exploited their power over the funds, goods, raw materials, and even services allocated to Anaocha in the Anambra State government's budget. As I soon found out, for years the local government officials had been taking advantage of the system they were charged with upholding. When agriculture inputs earmarked by the state government for use by local farmers arrived at the local government for distribution, instead of reaching those in need, they were shared internally among local government staff who sold it instead.

The very caretakers of the well-being of the people were acting as the impediment to their productivity. It reminded me of the injustices of working for Mr. Nwokobia on his farm during the war.

When I asked questions, I was met with surprised and sometimes blank stares of confusion, replies that it was the way things had always been, and reminders that I too stood to benefit from the practice.

"If you play your cards right, you can make a lot of money in this job," said another director whom I had approached with my dilemma.

My battle was not with him, so I nodded in understanding, concluding that guidance was not to be found there, and that I had to chart a new course by reimagining the job as it should be done.

The situation was dire and the injustice flagrant. I couldn't help but wonder when such selfish acts had become the norm. My mind went back to the war and a conversation I once had over dinner during my time in London with my friend Emeka, a historian.

"Ever wondered why the civil war is not in any of our

school's history curricula?" he asked. "Carefully taken out. No museum or anything! Because the war was neither won nor ended. It was only moved from the streets and physical battlefields to the minds of the various tribes and passed on from one generation to the next. We are still at war, not in the battlefields but in our minds with ourselves."

A country that was once governed to ensure law and order and respect for human life and dignity had turned into a world of mayhem, of every man for himself. Too many had died and much atrocity had been committed in the name of war and of survival. Our ndị Igbo community, which had once thrived in recognition of the least of its members, and by curbing the excess of egos, had reversed its course.

There was no going back after the war. To echo Chinua Achebe, they had put a knife to the things that held us together, but we didn't fall apart; neither did we fall together the way we had for Biafra — selflessly, purposefully. Rather, it became ever more so every man for himself because *Onye m'echi* — "who knows tomorrow."

The war effectively created a new reality, and Igbos went from self-sufficient communities that cared for the well-being of all to disparate people concerned only with survival, believing that the only way to live was to fend for oneself and one's family. The Igbo people knew not to count on anyone, least of all on Nigeria.

I realized that the war was but the most recent wave of a quiet onslaught that had been at play for many years before. Before the destruction of the war, other layers of identity had been tampered with and distorted.

First, there had been the role of the English colonizers in

warping the Igbos' sense of self. The narrative was that Igbos needed the version of education and the knowledge that the "superior" West offered. Igbos became convinced of their own inferiority, forgetting that the colonizers didn't know things that they knew. Did they know how to tap wine from the trees of palm? Or how to honour ancestors through the holes of ants that stretch into the earth? Or how to set their market days in accordance with the moon, or to care for one another so that no one ever wanted for anything? Both sides had wisdom, but one side claimed this only for themselves and in so doing robbed Igbos of their own share.

And because we hadn't written down those things we knew to be true, and because the colonizers' knowledge was written, we ignored our own wisdom and began the journey of forgetting. We lost sight of why we had thrived for centuries, and wondered why in the last decades we flailed.

With the spirit of community replaced by "I," and the latter insecure in the truth of its identity, we were left with a fragmented society where the parts didn't believe that they mattered, or that their individual actions, positive or negative, could possibly impact anything.

And so, Igbos had forgotten something we had always known to be true, and it was easily apparent to me, especially during those years in the village: everything impacts the other. When the rains didn't come, we understood that our actions could have led to an imbalance. This was the extent of the local understanding of the interconnectedness between us and our environment. Individuals and our actions not only matter, they are critical. They are needed to till the soil, to capture the rains when they did come, to celebrate and share in the harvest, and to invite rains for the next season. And when one or more of the above was ignored, there would always be repercussions. Everything was connected in a loop, with humans at the centre as guardians. The same lesson was apparent in considering the generosity Papa received as a young man that allowed him to support so many others. The care I received from strangers in the village, especially in those days when I did not know my way around. The way villagers supported families with a failed harvest. How women came together to cook for weddings, births, and funerals, as if for their own immediate families. Supporting each other was the way of life, and this affected everything else.

No part of Nigeria had been spared from this self-serving moral that was the legacy of colonialism and then the war — that nothing else mattered as long as the "I" was cared for.

Deciding not to partake was insufficient, and partaking had never been an option. I could feel the fervour of my young heart. I vowed to actively reverse the trend.

On the specified day of a large delivery of farm supplies — fertilizer this time — I had given unequivocal instructions that the lorry carrying the fertilizer not offload its goods until I gave the go-ahead. In the interim, I had sent word for all representatives of communities within the jurisdiction of the local government to come with pickup trucks to our Neni offices.

Dozens of cars arrived on the appointed date and time to be met by "this woman," as they referred to me. I was ready and waiting under the shade of an avocado tree, dressed in a long red and yellow skirt and matching wax print blouse, and topped by a head-tie of the same fabric. I knew how important first impressions were, and I had every intention of making a statement.

Beside me was a parked lorry, bags of fertilizers stacked high and visible from the top. In my left hand was a piece of paper and a red pen in my right.

"*Ndị be anyị nnọọ,*" I greeted. I continued in Igbo to be sure that my message was clear. "The reason I have called you today is to share your government allowance of fertilizer for your farms." Blank stares met mine, and some whispers wondered about this unorthodox way of "selling" the fertilizer, not knowing that they had a right to it for free. One voice rose louder than a hushed murmur, wondering if perhaps I was hoping for a bidding war to fetch me even more money. Several nods and hisses met the speculation.

Undeterred, and even enjoying the scene, I kept my words to a minimum, knowing that the only way to communicate the way forward was by action.

"When I call your name," I announced, "please come up one by one and take your share of fertilizer allocated to you and to your people.

"Adazi-enu, Adazi-ani, Ichida, Akwaeze, Agukwu Nri," I read out, summoning representatives who in turn were handed the corresponding bags of fertilizer due to them and their community. Their body language was of surprise and disbelief, each quickly grabbing the outstretched bag and scurrying away before the surreal play turned on them and the bags were taken back by the same benevolent hands that gave them away so freely.

By the time the sun was making its way west, the lorry was emptied of all its wares and all village reps were well on their way back home with strict instructions not to sell in turn, or they would face future consequences. One representative's words stayed with me. "Madam," she said, speaking with a thick Igbo accent in English to buttress the sincerity of her words, "I have never heard of such a thing as free fertilizer, let alone from the government. I didn't even know that they know we are alive. Thank you, Ma." She thanked me profusely, hands outstretched to clasp mine, knees bending slightly in reverence.

I received her prayers and thanks with the humility of knowing that I wasn't doing her and the community a favour, but simply doing my job. This was the tragedy of Nigeria. We have everything we need, but it is stockpiled under the lock and chain of personal greed, complacency, and forgetting to be our brothers' keepers.

Back in the office, I was met with hostility. I made many friends that day but even more enemies among the rich and powerful in the local government whom I had robbed of extra income.

"Madam, this is not how we do it!" This was both a statement and an accusation, shouted on repeat, their voices wanting to overwhelm me with the extent of their indignation.

Once they grew tired of shouting, I responded coolly, only betrayed by the fire in my eyes, daring them to do their worst. "From now on," I said, surprising even myself with the sternness of my own voice, "this is how it will be done!"

True to my words, with the support of my team, we instituted co-operative societies through which seeds and fertilizers were shared with the people. It was seen both as a positive and a hostile revolution, depending on the viewer's perspective.

Between the friends and enemies, my reputation grew, as did my trust in my ability to serve the public. Various awards and board positions bolstered my work as well. One such recognition would change the entire trajectory of my life.

Thirty

"One who serves benefits by the service."

I WAS AT MY DESK when a call came through from the local government chairman to see me in his office.

Mr. Odenigbo's office was much larger than any other in the building and was cooler from the air conditioner, which combined with a large fridge in the corner created a constant and loud humming. He was seated behind his desk, and we greeted each other warmly.

He spent the first minutes asking after Chike and the children, then took on a more serious look. "Everyone is sharing the story of what they are calling 'Dora's revolution.'" Before I could react, he added, "And not all of them are, let's say, from a positive lens." At this he smiled knowingly, as if sharing a secret with me. "I am very impressed to hear about the work you've been doing here, and I want to make sure that others can experience you."

I was listening attentively, and assured of this, he continued.

"I want to plant you in places where you can continue to have an even larger impact, which is why I have recommended

you for a federal government position." He paused to let the
impact of his words sink in. "Have you heard of PTF?" he
asked.

I shook my head.

"PTF stands for Petroleum Trust Fund, and it has been
recently created by the federal government with a mandate
to use the oil riches of the country to accelerate development.
To do this, they need to hire people of integrity and devotion.
People like you."

Key to note, Mr. Odenigbo said, was that the applications
were due soon.

I said my thanks and left. With a lifelong belief not to leave
for tomorrow something that could be done today, I spent
the rest of the afternoon preparing my application, which I
sent the next day along with prayers for its positive reception.
I knew the doors that working for the central government
would open.

After an interview for the role of PTF secretary for Anambra State, I received a letter with the news of my acceptance.
In an unexpected turn, I had not been appointed as the secretary for Anambra State alone but as the zonal secretary of the
entire Southeastern region, including Abia, Anambra, Ebonyi,
Enugu, and Imo States. I would be based in Enugu. I was to
co-ordinate all PTF projects that stretched across investments
in roads and waterways, education, food supply, health, water
supply, and a long list of other social projects.

I can still see myself holding the letter in sheer disbelief.
For the first time I understood the need to pinch oneself to
be sure of not dreaming, especially given my proclivity for
visions. I was overjoyed and shared the moment with God

in thanksgiving, as always acknowledging the hand of Mary in supplication to her Son and God the Father on my behalf.

PTF WAS FOUNDED in 1994 by General Sani Abacha, a military head of state, following his 1993 coup and ascension to power. Although it was Abacha's brainchild, PTF was run by General Muhammadu Buhari, a former military head of state of Nigeria who too had taken power in one of the military coups. The trust fund was meant to counter a national fuel price increase that had angered the Nigerian public, who depended heavily on government subsidization of fuel. To placate the people, the government promised that the income from the price increase would be paid into PTF and used in turn for development projects to benefit all citizens of Nigeria.

I joined PTF in late 1996, intent on upholding the vision for which PTF was created. Eager to prove myself and believing in the potential impact of my portfolio, I threw my heart, mind, and hands fully behind the dream to bring development to the people. My blind idealism was short-lived.

It started innocuously enough. I observed stark differences in resource and budget allocations for the Southeast compared to the rest of Nigeria.

For example, why was the proposed depth of tar for road construction allocated to the Southeast inches less than the national average? It was an especially curious discrepancy given that heavier rain falls in the south compared with the arid north. And why was the budget allocation per capita for the Southeast the lowest in the country?

There were few answers for such questions, especially in the hierarchical structure of PTF, where orders trickled from above without explanation. So I did the best I could to ensure that every kobo earmarked for various projects, however limited, was appropriately directed.

As hard as I dreamed of supporting the development of a region that was still finding its feet, and as much as I strived, I was still just one part of a system that didn't always share my values.

One of the more painful examples of this was surrounding a scandal where twenty-eight billion naira's worth (US$1.3 billion) of expired HIV/AIDS drugs were supplied to several hospitals in Nigeria. I had signed the documents authorizing distribution in the region but had no way of knowing that expired drugs had been swapped in. The drugs had to be recalled, but not before many sick patients had already been impacted by taking pills with no medicinal value.

It didn't end there. Promises were made to communities that went unfulfilled because funds were never released. Projects were launched to great fanfare and press, only to be abandoned halfway as required funds mysteriously dried up with no means of holding the controllers of the purse strings accountable. And incompetent tenders were awarded large-scale projects they were incapable of carrying out.

Those years working with PTF as the zonal secretary exposed me to the intricacies of a large bureaucratic arm of the federal government, the crippling lack of transparency, and the cost of individual shortcomings of staff in such a broad group of society. Above all, it taught me what not to do.

Thirty-One

*"Tomorrow is pregnant; no one knows what
it will give birth to."*

THE MORE EXPOSURE I had to the government, the more I
feared for the fate of the country. But still I had hope. While I
had seen the underbelly of the system, I also had experienced
the best of its people.

I made a point over the years of not forgetting the woman
who sculpted so much of my values. I paid a visit to Nne in
Isuofia at least once every two months. Shortly after I took
on the new position at PTF, she passed on. This time I didn't
mourn but celebrated this woman who had been a rock for so
many. Some estimated that she was well past a hundred years
of age. For me her age didn't matter so much; what I dwelt on
was how important those years with her and since had been
for me, and on the power of role models.

In reflecting on my own childhood and the unique experiences that had shaped me, I began to wonder about my own
children and the society that was shaping them. In those years,
I made a point to educate my children in proper values so that,
at the very least, they would not become part of the problem.

I started by hosting the neighbourhood block rosary in our home in Umuezebi Street, attracting children from both the more affluent end of the street and the poorer parts, whose families lived in zinc-roofed shacks. My reasoning was to inspire in them all the importance of prayer and spiritual communion, as well as create a melting pot that cut across socio-economic barriers.

To ensure the children considered the fate of those in need, I also made a point of taking them with me to visit the leper colony in Emene. The visits soon became a tradition, and three times a year, over every school break, we all piled into my Peugeot for the hour-and-a-half drive to Oji leper colony. I saw these visits as an important lesson on the hardships of life. None of the people affected by leprosy had chosen the life they had before them, sick and cast off by society, and yet they needed support the most. I wanted to arouse the children's empathy, consideration, and generosity, especially for those most in need. And though they didn't buy the toilet rolls and bags of rice we brought with us as gifts, I encouraged them to personally give these to the leprosy patients.

But there was only so much I could do; even if they were not part of the problem, they would still be part of a challenged system whose failures impacted everything from health care to education, safety, and social security.

It was at about this time that I got wind of the American green card lottery through a good friend, an Agulu woman named Dr. Nneamaka Grace Obidiegwu. I am a believer in signs that come our way to guide us. The thing with signs is that it is important to listen for them. I have noticed over the years that it is in the silence of prayer that I hear most clearly. I had never been interested in the American dream for myself — only once, what seemed a long time ago, for Nwogo. One more time, with omens guiding me, I started to dream this dream, but this time for my children.

I learned that if either parent won the lottery, their spouse and all children under the age of eighteen would be covered as well. This meant that the most prudent investment of our application fees would be for both Chike and me to file applications, since all six children were still under eighteen (all of them, with the exception of Obum, were in boarding school). Either of our wins would ensure that all eight of us were covered. So I filled out our two applications, and with that, the rest was up to God.

For days and months, I alone or we as a family huddled in prayer around the living room, bedroom, churches, and chapels, eyes closed, bodies hunched over bended knees.

Chike was not as confident as I was about the benefits of the green card. He scorned its pursuit as unpatriotic, challenging my argument about the access to great universities it offered. But nonetheless he prayed with us.

The call came late at night from Mrs. Obidiegwu, whose address we had provided in the States, not trusting the local postal system. My scream of joy caused my children, who were home for the holidays, to pile into my room, their eyes wide with curiosity as I smiled and began to dance.

From a pool of however many thousands of applicants from around the world and around Nigeria, I had won the green card lottery.

They joined me in spontaneous dance punctuated by shouts of joy. Cries of "God is good," "*Chineke Igwe*," and "*Chi m oooo"* filled the physical space as much as our emotional one. Chike wasn't around that evening, which allowed for the celebrations to be even wilder and more unbridled as the children hopped on the bed and our shouts grow more boisterous.

There was one more hurdle to clear.

With the first part of the miracle complete, there was a second step of actually qualifying for the green card. Think of winning the lottery as akin to being invited for a job interview, with the second hurdle being the actual interview.

This interview was to take place in Lagos in three weeks. I travelled by road with Obum, who was about seven years old. The rest of the children were already back in Lagos, the girls all in secondary school at Queen's College, with Ijeoma soon to graduate, and Dozie at King's College in his final year. Chike, unfortunately, could not join me, as he had an emergency at the hospital with one of his long-term patients.

The plan was that I would meet up with the children at their auntie Mrs. Okoye's home. It was where they spent many short breaks over the years, and they knew how to get there on the complex and busy Lagos public transportation. Once all together, we crammed into Mrs. Okoye's spare bedroom, talking late into the night, too nervous to sleep. At 5 a.m. I was shaking the children awake. We had all showered the day before, so all we needed to do was get dressed, eat a laid-out breakfast of bread and tea, and get on the road before the monster that is Lagos's traffic awoke.

We rode past the already bustling Yaba neighbourhoods and onto the impressive Third Mainland Bridge running across Lagos's lagoons and connecting the commercial district of Lagos Island to the mainland section of the city. The American embassy was located in Victoria Island, an affluent neighbour-hood marked by lush gardens and large houses.

By 7 a.m. we were standing in line at the embassy in our Sunday-best outfits with fresh haircuts, hairdos, and plaits. We joined the queue, avoiding the lashes of an overzealous security guard tasked with maintaining order. And we slowly snaked our way around the block until we finally made it into the waiting room, where we were met with yet another line, but at least this time we would be seated.

I both anticipated and feared our turn with the white faces who spoke behind glass. There was little to do but wait and observe the interactions between the consular officers and the applicants, some of the latter departing with tears in their eyes; others breaking down in front of the window, pleading; others still raining insults and accusing the blank-eyed faces of ill will.

I had given my children strict instructions to be on their best behaviour, which meant to be quiet throughout the entire process and especially when we finally made it to the glass window. It must have been quite the sight to watch us all, me with thick files of paper, surrounded by six children standing in domino formation from the eldest to little Obum. I smiled in exaggerated deference and presented endless sheets of paper.

"Mrs. Akunyili," said the kind-faced man behind the glass. I didn't want to correct him that it was Dr. Akunyili, so I simply smiled and nodded. "Why do you want to relocate to America?"

My honest answer would have been that I didn't, I was doing this for my children, but that wasn't the answer he wanted. So instead I shared my best version of the truth, which included my quest for the American dream that provided options and opportunities for both me and my family.

The dialogue, which felt longer than the twenty minutes my watch showed, came to an end and I was handed over my papers, which I accepted with thanks, all the while ushering the children away and towards the door. So far, so good, and from my understanding we would receive the results of the interview and of our application shortly.

Only once outside, on a table by the wall of the building did I stop to rearrange my papers. One sheet caught my attention and I scanned it with disbelief. I quickly shoved it and the rest of the papers into an oversized envelope and continued walking, children in tow.

It was only after we were back at Mrs. Okoye's house that I could trust myself to share about the letter. "First of all," I began, "the letter had been addressed to the consulate officer. And you will not believe what it said: 'Due to discrepancies in the information provided, specifically referring to the date of birth of Njideka Akunyili, we advise against qualification for a green card.'"

"*Chineke!* Are you serious?" came Mrs. Okoye's incredulous voice, joined by the excited chatter of the children.

"*Sista*, even I can't believe it," I answered, adding, "See God, can you imagine that he not only missed this memo but he mistakenly handed it over to me along with the rest of the documents!"

The discrepancy in question was that Nji's date of birth on her birth certificate was different from the one I had entered on the form. It didn't help that Njideka's birth certificate itself was a replacement after we couldn't find the original. Between having six children so close in age, separated almost solely by the months of pregnancy, and over the years celebrating all six birthdays on one day, I found it increasingly difficult to recall whose birthday was when. My mistake on the form, on top of the oddity of a new birth certificate, must have seemed very suspicious.

It was miracle enough that the consular agent missed the memo, but the finish line would be the final approval. "What if they get the memo when processing?" I worried ceaselessly. "The devil is a liar," I reminded myself as a way to dispel the relentless doubts that screamed in my mind. I intensified my prayers inviting God to show His full might.

The day we got the news, I was alone in my office. I knelt down in tears and thanksgiving. In that moment, I had a clear premonition that a window had just opened in the story of our lives. And it was all there in the words of a letter, the first words of a story that was still to be told.

Once celebrations were over and we had brought thanksgiving offerings of a chicken and ten tubers of yam to our parishes in Enugu as well as Agulu, I had now before me the task of raising the money needed to fly all six children to the United States.

Where we were to find money for such an endeavour, I wasn't sure, especially as it would not be one trip but several over the course of the years it would take for each child to graduate from secondary school in Nigeria. The intention was to honour the green card's rule that a card holder must not spend more than one year living abroad outside of the United States or risk losing one's status. As I didn't want to interrupt the children's education, I had in mind that their full relocation would be after their studies, at which point they could transition to university in America.

Thirty-Two

*"A well-travelled child exceeds a grey-haired
person in knowledge."*

MY YOUNGER BROTHER, ANAYO, was now a man, married
and living in a house with his wife, Sylvia, whom naturally I
had helped him find, and children. He had put on some weight
since his return to Nigeria, causing his lazy eye to seem even
more pronounced.

Over the last years, my job at PTF meant that I could do
what I had always desired, which was provide for my family,
including my brothers and sisters. In those years, as much as
I was a support for him, I had come to lean very heavily on
his support.

To call him a brother, especially in a country where every
other person is called a brother or sister, is not enough to
capture the depth of our relationship. He was a business partner, a confidant, and my most trusted companion. Those years
at PTF also greatly strengthened our bond, as we started to
work closely together.

Over the years, he proved himself to be a natural with
negotiations, and I encouraged him often that he had our

father's knack for business. Over time, Anayo himself would become a contractor working with various state and government agencies.

It was with his help, as well as Chike's and that of a good family friend, Arthur Eze, that we were able to acquire the funds needed to purchase tickets to the United States for all eight of us.

Chike nevertheless continued to be critical of the investment in a green card. He was particularly focused on how our first daughter, Ijeoma, had just scored the best JAMB result in the country, which is like saying she got the best SAT or any comparable university entry result out of at least a million others. She only had to point at the university of her choice, and she would be enrolled in the highest degree program — that being, of course, medicine.

"Ijeoma didn't need a green card to access the best universities in this country," Chike said, "and we cannot be assured of the same plethora of choice in the States."

Convincing Chike once his mind was made up was like trying to dry up a lake with a hair dryer. We were similar in that way.

Those months taught me to focus on the silver lining, on the opportunity it signalled for the rest of the family.

OUR FAMILY'S FIRST TRIP to the United States was the American summer of 1996; tickets had been booked months in advance to correspond with the beginning of the school vacation. More than one of my children had created a countdown calendar. They were absolutely vibrating with excitement.

I was to fly with the children. Chike would join just days later. At the Murtala Muhammed International Airport in Lagos, the only international airport in the country at the time, we presented our green cards at check-in with smiles and some anxiety that everything would actually work out. It was only once we were settled in on the plane that we could fully trust that we were all indeed flying off to America. There was a lot of excitement already in the sheer novelty of us all being on a plane together.

That plane stopped over at Amsterdam Airport Schiphol for about fifteen hours. The children had never seen any single structure so big and impressive. They refused to sit still and spent hours walking around the airport, in awe of the many marvels that every other traveller seemed to take for granted. Name it, and they were impressed: the sparkling clean toilets; the large glass windows with endless views of airplanes landing and taxiing; the free video game stations; and, my personal favourite, the duty-free shops with endless testers of perfumes and expensive creams. A lifelong lover of perfumes, and with only one body with finite parts to spray upon, I put my half-dozen brood to good use, inviting wrists, backs of hands, and crooks of necks for testing. Once parts were exhausted, we spent time smelling each other, trying to decide which scents were universally preferred as well as which bottle they corresponded to.

Our port of entry in the United States was JFK Airport in New York. We were not strangers to large crowds, especially having spent time in Lagos, but this one was made up of people of all shapes, colours, and backgrounds. It was like the world had been placed in one building, and we had a front-row seat.

We were picked up by our host, Dr. Joseph Obunike, an old friend of ours from our university years. Joe drove us through New York traffic and past the famous skyline to his two-bedroom apartment in the Bronx, where the children would spend the entire summer. I was not sure if Joe understood what he'd signed up for, as six children, however independent and mature, were still quite the responsibility.

Chike and I spent just over a week with them, enough time to stamp our passports and activate our green cards before we had to go back home to work. The children were all too happy to stay on and explore America, a point that was not lost on me whenever I called to check in.

America was for them indeed the land of plenty. They couldn't get over how accessible chocolate bars and cookies were. Or how soda, usually a treat, was so readily available, made further possible by their clever ruse of hanging on to used McDonald's cups, which meant a lifetime of free refills.

Similarly, they marvelled that no one simply took all the newspapers out of the coin-operated newspaper stands to sell them for, say, five cents less. Such a contraption, they mused, would surely never have worked in Nigeria! Still so young and they had already learned to see the hustle in any situation. They shared another marvel that made me laugh uncontrollably: all-you-can-eat Chinese buffets. My children would go to the neighbourhood Chinese buffet for lunch, and once they had fed to their fullest satisfaction, they remained seated, nursing a glass of water over a good book until dinnertime rolled around, at which time they would have room to once again fill their bellies.

In those years I concluded that you can take a child out of the village, but you cannot take the village out of the child. No matter how much they acquire over the course of their lives, they are shaped so much by their initial scarcities.

Winning the green card had opened the world to us all, especially my children, who had their entire lives ahead of them. My job also meant more disposable income with which we could dream bigger. Much was still becoming clear, but one thing was certain: life was changing very quickly for me and for our family.

Thirty-Three

*"If you pick up one end of the stick,
you also pick up the other."*

OUR HOME IN UMUEZEBI, now sprouting mould and green moss, had begun to feel like a shell we had outgrown. By mid-1997, we moved to a new house in a middle-class neighbourhood called Independence Layout in a shanty-free part of the city.

Enugu had grown over the years into a sprawling city, attracting Igbos from across the country. Even New Haven, with streets like Umuezebi that had been a mixture of houses and shacks, was becoming gentrified, with fast-food eateries replacing the various open-air structures in which petty sellers and hair weavers worked.

Independence Layout not only boasted the old charm of Enugu but was also the site of many of the mansion homes being erected across the city. Ours was a humble four-bedroom. I loved making a nest there and I spent the first weeks commissioning new furniture and outfitting some older pieces with new upholstery, each patterned in various tartan colours of blue, green, and grey. For the walls, I ordered a fresh coat of paint; it made for a very different space than the dirty walls of our former home, which were so grimy that the children didn't think much about rubbing their snot on them.

And to complete the change of fortunes for our family, we now had a cook, Peter — a signal that we were part of the Nigerian upper middle class. Peter was a light-skinned man of slight build, with one eye blinded by a childhood accident. He hailed from the Southwest of the country, known for delicious foods. I liked his quiet strength, which, mixed with his professionalism and efficiency, meant that we got along.

One of the first things I did was to teach Peter how to cook some of my favourite dishes from the village, such as Congo meat, a delicious, spicy delicacy of roasted snails the size of tennis balls, or onugbu, a soup of bitter leaves, which had to be carefully washed and scrubbed to temper the very harsh taste while leaving just the right amount. He also learned to make my famed Chapmans drink, which visitors had come to expect.

The children had just returned from their second of yearly trips to the United States and were soon to return to school. Chike had softened his stance and Ijeoma, who had since been admitted to Howard University, was to fly back to the States. To celebrate our new home, at the tail end of their holidays, we gathered for our very first movie night as a family.

The film of choice was *Titanic*; we had a bootlegged VHS of this film that was making waves all over the world. Though there was ample space to sit on the couches that flanked the walls of the wide living room, the children and I huddled close to one another, some choosing to sit on the floor from habit, leaning against couch edges and thighs. The room went very quiet as we watched Dozie manipulate the video player and the TV screen turn black before the opening scenes began rolling.

We watched mostly in silence but for my questions and interjections. "Why are they sleeping at the bottom of the ship?" I asked, oblivious to the quiet sigh of one of my daughters before answering the question. They seemed to have a skill I lacked to fully follow the details of the film.

"They said God himself could not sink the ship?" Alarmed by this statement, I repeated it again and again, snapping my fingers, surprised by the audacity of their blasphemy. Even I could tell that it would not bode well for anyone to make such a statement.

When Rose took off her clothes and steam filled the screen, my children averted their eyes. This was out of habit, as their father, the usual enforcer of strict morality in movies, was not around. Under his watch they were not allowed to watch films with violence or kissing scenes, let alone nudity or sexuality. I sometimes wondered if it was healthy that a simple kiss took on such a mythic quality, particularly since they didn't see Chike and I partake in this foreign forbidden pastime.

When the ship hit the iceberg, I went into overdrive. My cries of "*ewooo*" and "Jesus" played as an accompanying soundtrack to the hectic final scenes. When passengers seeking lifeboats were told "first-class women and children first," my sound effects became pained cries. Though it was just a film, I was deeply troubled by the discrimination against the passengers in the lower deck.

Towards the end, when Jack slipped into the water, with a forlorn Rose calling after him, my children shed their tears for the love that was so short-lived and the tragedy of such a cold end, while I cried for the blatant disregard of the poor in favour of the rich.

Many years later, my eldest daughter recalled her memory of us watching *Titanic* together as an apt encapsulation of my personality: "a woman who asked lots of questions, was fully engaged, and did not tolerate unfairness."

Thirty-Four

"He who tells the truth is never wrong."

AT PTF, THERE WAS always a fire to put out, always something that needed to be done. When life is that busy, something always ends up being sacrificed. I saw increasingly how that was true for both time for myself as well as time with my family.

This was exceedingly clear for me when Dozie fell sick. He was a first-year student at Penn State. The meningitis of years before had turned out to be a bone disease, which had gone to his spine and was eating away at the bone in his neck. The doctors said that, had he waited any longer before coming to the hospital, he would have ended up paralyzed. He had surgery to replace the degenerating bone with one from his hip. For almost six months he was in recovery. Chike took time from work and managed to be with him throughout, cooking for him and taking him to appointments. Unfortunately, after six months of rest and heavy medication, the surgery was deemed a failure. This time, I took a week to be with him as he underwent yet another surgery. It was also the same week of Ijeoma's graduation from the University of Pennsylvania after a transfer from Howard. This meant that I couldn't make it — a necessary but also costly choice.

By the grace of God, this time the surgery was successful.

To make sense of everything that was happening, for myself as much as for Dozie, I told him, "What happened to you is a sign that God wants you to be a doctor. Your injury and recovery are a sign that God wants to do great things in your life." My relationship with my son was built on trust, not unlike the one with my father. I noted how much strength my words gave him.

It was at about this time, when so much was going on, that my stomach pains began. One morning, back in Enugu, soon after breakfast, I felt a slight cramp. I thought perhaps it was something I ate and dismissed it and left for the office. Later that day, the pain returned more sharply.

It started innocuously enough with sporadic yet painful discomfort. I continued to assume it would eventually go away, but the pain lingered and ultimately forced a trip to the hospital, where I did some tests. A week later, I received the results: I was diagnosed with a malignant tumour. The diagnosis was too close to the dreaded C-word.

Not to alarm the rest of the family, including my siblings and children, Chike and I kept the details of my diagnosis private and focused on how best to proceed.

To carry out an operation to remove the tumour in Nigeria, as opposed to a country with better medical facilities, was undesirable for anyone with any option. I had options, including medical coverage as part of my PTF package. I chose to go to the United Kingdom for a second opinion, to be followed, most likely, by surgery. PTF, as per my benefits package, agreed to cover the cost of my travel and medical care, which amounted to an estimated seventeen thousand pounds, signed over in an open cheque.

My trip to the U.K. was hardly as joyous as other trips abroad, but I stayed positive and filled with the conviction of God's protection. The visit to a PTF partner hospital in London was smooth. When I met with the doctor after tests, she informed me that my results all came back negative and they did not find any signs of a tumour. I broke into prayer, calling on the many names of God: "God of Abraham, God of Moses, God that changeth not, You have done it again."

I was diagnosed instead with minor bowel obstructions easily treated with prescription medications and a temporary change in diet. The most important news was that no surgery was needed. The doctor congratulated me, excusing herself with a handshake, but not before directing me to another room where I was to discuss the balance. I thanked her again and I followed the directions to an office where I met with the same red-skinned portly gentleman who had welcomed me when I had arrived at the hospital.

He proceeded to check on my experience as well as inform me that I was in good hands, given the government partner relationship with the hospital.

"We have had a chance to treat several patients from government institutions across Nigeria," he said, and I answered with a gentle smile, not fully sure what he was getting at.

"In view of the misdiagnosis and you not requiring surgery, you have a balance of twelve thousand pounds." He paused for my reaction, but I had already expected as much.

"You have ample change to spare and as such, madam,

if you'd like, we can provide you with a receipt detailing the full expenditure of the available funds of seventeen thousand pounds." He paused to make sure I understood his proposition.

His expression was that of contained shock when I responded, "No thank you, and please instead make out the receipt for the proper five thousand pounds."

"But, Dr. Akunyili, are you sure? Everybody does it." His eyes and tone communicated that he was referring to Nigerians. At this point I started to wonder by his insistence if he too would gain from this scam. He wasn't done. "We just recently received a minister, a commissioner, and even the zonal coordinator for the Petroleum Trust Fund, and they all did it. There have never been any issues. You really have nothing to worry about."

Now fully alarmed by what I was hearing, I responded in a sharp tone matched in pitch and loudness, "So, that's how you want to add my name to this list? I am not interested in money that isn't mine!"

"Are you not a Nigerian?" came his surprised and indignant response. "I am sorry if I have offended you, madam," he added quickly. "We have been made to understand that this is an acceptable way of doing things back in Nigeria, and we have been happy to oblige our clients."

To which I answered, "It depends on the type of Nigerian you have seen. You have seen some; now you have seen others!" At this, I stood up to leave, but not before asking for a cheque for the remaining balance made out to the federal agency. I returned all twelve thousand pounds to PTF.

My honesty didn't make me any friends. Many of my colleagues were predictably livid. "Are you trying to make us look bad?" "Didn't they tell you how it's done!" "Don't you see that they might start to wonder how come no one else returns money?!"

Not a stranger to making enemies on this path, I didn't flinch and carried on with my life and with it my responsibilities, ignoring the taunts as a distraction.

I trusted that as long as I stayed true to my values and faith, I was on the right side of my conscience, which mattered above all else.

AS THE ZONAL SECRETARY of PTF, I had the opportunity to impact the lives of thousands of Nigerians, mostly Igbos across the Southeast. I also had a front-row seat to how the system discriminated against precisely those in need. Millions of naira siphoned out of the funds earmarked for social projects fattened the already heavy purses of the rich.

The whole system, not unlike the sinking *Titanic*, had it backwards: help must be given first to those in need, not to those with means.

Powerless beyond my small pond, my frustration in those years was to see how much more could be done, and how little ultimately was. My rebellion was to do my job to the best of my ability, controlling what I could, unwilling at any costs to take that which was not mine.

Thirty-Five

"Every door has its own key."

A YEAR AFTER THE INCIDENT with the hospital, Nigeria
went from the leadership of a military regime to a republican
government under the presidency of Olusegun Obasanjo, the
second democratically elected president of Nigeria following
almost two decades of military rule. Incidentally, Obasanjo
had also been the first military ruler to hand power back to
the first democratically elected civilian government in 1979.

In his 1998 campaign, Obasanjo had promised to clean up
what was widely considered to be a broken country, ravaged
by the unprecedented corruption and brutality of a military
regime, notably under General Sani Abacha — a man so
ruthless that many Nigerians celebrated his death. Perhaps
the country needed a reformed former military man like
Obasanjo — someone who intimately knew both the old and
new — to mop up the years of oppressive military regime. So
we welcomed democracy with open arms, and with it, our
fearless leader.

A seasoned politician, keen to deliver on his election

promise to fight corruption and usher in an open, fair, and transparent government, Obasanjo knew how important it was to move fast and show results.

Discussions to dismantle PTF began soon after he took office. By late 1999 it had closed its doors for good, and I found myself once again a lecturer at the University of Nigeria and a part-time lecturer at the West African Postgraduate College of Pharmacists.

In those years, the very last of my children, our no-longer-so-little Obumneme, who had turned ten, had left for secondary school, and I was left to focus on my work as a lecturer. I poured my experience and passion into training the young minds of the future. My dedication paid off and earned me in the year 2000 the title of professor of pharmacology at the University of Nigeria Nsukka. Less than a year later, my life took a turn fit for a saga.

The incidence of fake drugs in the country was at its peak following years of mismanagement by and apathy from the military government. All manner of adulterated, fake, and substandard food and drugs were dumped into Nigeria; the majority of drugs in circulation were reportedly fake. The result was the death of millions of unsuspecting citizens.

President Obasanjo, whom everyone called Baba in fatherly reverence, was intent on curbing this epidemic and was on the lookout for a trustworthy individual to manage the National Agency for Food and Drug Administration and Control (NAFDAC), responsible for regulating the safety of all food and drugs in Nigeria. He shared this with his advisers in a meeting whose content was retold to me so often that I felt like I was a fly on the wall watching it all unfold.

"I'm looking for somebody to work hard in NAFDAC," the president said. "That old man currently in charge does not impress me. I am looking for an honest and hardworking man to do the job."

Mallam Adamu Ciroma, minister of finance at the time and a close confidant of President Obasanjo, was listening intently, and his eyes lit up. He had heard the story of a pharmacist at PTF who had returned thousands of pounds that had already been signed over to her.

"Baba, there is an Igbo woman," the minister spoke quietly and quickly, his accent peppered with the lyricism of his native tongue of Hausa. "She went to Britain for a medical appointment and when she finished, she said whatever money was left from what had been deposited by her department should be sent back, *Wallahi tallahi.*"

The president was intrigued by this, that much was clear by his narrowed eyes and quiet contemplation. "So, there is a Nigerian woman like that? Where is she? I want to meet her."

Other advisers in the room had ideas of who they wanted in the job and were alarmed by the direction of the conversation.

"But, Baba, she is a woman," one said. "You know how hectic this job is. The director general deals with a lot of stress!"

Another said, "She is also an Igbo woman, at that." This would be a disadvantage because, according to them and in truth, Igbos were the main culprits in the production and sale of fake food and drugs. "It can be so hard to stand up to your own people, especially as a woman."

They weren't done yet. "Also, don't forget that the health minister, Dr. Menakaya, is an Igbo man, and having two Igbos overseeing everything pertaining to the health of the nation . . ." The speaker paused, searching for the right words. "Perhaps too many Igbos, *ehh*, don't you think, Mr. President?"

At this point, with his signature slow and measured delivery, the president said, "Well, I don't know that a woman cannot do even more than a man. And as for her tribe, maybe it takes a person who knows the minds and hearts of their people to do the job."

This was not the response his advisers were hoping for. After a brief pause another voice joined in. "Baba, I didn't want to be the one spreading rumours, but I too have heard of this woman and I think it is important that you know that some say she is not even a pharmacist. They say that she forged her qualifications. It wouldn't be the first time we've seen this." He was referring to a recent scandal where a high-ranking official was caught forging his credentials, casting a shadow on all other supposed certificates of officials.

Baba turned to one of his aides seated behind him. "Look into this personally." And that signalled the end of the meeting.

I would find out later that Baba would confirm with his relation Jokoo, who was a colleague at PTF, the story he heard about me. It would also be Jokoo who made my number available to the president.

Thirty-Six

"If the rain permits, the moon will shine."

IT WAS A SUNDAY afternoon and Chike and I were spending it in Enugu. We had just come home from church and I was about to change into a loose orange and dark-brown bubu before settling in to read the Sunday papers when the phone rang. On my way up the stairs, I picked up the call.

"Akunyilis' residence."

"My name is Obasanjo." Upon hearing this, I nearly collapsed. The voice of the president was so distinct that it would be very hard to imitate so expertly. "Are you Dr. Dora Akunyili?" he asked.

I nodded until I realized my own folly. "Yes," I answered.

I could feel Chike's eyes watching me. He must have noted my shock. At some point in the mostly one-sided exchange, I reclaimed my composure and mouthed at Chike, "It's the president, it's Obasanjo."

"I heard about what you did. The money you returned. I didn't know there were Nigerians like you." He paused and I wondered if he was expecting an answer.

"Thank you, your excellency."

"I want to see you in Aso Rock. There is a proposal I would like to discuss with you. Are you interested?"

"Yes, yes, I am. Thank you, your excellency," I repeated.

A voice in the background was demanding his attention, and he made excuses, muttering quick words about his special assistant being in touch. I hung up, still in shock.

I went to see him in Abuja the following week. The gates of Aso Rock were heavy and built to impress. Security guards asked my name, which they verified against my passport. Once they were satisfied, the gates opened to a grand driveway. My heart was beating fast, not from nervousness but a building excitement.

I was welcomed at the equally impressive entrance by a special assistant, who handed me over to another assistant, who led me to a living room with two large flags at each end. It was here that I sat waiting for my life to change.

Obasanjo came in, his presence filling the room beyond the reach of his title. He was very kind in a fatherly sort of way, his face crumpled in attractive folds and sags. It was the face of a man who was content with his advanced age. The visit lasted about an hour and felt like a friendly interview, with me answering various questions about my family, my husband, my background as a pharmacist, and my PTF experience.

I answered him with the ease of truth, unsure what to emphasize, not knowing what exactly he needed me for.

"Why did you return the money?" he asked.

"Because it is what my father taught me. It is what my mother taught me. It is what my grandmother taught me. To never take that which isn't mine. It never even crossed my mind to keep it. That this action stands out gives me pause about a world we have created where we assume it's normal for everyone to take advantage of the other. I want us to challenge what we have accepted as a part of life. Because whether we acknowledge it or not, to steal, especially from the poor, will destroy everything and everyone."

I paused in reflection and continued. "Growing up in the village, I imbibed a culture of contentment with what I have, however simple, and zero tolerance for corruption. This is because in our traditional village setting, corruption was completely unacceptable. It was taboo; it destroyed both the culprit and their lineage. In fact, there is no direct translation for the word *corruption* in Igbo. Entire families were ostracized for one family member's crime of stealing, embezzling community funds, or cheating. Individuals who stole were barred from taking any chieftaincy title, and their children would neither marry nor be married in the village, and the story was passed on from one generation to the next."

There was silence during which he seemed to weigh my words.

"Have you heard of NAFDAC?" he asked.

I searched my brain and nodded, recalling a recent article in the papers about the dismissal of its former director general.

"Are you interested in being the director general of the agency?" he asked, observing me very closely.

A master of my emotions, with years of training at masking them, I didn't betray excessive surprise, even though in my mind I was screaming my disbelief. "Me?! A director general of a national agency? But why? What? How?"

"Yes" was the only answer I gave him, firm and short, to

betray nothing and expose even less. "But please," I added, "I'll have to discuss this with my husband and family."

"Of course," he said, smiling, seemingly satisfied with my answer.

The rest of the meeting was spent in what I can only describe as story time, as he shared with me the opposition he had faced around hiring me, including from his cabinet.

In a turn of events that showed just how alive my Chi was, one of the things that worked in my favour was a cabinet reshuffle in 2001, which brought in new advisers and a new minister of health who was very much in favour of my appointment as the director general of NAFDAC.

I listened quietly, sensing that this was important to him, and personally appreciating the space it gave me to be in gratitude, as well as to find my composure from the shock of his announcement.

Once he signalled that the meeting had come to an end, I thanked the president with a conservative profuseness for the offer and his candour, and promised to be in touch.

The next day, I called the number he gave me to his personal line. "Mr. President, Baba, sir," I said in greeting, "this is Dr. Dora Akunyili. My answer is yes."

The task at hand was to safeguard all food and drugs coming into, going out of, and circulating within the country. At that point, according to a NAFDAC report, about 68 percent of drugs were unregistered in Nigeria. And an overwhelming percentage of drugs in circulation were counterfeit, which was defined as when a drug is not what it purports to be, including when labels misinform as to the drug's content or use.

When the news of my appointment was made public, some

people complained that I had no experience working on a federal level. They were right. They also thought that at forty-seven, I was too young for the job. Others argued that I might not have the capacity to tackle the Hydra-headed monster called counterfeit medicines. On this point, they were wrong.

While I was overwhelmed by the weight of the responsibility, I trusted that it was the will of God and as such I was not going into it alone. God, I knew, would never send anything my way that I could not handle. The appointment did more to convince me of this than anything before.

From zonal secretary — a small fish in a big pond — back to a lecturer in the university — an even smaller fish — on April 12, 2001, I became the head of the most important regulatory body in the entire country, in charge of ensuring the safety of food, packaged water and drinks, and medicine for over 160 million Nigerians.

Thirty-Seven

"The load is not too much for ants."

PROTECTING THE SAFETY of the food and medicines for citizens is one of the more basic roles of government. NAFDAC was created in 1993 by the federal government to do just this, by regulating the manufacture, importation, exportation, advertisement, distribution, sale, and use of food and drugs, as well as medical devices, cosmetics, detergents, chemicals, and all packaged drinks.

The ineptitude of past administrations — all of which, up until the new government of Obasanjo, had been military governments that held onto power by brute force — resulted in many years of ineffectiveness. In spite of its significant role, NAFDAC remained a relatively obscure organization with little power or will to uphold its mandate.

This vacuum opened the door for the production, importation, and distribution of counterfeit drugs, tainted food, and other dangerously substandard products. The key players were cartels of counterfeiters, usually made up of Igbo traders, in a natural continuation of their dominance importing and supplying goods across the country.

This was the environment I entered as the director general. The role required me to relocate to Abuja. All my children had left home, making it a much easier decision. Obumneme had been the last to leave, just the year prior, for boarding school in Benin. Chidiogo was in her final years in boarding school at Queen's College in Lagos, following in the footsteps of her three sisters, who had graduated from the same secondary school. Somto and Nji were at the University of Pennsylvania and Swarthmore College respectively. Dozie was in his final year of pre-med at Penn State, and Ijeoma, who had at that point decided against medicine, was working at the World Bank in Washington, DC, following graduation from Harvard with a master of public administration. I was no use to any of them in Enugu.

Everyone was happy for me to gain the NAFDAC position, Chike most of all. In the days before I left for Abuja, he repeatedly told the story, with his usual ability to hypnotize an audience, of how there were so many people questioning him about allowing me to go, and his dismissal of their worries. I could hear him wanting me to note his generosity for having no opposition to me saying yes to the opportunity. His care for me and for the family was a point of pride for him, and he wanted it to be noticed.

In accepting the role, I had to once again face the voices of fear and concern, this time internal and external, questioning how exactly I planned on achieving the mammoth task of curbing an epidemic with so many faces. I knew to expect the worst. But even this could not have prepared me for what I witnessed.

In my first days, I undertook a familiarization tour of NAFDAC's facilities in Abuja and Lagos, including offices and laboratories. The Abuja offices, which served as the corporate headquarters, were in shambles — old, dirty buildings with dusty files and bored-looking staff. The situation in Lagos, the operational headquarters, was even worse. In both cities, the laboratories were derelict, filled with obsolete non-functional equipment, and the general environment was depressing. I became quite nervous. The level of decay was unbelievable, and the scope of the work that needed to be done became even more apparent.

And to further compound the dire situation, there were no handover notes from the former director general. I was to start from scratch, but for the incredible support of a Mr. Tubosun Odusanya, the personal assistant to the former director general, who stayed on, working around the clock to acquaint me with the system.

Undaunted, I rolled up my sleeves. With the sheer volume of work that needed to be done, I knew I couldn't do it alone. I needed to surround myself with individuals who believed in the mission and shunned the lure of bribes and other traps. I reached out to old and trusted colleagues from my time at the local government. Key among them was a fellow local government director, Mr. Kalu Ugwumba. I'd always admired his eye for detail and his ability to get things done. He was my first special assistant. For my second special assistant, I chose a certain Mrs. Lizzy Awagu.

I also leaned on the general wisdom of my old friends, such as Stella Okoli, a pharmacist and CEO of Emzor Pharmaceuticals, with whom I spent many long conversations picking her mind for her in-depth knowledge of the drug manufacturing business. And for moral support and advice, I sought out Dr. Dere Awosika, a fellow pharmacist and a savvy politician with many years of experience who showed me the ropes of navigating a federal agency.

Within NAFDAC, we identified key individuals such as Dr. Andy Andem and Mr. Dioka Ejionueme to serve as directors. Together, we formed a core group to take stock and plan the next critical steps.

With minimum delay, we started by defining the very mission of NAFDAC and came up with our new vision statement: "To safeguard public health by ensuring that only right quality products are manufactured, imported, exported, advertised, distributed, sold, and used." Over time it became "NAFDAC — safeguarding the health of the nation."

Understanding the importance of breaking a large task into smaller, more manageable pieces, we resolved to focus on one goal at a time, starting with those at the marriage of greatest potential impact and realizable within a short period. The measure of success was always the same: to eradicate fake drugs and other substandard regulated products.

I knew that nothing could be done without the support of the existing NAFDAC staff, numbering about three thousand. A few months before I took on the role, with the former director general relieved of his appointment and little or no leadership in the time since, staff had become fully disengaged from service. Morale across the agency was non-existent and many didn't even bother to show up, not even on my first days in the office. This apathy was compounded by the lack of accountability that had been exacerbated by the leadership gap of the last months.

The only way to get people to step up, we reasoned, was to target the existing staff mindset — inviting individuals who made up the staff body to know that their efforts mattered.

In Lagos, which housed most of our staff, I called the first general meeting for all staff. I wasted little time reintroducing myself before getting straight to the point.

"Do we allow the evil to continue?" I asked the fully packed room. "Do we keep quiet and allow business as usual?" I had decided to speak to their sense of fairness and justice. "The evil of fake drugs," I added with great conviction, "is worse than the combined scourges of malaria, HIV/AIDS, armed robbery, and illicit drugs. This is because malaria can be prevented or treated; HIV/AIDS can be avoided; armed robbers may kill a few at a time, if at all; and cocaine and similar drugs are taken out of choice and by those who can afford them. But fake drugs are taken by all and kill en masse, and anyone can be a victim."

I ended my talk by reminding them that each person in the room could be a victim of this plague, as my own sister had been a victim. And so, each person had a critical role to play in safeguarding the lives of the people.

"We cannot change this country without you," I said, "and this is what we aim to do: in saving lives, we can transform the face of the country. I invite you as such to join the new NAFDAC and give faking, counterfeiting, and other regulatory anomalies the frontal attack for which the agency was established."

I felt the energy shift in the room as staff sat up straighter. While my talk had been effective, I knew much more was still to be done. We spent the rest of the meeting discussing how to tackle the barriers that prevented staff from delivering on the mission. Again and again, corruption came up as the greatest impediment to efficiency.

We all agreed that the most critical step to address staff mindset was tackling the cankerworm of internal corruption. This was no easy task in any scenario, least of all when corruption is fully ingrained from years of past leaders of the agency and the country at large turning a blind eye to the dumping and manufacturing of substandard food and drugs.

Thirty-Eight
"One should sip hot soup slowly."

HOW DO YOU ASK a person to refuse a bribe in exchange for registering a medicine when they believe that the next person will accept it, or when it has been the way of things for years prior?

You do so by sending the clear message of zero tolerance.

Not unlike my days at the local government and at PTF, in confronting recalcitrant staff, I endured rebuttals that I was now all too familiar with: "We have been here a long time and this is not how we do things here." To which I responded with what was beginning to feel like my signature statement: "This is how things will be done from now on."

Those found unwilling to comply with the resolution of transparency were let go, and we were left with a group that was relatively willing to heed the new mandate. The second phase of the strategy was to fuel and reward passion and dedication to the mission.

NAFDAC embarked on extensive local and international staff training. This equipped staff with the relevant skills required for effective regulation and control of food and drugs, and also served as a reward mechanism. Staff who displayed a passion for their work were prioritized for business trips to conferences and training programs regionally and overseas.

With a belief that the environment should reflect the spirit of the agency and its staff, we set out to refurbish NAFDAC staff quarters, offices, and laboratories, repairing or replacing dilapidated staff vehicles and properly equipping the offices with telephones, photocopying and fax machines, and computers. We also purchased power-generating sets for offices nationwide to resolve the irregular power supply and increase efficiency.

Next, we focused on addressing staff well-being, knowing that you cannot give what you don't have. We paid all outstanding arrears and introduced staff welfare packages that included allowances and end-of-year bonuses. Within this, we acknowledged the disproportionate challenge on young working mothers, which led to the establishment of a daycare centre. We improved health care access for staff by building relationships with various health care facilities across the country, and we harmonized the banking system so that NAFDAC staff could enjoy fast-track bank services anywhere in the country. It was a perk that made them feel a sense of importance and belonging.

We didn't stop there. Conscious of the financial stress life events impose on families, we set up an allowance system to help with high-cost occasions such as burials and weddings.

Furthermore, we encouraged staff to take initiative. Take, for example, the story of a new employee who, only three months into his NAFDAC employment, became an unexpected vigilante. Acting on a tip, he followed a vehicle he suspected was carrying counterfeit medicines across the Nigerian border to the neighbouring Republic of Benin. He followed steadily until the suspects stopped for gas. At this opportune time, he scurried over, unobserved, and carried out a quick review of the vehicle, confirming by sight some of his suspicions. He slashed the tires of the suspected vehicle, after which he called the police.

The smugglers were arrested on the spot and extradited back to Nigeria, where they were charged and apprehended, along with the car filled with fake and unregistered medicines. Though his method was unconventional and rather dangerous, he saved many lives by his actions. I swiftly promoted the young man for his bravery in the full belief that when hard work and integrity are not rewarded, corruption is promoted.

Within a few months, we could see the fruits of the staff rejuvenation. The agency was growing in reputation as a coveted place of employment. Once we had our house in order, the next line of action was for the agency to take stock of the extent of fake drugs. Even I was not ready for what the data uncovered.

Thirty-Nine

"When the food is properly done, soft enough
so that crumbs fall, it reaches the ant."

WHEN WE BUY AND CONSUME a pill, most of us trust that it has all the active ingredients promised. What if you couldn't trust that it would work? What if you had no way of knowing the difference between a capsule filled with medicinal ingredients and one containing chalk, milk, talcum powder, or vegetable oil?

This was what people in Nigeria were living with every day. This was what killed my sister.

Nigeria was rated globally as one of the countries with the highest incidence of fake and counterfeit drugs and other unregulated products. We found in an initial study that as much as 50 percent of medicines in circulation fell under the broad umbrella of counterfeit; about 70 percent of drugs were unregistered and undocumented by the regulatory agency. And to further compound this, the general public was ignorant of the existence of NAFDAC, the pervasiveness of fake drugs, or their right to good-quality, regulated products.

In the food category, expired products were widespread, along with contaminated packaged drinks, deceptively labelled foods and drinks, foods processed with toxic chemicals, and improperly preserved fresh products.

The very water Nigerians were drinking was not safe. Water, our most basic need, was causing so many to fall ill. We found that over 95 percent of bagged sachet water, known colloquially as "pure water" and marketed to millions of low-income groups, was contaminated with either microorganisms or chemicals. The effects were constant outbreaks of cholera and other water-borne diseases.

Tins of infant formula were filled with a mixture of cassava flour, sugar, and powdered milk and consumed by thousands of unsuspecting infants, leading to countless deaths. Imported sand was labelled as milk powder, and unpasteurized milk and yogurts were packaged, stored, and sold under unsanitary and unsafe conditions.

The situation with counterfeit medicines was even more alarming.

The World Health Organization (WHO) defines counterfeit medicine as "one which is deliberately and fraudulently mislabelled with respect to identity and/or source." Counterfeit products may include products with the wrong ingredients, without active ingredients, with insufficient active ingredients, or with fake packaging. For example, we found 47 of the 149 brands of water for injection were unsterile or simply filled with tap water. Fake adrenaline, a cardiac stimulant used for open-heart surgeries, was widely available and indistinguishable from authentic adrenaline. The market was also awash in fake antibiotics, leading to many preventable deaths from infections.

It was bad enough when the drug was completely devoid

of any benefits, but what if it had just a little, enough to fool you into believing it to be real but not enough to be potent? Such counterfeiting of drugs with insufficient active ingredients was most rampant with popular and fast-moving medicines, such as antimalarials and antibiotics; sometimes as much as 75 percent or more of the active ingredients were sacrificed in order to produce increased quantities of the drugs at low cost.

Other times we found that drugs contained active ingredients that differed from those stated on the label. This was especially prevalent with scarce or expensive drugs, which sometimes were counterfeited by mislabelling another product.

There was also the issue of clones of fast-moving drugs whereby fakes are packaged to look exactly like the original brand and sold in large quantities to an unsuspecting public.

Expired drugs, drugs without any expiry date, or drugs relabelled to extend their shelf life were another challenge. Due to the weak regulatory environment, large consignments of expired or about-to-expire drugs were regularly shipped into Nigeria, where they would be relabelled, or not, and sold to consumers.

In Nigeria, especially in rural areas, herbal remedies were a significant component of health care, with increased demand from consumers wanting an effective cure when Western medicine failed. This market too was not spared, and herbal preparations were sometimes mixed with dangerous narcotics, such as heroin, in an effort to inspire a supernatural reputation and increase demand.

The challenges extended as well to medical equipment: syringes with poor calibration, unsterile syringes packaged in unsterile environments, blunt needles, adulterated blood bags and infusions, even condoms with poor tensile strength. And the list went on.

Anything that could be faked was, even things you would never expect. Cosmetics were not exempt, and the market was awash with skin-bleaching creams with toxic and sometimes carcinogenic ingredients that had deleterious health consequences to its users.

The entire situation was exacerbated by the lack of traceability, with no manufacturer name or contact to identify the counterfeiters.

And while all this was bad enough, no one could fully comprehend the damage, given inadequate data due to poor recording systems. Over the years of battling counterfeit medicine, only few recorded examples of its impact existed, including the 1990 death of over two hundred children in the North and Southwestern cities of Ibadan and Jos after being given paracetamol syrup produced with highly toxic diethylene glycol solvent.

The problems had only got worse over the years: the supply of genuine products was so heavily crippled by the unfair competition from fake medicine that honest manufacturers shrank in the market while the sale of counterfeits soared. Unhealthy competition from fakers meant that legal manufacturers who were employing workers, producing genuine products, and boosting our economy could not break even. Many multinational companies had long divested and left Nigeria out of frustration; local pharmaceutical companies could hardly cope where these giants had failed. By the early 2000s, the situation for local manufacturers worsened when,

due to the high volume of counterfeit medicines in circulation, most made-in-Nigeria drugs were banned across many
countries in West Africa.

Hospitals, clinics, and pharmacies across the country could
not be sure that the drugs dispensed to their patients were
genuine. The same was true for consumers, especially given
that in Nigeria prescription medicine could be purchased over
the counter, further placing the burden of discernment on the
consumer, who had little or no way to identify fake drugs.

The consequence of fake drugs was mass murder.

With holy rage at what I saw before me — an environment
laid waste by years of mismanagement and the unchecked acts
of counterfeiters — I set out on a crusade or jihad (depending
on which demographic I was speaking to) to eradicate fake
drugs in Nigeria.

My furor was fuelled by my own experience of losing
Nwogo. I knew all too well the pain of avoidable loss of life
and didn't want anyone else to experience what my family had.
In addition, I was buoyed by a pact I made with God when I
got the job to do everything in my power to serve the position.

I saw the way forward as having two branches: one, eradicate ignorance; two, eradicate fake drugs. These battles would
have to happen in tandem, the success of one supporting the
other. We had work to do.

Forty

"Sticks in a bundle are unbreakable."

TWO OR THREE TIMES a month, I got away from Abuja to visit Chike. For hours, we sat in the living room in our new home in Enugu, which I had contracted Anayo to build. In those evenings, with CNN playing in the background, we went through mounds of "point and kill" — fire-roasted fish — and plantain washed down with juice made from freshly squeezed oranges that Chike had brought over from the village. I appreciated his attention to my needs, and that extended to his willingness and even eagerness to explore the intricacies of the world of NAFDAC with me. It was in this room, surrounded by framed family pictures, that we discussed and planned.

"Ugogbe," he would tease, "or should I call you *Ochiri ozua*," referring to my new title that meant "the mother of all." "You are taking care of everyone but me, oh."

"Mschew," I would hiss jokingly before sharing the latest developments of NAFDAC to an attentive Chike.

I always came back from these trips rejuvenated, helped by

sleeping aids, which had become indispensable for me over the years to quiet an overactive mind. For all I knew, half the time I was taking fake valium, but I found it hard to sleep without it.

With a belief in the people working together to enact change, the first line of business was to raise public awareness. We knew that getting consumers on board was key, especially given the difficulty of differentiating between real and fake drugs, thanks to the ingenuity of the counterfeiters.

We embarked on a nationwide enlightenment campaign via town-hall-style workshops; radio, TV, and newspaper ads; and interviews to inform Nigerians of the dangers of fake and counterfeit products, as well as the role of the citizens as active contributors to the eradication of counterfeiting. We highlighted the most commonly faked products and the telltale signs of inauthenticity, such as a blurred or missing expiration date, packaging colour inconsistencies, and misspelled brand names that mimic another.

In all these interactions with the public, we had one key message, which we repeated over and over again: "Counterfeit and substandard drugs and other unregulated products are killing Nigerians and wrecking our economy. Join NAFDAC to safeguard the health of the nation."

We set up hotlines for citizens to report any individuals, factories, or warehouses where counterfeit drugs, unwholesome food, or other substandard regulated products were suspected to be manufactured or stored. Citizens began reporting suspicions or knowledge of drug, food, and water counterfeiting businesses. Others called to confirm whether a drug or food was safe for their consumption.

Some such tips would be sent directly to my personal cellphone, which meant that at any given time, one or more of my five phones was always buzzing. No message went unread and unanswered, and the same was my expectation of the rest of the NAFDAC staff.

I knew that the current approach, however effective, was not sustainable.

One night I was dreaming of rain, the heavy type that drowned out everything else, and I woke up with an urgent idea: that we revamp the concept of the NAFDAC registration number. It was to be a simple set of numbers printed on packaging to signal to the consumer that the product was registered, and hence approved by the agency.

As with every idea I had in my sleep, I got up and scribbled this one down in a small notepad I kept on the bedside table beside my rosary, which lay on top of my Bible.

Our first area of focus in enacting this idea was with pure water, the drink of Nigeria's poor and middle-class populations, sold in polyethylene bags at a fraction of the cost of bottled water.

We started by requiring all pure water producers to register for a NAFDAC number. The process required manufacturers to prove the water sourcing and filtration in facilities that met cleanliness standards. Once we had created a standard, we expanded to the producers of bottled water. Over the course of a few weeks, we further expanded the registration process to include foods and drugs. To ensure compliance, we mandated that by a deadline of January 2003, all products for the Nigerian market must have NAFDAC registration numbers.

Now, in addition to being empowered to spot fakes and report any suspicions of counterfeiting, health care providers and citizens alike had an easily verifiable number to check the authenticity of food and drugs. This approach was a resounding success.

In bringing average Nigerians on board as critical actors in the crusade, we showed the importance of citizen engagement. With every anonymous report and action taken, the power of the people and the role they could play in effecting change and holding each other accountable were on full display.

We also called on pharmacists, patent medicine dealers, medical doctors and hospitals, bankers, airlines and courier services, the National Union of Road Transport Workers, bakers, millers, importers, civil society, government parastatals including the port authority, and international organizations to join in the battle. Our message was consistent: the merchants of death must be stopped.

Doctors were a critical ally, given their proximity to patients. Suspicious deaths that previously would have gone unrecorded were now tracked. It was doctors who reported the high cases of kidney failure, diarrhea, vomiting, fever, and convulsions in infants that, upon investigation, we found was the result of a teething mix that contained diethylene, used in antifreeze. It killed several children before it could be recalled.

It was following their medical advice that NAFDAC closed bakeries that failed to heed the message that carcinogenic potassium bromate was no longer a welcome ingredient in bread or other baked goods.

In collaboration with medical associations, NAFDAC introduced the need to fortify flour, sugar, and edible vegetable oil with vitamins and minerals, measures that positively contributed to the nutrition of the people. The agency called as well for the iodization of salt, an important step to support the body to produce thyroid hormones, critical especially in an infant's brain development.

Critical as well were members of the private sector, notorious for distancing themselves from anything related to the government. Banks, the artery of all financial transactions, following negotiations and an official policy directive from the Central Bank, came on as a partner. The agreement was that banks could only process financial documents for drug importation after validating the imports with NAFDAC.

Border porosity had always been a great challenge. In cooperation with the Ministry of Aviation, NAFDAC issued new guidelines that prohibited aircrafts from carrying drugs into Nigeria without obtaining NAFDAC authorization from their clients. Failure to do so would result in the grounding of the flight. Shipping lines were required to furnish NAFDAC with all their cargo manifests, as was the Nigeria Customs Service, which controlled the movement of cargo across the country.

These partnerships proved to be immensely effective, as with more hands on deck, no one was spared the wrath of the crusade, not small-scale counterfeiters nor international giants like Nestlé.

NAFDAC intercepted and seized a shipping container of expired milk earmarked for baby food production by Nestlé Nigeria PLC. The following weeks were spent in legal battles between NAFDAC and the world's largest food and beverage company, with the latter claiming the safety of its product in spite of the shipment being expired. Against all odds, NAFDAC won the battle and over six thousand 25-kilogram bags of expired milk, worth one hundred million naira (US$830,000), were destroyed.

Through tip-offs from medicine sellers and the general public, the agency located many warehouses containing fake products, all of which were destroyed, alongside those voluntarily handed over by the repentant traders. This activity resulted in the destruction of almost two billion naira's worth (US$16.6 million) of fake products in Onitsha and Lagos, in July and October 2001 respectively.

Over the years, we carried out over eight hundred raids on drug-distribution outlets and up to ninety destruction exercises on counterfeit or substandard medicines — millions of dollars' worth of counterfeits piled into heaps as high as a five-storey building in open squares awaiting their fate: destruction by fire. Between April 2001, when I took the helm of leadership, and August 2004, the agency destroyed over 7.57 billion naira's worth (US$59.6 million) of unregulated products.

The success of NAFDAC took the country by storm. Nigeria watched with varying degrees of awe as counterfeit products burned, the images displayed on television screens and newspaper pages. The reputation of NAFDAC and, with it, mine as the director general leading the transformation of the agency grew to dizzying heights spurred on by the excitement of Nigerians and the media to behold a force like ours. NAFDAC's crusade against fake drugs touched the hearts of the people.

A baseline survey repeated in 2002 and 2003 showed a reduction of 67 percent and 80 percent respectively in the incidence of unregistered drugs.

We were doing more than was expected of the agency —

so said President Obasanjo, who made no secret of how impressed he was by our work.

The counterfeit food and drug peddlers had been targeted and punished, but they would not give up on a multimillion-dollar industry without a fight.

Forty-One

*"If you think you are too small to make a difference,
you haven't spent a night with a mosquito."*

ONE AFTERNOON, I RETURNED from a strategy meeting to
see that the door of my office was ajar. This was not unusual,
because my assistant Noreen went in and out often, but what
didn't make sense was that the office had just been sprayed the
day before with Shelltox and Noreen knew just how much I
hated mosquitoes. That she would leave the door open, though
an annoyance, should not have been alarming.

I tentatively opened the door, and though nothing seemed
out of place, nothing felt right. Then I noticed there was something on my desk. I moved closer. Lying there was a clump of
feathers dripping what looked like blood and wrapped with
a thin rope.

I was shaken but not surprised. Counterfeiters were rich,
connected, and powerful, and they had gone unchallenged
for almost three decades. I was the definition of a thorn in
their side. NAFDAC's crusade was costing them millions of
dollars in lost revenues, and as the chief troublemaker, I was
bad for business.

Many such producers of counterfeit medicine, when their business was hurting, had approached me since I had taken office with various temptations — offers of cars, boxes of trinkets, and bags of money. It was a rude shock to them when I always refused.

This was not the last fetish object that would be left on my desk. Two weeks later, I found another. Blood-stained feathers, coral beads, cowrie shells, and even a dead tortoise. The intention was clear: to plant fear in my heart. As fearless as we Nigerians are, the one thing we don't play with, along with open waters and extreme sports, is juju.

What they didn't bank on was that this Nigerian had her own juju in the form of holy water, which I sprinkled on the objects, all the while chanting my own incantations of "I bless you in the name of Jesus." Afterwards I simply had the items removed, trusting that I couldn't be harmed fighting God's fight.

They didn't stop there.

Six armed men stormed my residence in Abuja. Luckily, I was on an emergency trip to Lagos; after much intimidation of my staff regarding my whereabouts, they realized that I would not be coming home and departed.

After that, my only desire was to be in the quiet of my home with Chike. Instead of a return flight to Abuja, I made my way to Enugu. I enjoyed the familiarity of our upstairs living room, which was where I spent the majority of the time whenever I was in Enugu. Chike had just come back from tennis and gone into his room to take a shower. I was dressed in my brown and orange bubu, waiting for him to join me in the living room that we might share a breakfast of fried plantains and stew that had been brought up as soon as he returned home.

Time does not heal all wounds, but it does inspire wisdom. Chike over the years had continued to support me every step of the way, defying any expectations that he would feel my success undermined his. I had learned to let go of the expectations of marriage I held in my youth, to instead appreciate the life we had, blessed by six healthy, wonderful children whom I knew Chike loved, however harsh his disciplinary tactics. My own journey towards finding peace allowed for just enough space to build a friendship.

I looked up from the paper as Chike walked into the living room wearing a wrapper over his midsection and a serious look on his face.

"*Kedụ,* Daddy," I greeted, calling him by the same name our children used. Upon observing his serious demeanour, I asked, "*Ọ dịkwa mma?*" Is everything okay?

"*Achọọ m ka anyị kpaa nkata,*" he said, sitting beside me. "You know I have no problem with your work or you leaving me all by myself here."

I smiled ruefully at his slight jab.

"On the contrary," he said, "*a na m asupport gị.*"

"*Ama m,* I know," I answered dutifully, willing him to continue.

"There is only one of you, and many other people who can be director general. Please, I am not ready to lose you completely to this work."

I smiled at the concern written all over the face, and before he could conclude that I wasn't taking him seriously, I said, "*Ọ ezi okwu,* it's true, Chike, but I am fine."

"Dora, *Nne*, listen to me, I know your heart is in this, but please take it easy. Your life is more precious than any job," he said, his eyes full of tenderness.

"This isn't just a job, Daddy. I cannot allow these people to continue to harm innocent Nigerians."

I knew he would never go as far as to suggest that I give my notice, since he knew how important the work was to me, but his concern registered. I had long been unfazed by the prospect of sacrificing my own life, but I hadn't fully considered what it would mean for my family if something happened to me. With his words, my perspective shifted.

Just a few weeks after that conversation, approximately thirty armed men attacked and vandalized the newly refurbished NAFDAC laboratories in Oshodi, Lagos. While no lives were lost, they harassed and stripped naked all the security men on duty and destroyed the building, equipment, samples, and files. The cost of the attack was 438 million naira (US$3.65 million).

The loss was a blow, but we were not thwarted. Neither were the counterfeiters.

Forty-Two

"One who holds me to the ground holds himself."

CHRISTMAS WAS THE ONE time of year that our entire family would be reunited, and in December 2003 we were all together, with five of the children flying in from various parts of the United States and my youngest joining by road from Benin City. After so many months of being fully focused on work, having my family around was even more special.

That Christmas break, unlike all others since Chike and I were married, we made the decision to stay in our home in Enugu instead of spending the holidays in the village.

For one, I needed a pause from the breakneck pace of NAFDAC, and the village, one of several where millions of Igbos would be returning home for the holidays, seemed to offer the opposite. But there was another reason for this decision, one I was less inclined to share with Chike or the children: my own intuition cautioned me against making a trip that year for my safety and theirs, buoyed by intel.

We had received a tip that a certain Igbo counterfeiter and member of the mafia had put a price on my head. Though I had armed police escorts assigned to me ever since the threats began, with the crowds and chaos of celebrations of the holiday season, ensuring my safety and that of my family was going to be particularly difficult.

However, after Christmas, on Boxing Day, against my better judgement, I decided to make a trip from Enugu to the village. I had received a call the night before from an important ally in the fight against counterfeiters cajoling me to attend his chieftaincy at Orlu in Imo State. He was insistent and I knew how critical his support was, as well as the significance of me missing such an important event. We would make it a quick trip, I reasoned, and since we had decided against going to the village, no one would be expecting us.

As is customary given the time of the year and the type of celebration, it was important to come with my family. I also wanted my daughter's friend Leila, who was visiting from the United States, to enjoy her holidays beyond the walls of our home in Enugu, especially as the city is like a ghost town during the holidays, with most of its residents departing for their various villages.

I had decided against telling Chike about the threat of an attack; had he known, he would never have agreed to us all going to the village. For moral support, I invited my brother Anny along as well, knowing that he also stood to benefit from the connections at the event.

My children were happy for the adventure, although they didn't like that they had to dress up, the girls in tight head-ties and lace tops and skirts they complained were either too itchy or too heavy, trapping sweat and amplifying the dry heat of the season. For the boys, it was loose cotton ankara tops and tailored trousers in coordinated colourful patterns. I matched the girls, choosing an equally elaborate and heavy lace outfit complemented by a gold jewellery set.

The drive to Orlu was about an hour and a half, which we made in a convoy of five cars, sirens blaring in the front and back. It was President Obasanjo who had directed that I receive a security detail after the last attack on NAFDAC. The first car in the convoy was a police escort pickup, clearing the road and setting the pace for the cars behind; in the second, a small luxury car, sat Chike, Anny, and me, with a policeman in the front passenger seat; the two cars directly behind us carried the children, all seven, including Leila, piled into two Jeeps; and behind them was another police escort.

I had given strict instructions that the convoy move quickly and under no condition were we to stop. They took this seriously, for we were moving at a deadly speed, sirens blasting as if daring any car or hawker to stand in our way. Normally, once I decide, I stick to it, but this time, I started to doubt the wisdom of this trip.

The chieftaincy event itself was a blur, much like the hundreds of other such events over the years. Loud music blaring, accompanied by drums and ọja; dancers and masquerades; stylish and colourfully clad guests; unending greetings of hugs, pats, and smiles; heat; sweat and running makeup; and a headache from too-tight head-ties.

At around 5 p.m., we were to head back to Enugu, but not before stopping by our family home in Agulu to say goodbye to my paternal grandmother and the rest of the Akunyili family. However, as it was getting dark, and not wanting the increased security risk of a night journey, I gave the drivers the last-minute instruction not to stop at the Akunyili family compound but to continue straight home to Enugu.

A few seconds past the gate that led to our family compound, I noticed the car in front of us swerve dangerously, then speed off as if pursued by fire ants. Then the commotion started. Gun shots could be heard overhead and all around. No one needed to tell us to crouch down. I was just getting down when I felt a sharp pain like hot water being poured on my head. Everyone in the car was screaming, and their voices drowned out mine. Sander, my personal police escort, was shouting, "Don't stop, don't stop!" in quick barks. "We are under attack! We are under attack!" I thought we had been driving fast, but now we experienced a whole other dimension of speed as the driver revved the engine to its maximum.

From our place as low in the car as possible, all were still screaming, my voice now laced with prayers, fear clawing at my heart. In those moments, I prayed for my life, and I prayed for God's love and protection of my family and everyone with us.

We stayed low until we hadn't heard a gunshot for a few minutes and Sander informed us that everybody was safe. I instructed the cars to head to the police station in Awka and under no condition stop. Chike lent his voice to the order: "Hurry, hurry!"

We arrived in Awka, normally a thirty-minute drive, in ten minutes. The policemen in the station were standing by, and once we pulled into the station, they hastily closed the gates behind us. With the coast clear, everybody emerged to share and check in on each other, robust Igbo emotions in full display. I was surprisingly calm, saying little, but for the shock in my eyes. Surrounded by my family, everyone looking to me to say something, I kept running my fingers along my scalp.

"There is a bullet in my head" was all I said. This seemed to be the comic relief everybody needed, for they all burst into a chorus of laughter.

"Mummy, that's impossible," said my son Dozie.

I ignored him and insisted; I knew what I'd felt, and I had no doubt I had been hit.

The officer on duty, who had been quietly observing the exchange, in broken English said, "Madam, if bullet entered your head, you will not be talking."

I didn't dignify his answer with a response but simply reproached him with my eyes. "There is a bullet," I said again, this time raising my voice to its usual authority. I motioned for my brother Anayo to come over to check the spot I was rubbing.

Anny's "Oh my God" got everyone standing straighter. "*Ọ metụkwaa ya n'isi*, the bullet *grazi* your scalp."

"*Ewoo*," I cried, in anguish and alarm. "It did not go in?"

Anny shook his head. "It didn't, but your hair is burned."

Everyone took turns looking at the singed track across the top of my head. Someone quickly produced my head-tie, which I had been wearing at the time of the attack, and lo and behold, there was a hole in it. The semi-shattered back windshield of the car, which on closer examination bore the hole of a single bullet targeted at my head. The attack went from being a very scary experience to a deeply humbling celebration of the miracle of life. I was so grateful for God's protection, not only of me but of my children and all of our companions.

We later found out that a bus driver, Mr. Emeka Onuekutu,

had been fatally shot by a stray bullet in the crossfire between the assailants and the police escort. That another died in the attack, leaving behind his wife and children, deeply saddened me. I promised justice for the family and the memory of Mr. Emeka. No matter what it took, I vowed that the assailants would not get away with it and I had every intention of finding the perpetrators, notably the main boss behind the attempt, and bringing them to book.

Every single newspaper's headlines the following day were about the assassination attempt, painting a graphic image of how the assassin's bullet narrowly missed my skull, scorching my headscarf. In the coming days, especially given the lull of the holiday period, the articles and news coverage continued, with pictures of my headscarf with arrows pointing to the dark shadow of a hole against the golden fabric.

I received hundreds and thousands of calls and text messages from colleagues, friends, family, and well-wishers sending their thoughts, praying with me in thanksgiving and for my continued safety. Others shared their lingering concern, for though I had two cars full of security, the attempt would have been successful had we stopped at our Agulu home. We concluded that we had a spy in my detail who was sharing information about our movements, but the challenge and cause for concern was that even if they were found and dismissed, there was no way of ensuring that another hire would not be equally compromised.

So, although my security detail increased to ten policemen with me around the clock, this did little to quell fears, especially my family's, about my safety and well-being. Fetish objects, threats, and vandalism were one thing; an assassination attempt was quite another. That the attack was unsuccessful meant that the masterminds behind it would want to ensure they finished what they started and cover the tracks of their initial failure.

The one bright point was that the police were able to track down and capture the assailants, who identified in their confessions a rich Igbo businessman as the mastermind behind the attack. We promptly took the case to court with every intention of pursuing justice, and he was charged with attempted murder. Now to get him convicted.

Forty-Three

"There are no shortcuts to the top of the palm tree."

THE COUNTERFEITERS, FRUSTRATED by NAFDAC's effectiveness and thwarted by increased security around me, continued
to target NAFDAC facilities.

The next attack came just months after the assassination
attempt on my life. In March 2004, the Lagos operational
headquarters — a key artery of NAFDAC's activities — was
reduced to ashes. Everything was destroyed including office
equipment and sensitive files with data on registered products.
Someone wanted to cripple the agency and erase all its records.

On March 10, 2004, barely seventy-two hours later, the
laboratory complex in Kaduna, which was critical for testing large quantities of medicine and food, was set ablaze and
also razed to ashes. The entire building, laboratory equipment,
chemicals and reagents, furniture, and office equipment were
destroyed by the fire. The destruction was valued at about 228
million naira (US$1.8 million), a colossal loss to NAFDAC and
a setback to our operations.

A few days later, a building adjacent to our Benin office was burned down. We had cause to believe that the NAFDAC office was the real target of the arson. Shortly thereafter, criminals broke into the premises of a NAFDAC laboratory complex in Maiduguri, in the Northeast of the country, but they were foiled in the process.

Many at this point were questioning my sanity because I would not throw in the towel; after all, they said, "Your name is not NAFDAC" — it was just a job and not one that they thought I should be so invested in. Despite this rhetoric, I felt like my entire life had led up to this moment. Every obstacle I had faced was mirrored in the reoccurring challenges of keeping NAFDAC alive.

Newton's third law states that for every action or force, there is an equal and opposite reaction. This is true in physics and in life. For each attack we endured, we grew stronger as an agency, as did our sense of pride and purpose, which was buoyed by the support of the people. The attacks were the most vicious they had ever been, and yet NAFDAC was more powerful than ever.

With bribes never having made headway, and the combined attacks on me and on the agency failing to dissuade us from the war at hand, fake-drug manufacturers changed tactics. This time they targeted my family, specifically my youngest son, Obumneme.

Obum was no longer a baby but a full-grown teenager in his third year in Igbinedion Secondary School — a private school in Benin City. He broke from the family tradition of going to either Queen's or King's College, as neither school was as esteemed as it had been just short years before.

He was at school when a group of men, the type you know

have practised their menacing looks, approached him asking if he was Dora Akunyili's son. He said no, answering, "She's my auntie," and then excused himself to join the safety of the closest crowd of students. Obum promptly reported the incident to the school authorities. It was his teacher John Ekong who relayed the incident to me. A week later, Obum was on his way, accompanied by Chike, to St. Anne's Belfield School, a private school in Charlottesville, Virginia, in the United States.

The one thing that could break me was losing any one of my children. Contemplation of my own death was always made difficult by the thought of its impact on my family, but I had never imagined that the war against fake drugs could cause direct harm to my children. It dawned on me in those moments that history was repeating itself. I remembered my own parents' sacrifices, and how they wanted the most for me, which meant sending me away.

My own children had been so young when they left home and had never really come home since. All of me wanted only the best for them, and I had been willing to give everything to ensure this. I closed my eyes and tried to recall memories with them, but they were mostly of when they were much younger, with fewer opportunities to see each other in the last years beyond our Christmas gatherings. Always focused on solutions, I vowed to remedy this, instinctively reaching for my phone. A few rings later, I heard my daughter Ijeoma's voice. My plan was to call each in succession, in my usual fashion from oldest to youngest. I had every intention of reaching out more frequently.

Still with my gaze always on the big picture in those years I intensified my prayers to include the following prayer points:

1. Forgiveness of sins
2. Praise for God, thanksgiving
3. God's favour for me, family, relations, and friends
4. Good health and long life for me, family, relations, and friends
5. A good end to this job so that it gives me what is best for me in my future career
6. The best outcomes for my children's careers and spouses
7. Nobel Peace Prize 2007
8. Divine guidance and protection — do not allow me to be put to shame
9. Sound sleep
10. Peace of mind and body that surpasses all understanding
11. Unspeakable joy
12. Love for everybody
13. Spirit of discernment
14. A holy and prayerful life
15. A miraculous end to my court case
16. Solutions to other problems I have or may not even know I have

Forty-Four

*"We desire to bequeath two things to our children; the first
one is roots, the other one is wings."*

CHANGES ON THE WORK FRONT were happening parallel
with changes at home. The demands on my time were only
becoming more unforgiving and I did not see the pace relent-
ing any time soon.

It dawned on me that our family had never before taken a
proper vacation with all six of the children, and that even during
time together over Christmas holidays or life celebrations, we
didn't spend much quality relaxed time together. Even earlier in
the year, when Ijeoma had got married in Côte d'Ivoire, I had
been so busy catering to the needs of hundreds of guests flying
in from Nigeria as well as the dignitaries of the day, among
whom was the first lady of Nigeria herself, that I didn't even
have time for the bride let alone the rest of the children. Even my
fiftieth birthday celebration, for which all the children had once
again come home, was a blur of pleasantries and politics with
many of the hundreds of guests who joined the celebration. The
only time I had for the children was when I checked that their
chosen outfits for the event were appropriate and impressive.

I mentioned the idea of a vacation to my daughter Ijeoma, who to my delight had decided after her sojourn at the World Bank to return to medical school at the University of Maryland. She suggested a family cruise. It was a resounding yes for me.

She took care of all the details, booking us all a return trip from Fort Lauderdale and around the Caribbean Islands. We chose to make the trip during the final school break of 2004, so all the children could join. Unfortunately, the date did not work for Chike, who hardly had any time off given the demands on his time as a busy ER doctor.

We all met at a hotel close to the departure port, with each child joining from various parts of the world. Once on the ship I noted that Ijeoma had booked the most economical cabins for the rest of her siblings and a larger one for us two to share.

It struck me that despite how far we had come from the days at Umuezebi Street with the shared birthday parties, my children had an aversion to spending. I made a mental note that after all the years of teaching them frugality, it was now time to show them a different possibility, that some things were worth spending on.

The seven days together on the ship and docking at various islands was a gift for us all. I realized in the first hours after departure that my phones had no reception. Without my phones to respond to any of the hundreds of text messages I received every day, or to correspond with the office, I had absolutely nothing to do. I couldn't remember the last time I had dedicated myself fully to relaxation — it might not have been since before I left to live in the village. Over the years, many had teased me that I didn't know how to rest. It was only now that I understood how hard disconnecting from work was for me. However, a day or two into the cruise, I was thoroughly enjoying the therapeutic respite it gave me to hear my own thoughts, and to spend time, as if for the first time, with my children. In some ways I felt like a younger version of myself — carefree, making jokes of every situation, and keen to share stories. I was glad to know that my children could witness me in this way.

Each day, with hours spent undistracted by work or technology, we got to know one another. One evening, gathered inside Ijeoma's and my room, I found myself sharing. It felt like a story at first, of the pains I had endured at the hands of some members of Chike's family. With each word, it felt more real. As I shared, tears streamed down my face. I don't believe I had cried in front of my children before. And now, in this cabin aboard a ship, I allowed myself to feel and to weep for what had happened.

I could not have been happier with the decision to take this time together as a family.

Forty-Five

"When the elephant places his foot on the ground,
one sees his footprint."

BACK IN NIGERIA, NAFDAC'S war continued. With their efforts continually foiled, drug importers started to transport their counterfeit medicines in ingenious ways. Fake drugs were discovered concealed in containers filled with children's wear, duvets, shoes, electronics, and all manner of household objects. Mislabelled cargo containers were filled with counterfeit imported medicines, and counterfeit manufacturing factories went deeper underground.

While the battle on the ground was increasingly victorious, it was paramount to stop the epidemic at the source. Most fakes imported into Nigeria came from India and China. We realized that approaching these countries directly to prevent the counterfeits from leaving their shores was as important as, if not more important than, preventing them from coming into Nigeria. We quickly developed and rolled out a strategy to curb international export of fake drugs. It was primarily to employ diplomacy and appeal to the goodwill of foreign government officials, making them aware of the countless lives lost in Nigeria and across the region due to their internal regulatory failures. We also provided strong incentives and ultimatums for their co-operation.

In international speeches highlighting the dangers of counterfeiting, I shared anecdotes of innocent Nigerians who had gone blind, lost the functioning of internal organs, or even lost their lives or those of their infant children as a result of this epidemic. To communicate that these were not abstract stories, I always shared the very personal story of the loss of my own sister due to fake drugs.

The result of consistent interventions and international negotiations led to many success stories, such as the Indian government adopting a pre-shipment analysis of consignments for exports to Nigeria and working in tandem with a NAFDAC-appointed independent analyst based out of India.

We formed relationships with several leading Chinese pharmaceutical companies, to which we offered incentives to bolster the sales of their regulated goods in Nigeria. We also appointed a public analyst of all exports to Nigeria.

And lastly, we forged strategic relationships with international organizations such as WHO and UNICEF in order to garner international support, especially given the complex and interconnected nature of trade.

Now to tackle the problem of local manufacturers. NAFDAC had to go to the belly of counterfeiting — open-air markets across the country. Open markets in Nigeria are expansive sprawls with thousands of traders and buyers exchanging up to forty tonnes of goods per year. They include everything from fresh fruits and vegetables, groceries, jewellery, and clothing to household, industrial, and office equipment, not to mention fake drugs.

We concluded that our working practice of periodically screening market stalls was no longer adequate. Counterfeiters were getting very creative in evading NAFDAC inspectors. To avoid seizures, traders had created an alert system across each expansive market that allowed them to move counterfeit medicines, or even machinery, from one part of the market to another once news of NAFDAC's presence was sounded.

In order to carry out a full-fledged mop-up, we had to close down the entire market at once. The logistics of such an operation made it almost laughable, but we saw no other way of ending the war once and for all. We would close down three major markets in Aba, Kano, and Onitsha, with the latter being one of the largest in Africa.

The closure of Onitsha Bridge Head Market in Anambra State shook the country. The Onitsha market had existed for three decades and was the main culprit of counterfeiting, producing 20 percent more fake drugs than the rest of the country combined.

To achieve this monumental plan of closing a market of its size, we needed the full support of the federal, state, and local governments. In Nigeria, as in many other countries, it is very difficult to achieve meaningful change without support from the top. President Obasanjo had over the years been our biggest ally and a very vocal supporter of NAFDAC's progress. As such, getting his support was easy enough, as we had earned his full trust. Getting it from the state governor, Peter Obi, was slightly harder, as he feared the impact the closure would have on the economy and his polling for upcoming elections. We had to convince him of the lives that would be saved by such an intervention, and with them the unforeseen impact on the social and economic well-being of the people and on the polls — we soon had his support. And together we sought a green light from the Obi of Onitsha, the traditional leader, who, knowing the harm the drugs had caused his own people, gave his blessing. Only once I had all three layers of government on our side did we proceed.

At 3 a.m. on March 6, 2007, 350 police officers, 150 soldiers, and 150 NAFDAC staff mobilized to do what no one believed possible: close down the Onitsha market.

The entire operation had been so covert that even the police and army force NAFDAC had at its disposal did not know what exactly they were mobilizing for. We had chosen the route of secrecy for fear that someone might tip off the powerful and well-connected traders. Over the course of a month-long, shop-by-shop screening of the market, NAFDAC discovered, removed, and publicly destroyed 104 truckloads of fake, counterfeit, expired, banned, and smuggled drugs worth over 6.5 billion naira (approximately US$553 million). This was in addition to destroying illegal manufacturing factories, as well as clinics where unsafe injections and infusions were administered and even illegal and unsafe abortions performed.

Other major counterfeit markets met with the same fate. Between April 2001 and October 2008, NAFDAC led the destruction of counterfeit and substandard products valued at over 24.8 billion naira (US$21 million).

By June 2006, NAFDAC had secured a total of forty-five convictions against counterfeiters, with fifty-six other cases pending in various courts in Nigeria. The ripple effect of

NAFDAC's efficiency was felt in neighbouring countries with food and drug regulatory agencies, including the Medicines Regulatory Authorities in West Africa, the West African Regional Program for Health, the regulatory authorities of South Sudan, and the Ugandan National Drug Authority, which all reached out to learn from NAFDAC. Nigerians were also beginning to ask their political representatives to live up to the same values and efficiency as NAFDAC.

With the head of the snake cut off, the number of unregistered and unregulated medicines in circulation across the country dropped from as high as 70 percent in 2001 to lower than 20 percent by 2008, almost a 75 percent reduction.

The efforts did not go unnoticed and earned me in July 2006 an honorary doctor of laws, *honoris causa*, degree from the University of Bristol along with hundreds of awards, including as one of the Heroes of our Time by *Time* magazine and the International Service Human Rights Award, which I received at the House of Commons in London.

Part IV

2008–2012

Forty-Six

"The forest that denies you firewood has massaged your neck."

EVERYTHING HAS ITS TIME, this much I had always known. In all my years at NAFDAC I never expected that I would stay in the position longer than needed. It had been over seven years since I accepted the position; in that time, every day has been as much a triumph as it was a constant depletion of energy. This feeling was further amplified when my younger brother, Anayo, was kidnapped for ransom because of the perception that he was linked to power and by extension to money. Through intel, he was found a few days later by the police, badly beaten and shaken but alive. How many people around me had to suffer?

The fork in the story appeared when the newly elected president, Umaru Yar'Adua, who took power in 2007 following President Obasanjo's two terms, shared his intent to offer me a ministerial position, presumably minister of health.

I was very pleased. The health ministry portfolio would be a natural evolution of my work at NAFDAC; the agency fell under the mandate of the health ministry. It would be a new challenge and an even greater opportunity for me to be of service to ensure the health of a nation. I was already busy drawing up a mental strategy for all the ways I planned to revamp a failed health care system.

Soon it was time for announcements — a live event. All the candidates for cabinet positions were gathered on the afternoon of December 17, 2008. My daughter Ijeoma had flown in from the States to be there and was beside me in the large chamber. The suspense in the room was tangible, and heightened as brown envelopes were handed out to candidates containing the name of their cabinet position.

Ijeoma, looking on eagerly, noticed the writing in my envelope was far too long to read "Minister of Health." None of us could have imagined my envelope would contain the words "Minister of Information and Communication." She discreetly laid her hand on mine in comfort, conscious of the curious camera lenses capturing the reactions in the room. At that moment, I was particularly grateful that she was with me.

That I was disappointed was an understatement. If not health, then I would have assumed another ministry that needed transformation, such as education. The consensus was anything but information and communication, a portfolio that many, myself included, didn't know the function of, beyond communicating the government's propaganda. And a portfolio with technology in its description! I still had my emails printed out, and I handwrote my responses to be typed and sent back. The same went for the majority of my text messages. Prowess with technology simply was not one of my superpowers.

It was as if I had been jarred awake from the fairy tale I had dared to dream: director general, then minister of health, then head of wHO, and someday maybe even president of the country. That was to have been my trajectory. I had been so sure of God's plan. He was to have worked through me, and I had been so ready to step up to the responsibility. Seated in the room, I felt like the subject of an unkind joke. The name of the portfolio before me on a white sheet of paper with the seal of the republic made no sense.

I imagined the faces of unknown men laughing as they selected the portfolio that would humiliate me the most. They succeeded. I felt a deep sense of shame. To be minister but no better than a propaganda announcer.

Through my embarrassment, I tried desperately to find the bright side. My mind came up blank again and again. What did the ministry even do? The information and communication portfolio was essentially the mouthpiece of the presidency. All signs pointed to Yar'Adua wanting to leverage the trust I had built up in the hearts and minds of the people to deliver his messages.

Under the continued scrutiny of watching cameras, I smiled softly, first to dispel my sadness, then for the cameras pointed at me. It was a small smile that I invited with great effort to reach my eyes. I imagined my friends watching on the other end of the lens smiling back at me. I smiled again, and this time it reached my heart. Everything was going to be okay.

I made time to be silent but for the chaos of my own emotions. I listened to the harsher voices in my head. "What were you expecting?" was a recurring question; another reminded me of the dangers of flying too close to the sun, like in the Greek myth of Icarus. I was surprised by the vile voice that took on the tone of those who had worked hard in the past to pull me down: "Who are you to think you could inspire a different Nigeria, you! Nothing but a mere woman." Giving in to the alien textures of my own disenchantment, I concluded that this, after all, was Nigeria, and here, fairy tales don't come true. For now, I had been given a loudspeaker to share only the news that pleased the office of the presidency.

In the following weeks, I wrapped up at NAFDAC. My fear in those days was that all the hard work of the last eight years would be in vain. This fear was made even worse when I got the news that I would have no say in who would succeed me. My practised stance of many years when life got overwhelming was to surrender to the will of the Almighty. This time it felt harder to do than ever; nothing seemed to make any sense.

As usual I made my way to the one place I could find peace: home to Enugu.

Chike was angry on my behalf, but tempered. The way he saw it, being a minister, though not with the portfolio I desired, was still a powerful position.

The first night home, I lay in bed, heavy curtains shutting out any light, the room illuminated by long fluorescent lights overhead, my rosary wrapped around my hand. Chike was lying beside me. We had been talking in this position for almost an hour.

"Dora," Chike said, "you can change the world from anywhere."

"It's true, but my fear is that they want to use me to do the opposite."

"Yes, Nkem," he responded, "but since when has anyone made you do anything you don't want to do?"

It felt like he had reached into the core of my fear: of not being able to be useful. I was then able to see how unfounded it was. With this, I recovered from disappointment to trust.

I didn't have to fake my positivity with the many who called on me, checking in to see if I was all right, wanting to console me or wish me well. I could in all honesty share my belief that everything was going to be exactly as was written. I was ultimately responsible for my actions, and I had no intention of being compromised.

Forty-Seven

"I am because we are."

THE FEDERAL MINISTRY of Information and Communication was housed with the Federal Radio Corporation of Nigeria and the Voice of Nigeria in a low-rise white building in an 1980s style of simple lines, small windows, and a large entrance leading into wide hallways of terrazzo floors. It was through these corridors that I walked on my first day, the sound of my heels amplified by the open space, the sparse furnishings, and the quietness of everyone who stopped to watch me walk by. The only other sound was the occasional exuberant greeting of "Welcome, Ma."

Once in my office of lush carpet and heavy tables, I called a meeting of key directors from across the ministry and various departments who were tasked with overseeing the news, the flow of information, and all telecommunications, including TV and radio.

After several days of introductions that served as an onboarding, I had a clear sense that, given the wide reach of the ministry, a consolidation exercise was needed to understand the opportunities and gaps. In studying past interventions of the ministry, we quickly deduced that while we could bring more efficiency to several processes, notably the telecommunications industry serving millions of Nigerians, to truly impact lives, we needed to explore uncharted waters.

My father's voice and lessons had been very present with me in these early weeks, as were his stories. They were coming back to me in the form of questions. What if we could inspire and reconnect to values and principles that serve the whole? There was a shared sense of disappointment in a country that had so much to offer, yet repeatedly failed to live up to its potential as the "Giant of Africa." A country that fails to live up to its potential is a country whose people are not living up to their potential.

My intuition guided me to see my role as the chief image-maker of the country, to inspire Nigerians to find a renewed sense of pride in themselves anchored by a sense of responsibility to each other. It was time to revisit the stories we were told and those we told ourselves.

We started by reviewing past efforts that had a similar goal of addressing Nigeria's image. Soon, with a growing team of staff who stood out as resourceful and efficient, ideas on how to change the trajectory of the country began to rise to the surface. This was the birth of what became known as the rebranding campaign aimed at ushering in a new Nigeria.

My experience as the director general of NAFDAC had taught me that Nigerians will rally around a cause if they believe in it. I was keen on designing a homegrown and people-centred campaign. Ownership was crucial.

To foster this, we created a competition for Nigerians both at home and in the diaspora to submit logos and slogans of their own invention. The winning slogan, selected from almost three thousand entries, was "Nigeria — Good People, Great Nation."

The rebranding campaign was formally launched in March 2009, just three months after I took office. The vision was to transform Nigerians' perception of self from negative to positive and instill a renewed spirit of hope in the heart of the people.

The greater aim of the campaign was that, in transforming Nigerians' belief in themselves, we might transform our global image from the "single story," as coined by Nigerian writer Chimamanda Ngozi Adichie, of a failed state filled with dubious citizens to a more robust story of a good people and a great nation.

I grabbed onto the rebranding campaign like one would a log in a fast-moving stream, and I was grateful to have purpose. I focused everything into this simple message of good people, great nation. In speeches and campaigns, to remind Nigerians of the truth of this slogan both in themselves and in others, we shared the many contributions of Nigeria, from its prominent writers, sports stars, and political figures to its successful movie, music, and fashion industries and its abundant natural resources.

The way I saw it, as things were, we couldn't take our citizenship as Nigerians to the bank. While we all want to bequeath to our children a country that they can count on, none of us could. This failure had its roots in corruption. When we talked about inefficiency in the education sector, health sector, political sector, and governance, everything boiled down to corruption. And corruption was not just about giving and taking money; it was about not doing the right thing—a selfishness that ensured everyone ended up losing out. And why were we corrupt? I often asked. It is because of a lack of understanding of how few our needs are. Our want was too much, but our needs were very little. In truth, I didn't even envy corrupt people, because of the shortsightedness of greed, with its potential to destroy them and their children, generations unborn.

Why choose such a path?

When we look at the way we have behaved, both to ourselves and to this country Nigeria, for we had no other country that we could call our own, it was all because of bad attitude—a corrosion from the top right down to everyone. Hence our message through rebranding was that we must change. For if we did not change, nothing would change; if we did not change, we would not achieve our vision. Because it was, after all, human beings who would have to work to actualize the vision for Nigeria. Change would not come from the air, angels would not come down, foreigners would not come to fix the country for us, as they had their own countries to fix. The change of attitude, which was a critical part of rebranding, was one we had to embrace for ourselves.

Rebranding was the key. As was reclaiming a different story about who we truly were, even if it was an aspirational journey.

No matter how staunch my conviction, the challenges with the rebranding campaign were multifold. "How do we as a nation hope to see the decay of several decades swept under a beautiful carpet of logos and catchphrases?" one article asked. Our efforts were further compromised in 2009, the year of our launch, when Transparency International ranked Nigeria

130th out of 180 countries in its corruption perception index. Unemployment was rampant at about 20 percent of a population of 160 million, 75 percent of whom were living below the poverty threshold.

Combined with a high crime rate, poor infrastructure, and inadequate education and health care, we were faced with the most unconducive environment to convince the country that in spite of what their eyes could see, and what their ears could hear, and what their bodies could feel, they were part of a great nation.

"How," Nigerians asked, "can we talk about rebranding a country where corruption still holds sway in all segments of life? How can we rebrand a country whose citizens cannot walk the streets safe from harm, sometimes even from the law enforcement agents meant to protect them?"

"What makes us good? What makes us great?" many asked, voicing their frustration at words that made promises but had no substance.

"You!" was always my response. The power of individuals and of the collective. The problem was that I was speaking to the potential of the people, not necessarily the reality. After years of too many of the same people failing to look out for the well-being of the whole, we were far too bitter to aspire to, let alone claim, the goodness of the people and the greatness of the nation.

No matter how much I insisted on a Nigeria of my dreams where Nigerians would be so changed in their attitude that we would tell the world who we were; no matter how much I reminded us how, for too long, other people had defined who we were and how we needed to evolve, when we could do this for ourselves; no matter how much I hoped for a Nigeria where we would have a sense of pride for our country, love one another, know who we are, and tell our beautiful stories to a global audience, appreciating all that we as a country have achieved; no matter how much I tried to remind us that together we were unstoppable — alas, my words did not find their usual mark.

Despite my best intentions, I had forgotten that the desire to change had to come from the people. And so, while we worked tirelessly to make the slogan a reality that would transform the country, it never fully took off, though I wanted to believe otherwise.

An *Economist* article dated April 30, 2009, titled "Good People, Impossible Mission," referring to the rebranding campaign, summarized the sentiment of the time: "Many Nigerians say their government should tackle the country's fundamental problems — power shortages, crime, and corruption — before worrying about its image. 'They [my ministry] have been sending texts to my phone, telling us about how to reorganize Nigeria, how to reorganize our minds, our heads,' says Olufemi Oyegun, an oil-and-gas man in Lagos, the commercial capital. 'But it's our leaders that are our main problem, not the people.'"

In my heart of hearts, I knew he was right. I felt such a deep sadness in those months, the type that comes from knowing you have done everything in your power but it is simply not enough. Still, I busied myself slaying what dragons I could, but unlike in NAFDAC, where the rewards of hard work could be seen and felt, in the ministry I felt limited by a portfolio that seemed not to allow for any real change.

Forty-Eight

"A lie has many variations; the truth has none."

MY TIME AS MINISTER of information and communication would be defined by an event that changed the trajectory of the nation.

In November 2009, President Umaru Yar'Adua fell sick and travelled to Saudi Arabia for medical treatment. Normally this would not have been cause for alarm, as no one expected the president to seek medical treatment from the country's broken health care system — even the minister of health wouldn't be caught dead in a Nigerian hospital.

When a month had passed and no word had been heard from the president of Africa's most populous country, many started to feel unease. Was he alive? Was he dead? And in either scenario, given the length of his absence and accompanying silence, who was running the country? As weeks rolled by and the president had still not shared so much as a statement, rumours, including that he was most certainly dead, filled the information vacuum.

Every week, as the minister of information and communication, I stood in front of journalists repeating the only
information I had, the gist of which was that the president
had gone for a routine checkup and sent his best wishes to
the good people of Nigeria.

Acting as a mouthpiece in this way was akin to pulling
teeth for me. I complained bitterly to Chike over the phone
or during my visits to Enugu. It had been almost a decade
since we had lived together under the same roof, and in
many ways, this allowed me to transition away from any
lingering disappointment to appreciating the strength of
our friendship and companionship. Chike shared my frustration and together we debated the best way to navigate
the situation. He advised me to say only the bare minimum,
and to preface it with the truth that I had not received any
updates beyond that which I was sharing, and none at all
from the president.

In those days that stretched into months, I grew increasingly frustrated with the deluge of conflicting information
from unofficial sources claiming to convey the wishes of the
president from his vacation spot in Saudi. These sources were
mostly friends and allies of the president, known in the hallways of power as "the cabals."

When trusted news finally came, it was that the president
was suffering from acute pericarditis, an inflammation of the
lining around the heart. His condition had required minor
treatment, from which he was recuperating in a hospital in
Jeddah, and he would return to the country as soon as he was
given the green light by his doctors. This was all well and good.

However, it meant that the country still had no leadership, and that could last for months to come.

In a normal situation, though the country was far from normal with the president unwell and already away for an extended period of time, there should have been an official transfer of power to the vice-president. Yar'Adua had failed to write the required letter, and it wasn't clear if he had been too sick to ensure this transfer or simply unwilling to relinquish power. Whatever the case, it was to the detriment of the country. Nevertheless, in spite of the lack of formal transfer of power, Vice-President Goodluck Jonathan was forced by necessity to oversee many of the president's duties.

This unconventional status quo continued until increasing criticism from citizens and politicians forced the federal high court, whose members had been appointed by the ailing president, to rule on the way forward. The court's conclusion in the early days of December was that, in the absence of an official transfer letter, the vice-president could not serve as the acting president. This ruling concluded furthermore that there was no constitutional requirement for the president to hand over power to his deputy; the latter could act on the behalf of the president but in an unofficial capacity. The high court also went as far as to declare that the president was in fact fit to run the country from Jeddah. It was all quite confusing. Their actions were clear: an unequivocal declaration of their loyalty to President Yar'Adua.

I found their ruling especially suspicious given that said "capable" president had yet to make any public appearance since being flown to Saudi Arabia in November, well over a month prior.

Our stories, and the stories of those who came before, are interwoven in an interconnected web of our shared humanity. These are the people from whom I come. From left to right: my father, a young Paul Young Edemobi, seated beside his wife and my mother, Grace, and her only brother, Romanus Okoli (Onye Nkuzi). Circa 1945.

They say it takes a village to raise a child. Our family enjoyed close ties with my mother Grace's best friend, Mama Bridget, seated to her right. In this picture you can see so much of our personalities — my mother's graceful demeanour, surrounded by her children, my beaming face on the bottom left, willing you to look.

The short dress, the afro, the dream of my entire life before me. Circa 1972.

Chike was every inch a GuyMan. His style, his smile, and his charm inspired mine. I was happy to be by his side and to have him by mine. Circa 1976.

Chike and me. White wedding, 1976.

My youngest daughter was just an infant, and I had just healed from a sickness that nearly took my life. I had a lot to be grateful for, not least of all, my children. Circa 1986.

If only a picture could truly capture the essence of another, but perhaps in her stance, and her easy smile, shy and bold, vulnerable yet strong, you can begin to know my little sister, Nwogo, *nwa mma*. To know Nwogo is to love her. Circa 1980.

I was weeks away from making the decision to leave for the United Kingdom for my Ph.D., leaving my five children behind. As always, I leaned on God to guide my choices. Circa 1988

The lab was a happy place. Here life made sense and fit perfectly
into predictable equations. Experiments were welcome, and my
mind could rest from the worries of life, lost in the possibility of
new discoveries. Circa 1989.

Upon receiving the news of winning the American green card lottery,
I had a clear premonition that a window had just opened in the story of our lives.
Even they, seated upon the stoop of their summer home in the Bronx, could not
have known that nothing would ever be the same again. Summer 1996.

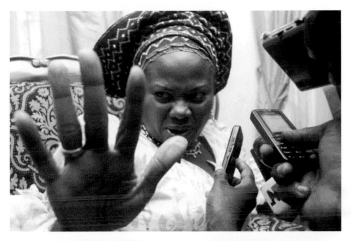

The evil of fake drugs is worse than the combined scourge of malaria,
HIV/AIDS, armed robbery, and illicit drugs. Fake drugs are taken by all, and
anybody can be a victim. We declared a holy war against fake drugs.
My NAFDAC years, 2004–2008.

"While the world saw Dora Akunyili at the peak of her strength...
I saw the complexity that was hidden from sight.
This is the story of her multiplicity: the story of my mother."
— Chidiogo Akunyili-Parr

This was the last portrait we took as a family. We were the picture of a middle-class Nigerian family, complete with the average five-plus children, all infused with maximum discipline and a clear focus on their education, and their career-focused parents. Circa 2004.

My first daughter was getting married. You would dance if you were me. The surprised look on my sister Ngozi's face on the left tells you that me dancing with such joy and abandon was not something she had seen in a while, if ever. I was happy to share this day of celebration with my daughter and so many who had flown to Côte d'Ivoire to celebrate with us. Circa 2004.

Igbos have a proverb: Ukwa ruo oge ya ọ daa — the breadfruit will fall when it is ready. I had always revered professors, and for so long nursed a desire to join their ranks. Receiving the honour of doctor of laws, honoris causa, from the University of Bristol in 2006 was a lifetime achievement for me.

"A society grows great when old men plant trees whose shade they know they shall never sit in."

This memorial statue stands in Agulu. Throughout history, stories have mattered. The stories we tell ourselves of who we are, and the stories others tell of us, shape us and everything around us.

They called me *Ugogbe mmụta* — mirror of wisdom. A mirror simply reflects truth.

I am proud of Nigeria despite the challenges... I love this country with a passion. Without this country, there would not be me. With this country, this is me, and the country has made me who I am.

With the commander-in-chief missing, key government, business, and civil service appointments were stalled or halted, with significant consequences. This was especially dangerous given that the country was in the middle of a crisis in the Niger Delta region, with militants growing more powerful by the day.

With no credible, trustworthy channel for news on the true state of the president, so that I might assuage the state of unrest in the country, I started to question my role in the farce. Knowing I couldn't continue this way, I made a personal decision to take time off, in self-preservation against the toxic role.

Chike was very happy to hear of my decision. It was one of the few things he and my brother Anayo agreed upon. Over the years, they had clashed more and more, as Anayo did not appreciate Chike's shortcomings, and Chike didn't appreciate my full trust in Anayo. My trust translated into a dependency on my brother, which Chike saw as an encroachment on his role as my husband. To see them in solidarity on something was a testament to how much the situation was affecting my mental well-being.

I decided to use the time away to visit my children and dedicate myself to penning the story of my years at NAFDAC. Over three weeks, between periods of writing, I criss-crossed the United States from Texas to New York City. I even made it to Beijing to visit ChiChi, who was living in China. I loved listening to her to speak the language of the country, a sound that always caused me to burst out in happy laughter, reminiscent of my tickled teenage self.

I was at my hotel with her when I saw from multiple alerts on my phones that the president had made a public statement. It was the first in over seven weeks. It was a muffled recording of what was supposedly his voice assuring citizens that he was in recovery and would be home soon.

That I was finding out in this manner did not even surprise me the least. I decided then that the status quo was unworkable, not just for me but for the country. As a first stance of rebellion, I would no longer report on the health of the president. Second, I planned to speak up and address the elephant in the room: Yar'Adua needed to transfer power to the vice-president so that the system could be stabilized.

Once back in Nigeria, the first part of the plan was easy enough. I declined to make further comments on the president, sharing plainly that I had no information. For the second, I drafted a memo which I planned to circulate at the Federal Executive Council meeting. I worked alone first, to find the limit of my boldness, holding nothing back, allowing truth to speak loudly. On the eve of the meeting, I worked through the night, conscious of the impact of each word.

In spite of the unseasonably cool temperatures, I had the windows of my bedroom closed and the air conditioner unit quietly cooling the room, allowing me to think. With the curtains open, I looked upon a dull half moon overhead, aware of the weight of my action.

In the morning, I reached out to Mr. Ugwumba, my former special assistant at NAFDAC, whose mind and opinion I trusted, to come to my home to review the draft memo. I watched him put on his half-moon glasses to read the carefully typed-out lines. When he finished, he looked up and without hesitation said, "They will persecute you." His response came as no surprise.

"It has to be done" was my indignant response.

In the last days leading up to the meeting, before circulating the memo, which at its core called for the empowerment of the vice-president as acting president, I tested the waters in various one-on-one conversations with ministers to know their thoughts, but I found no allies.

Undaunted, I recalled the words of Haile Selassie: "Throughout history it has been the inaction of those who could have acted, the indifference of those who should have known better, the silence of the voice of justice when it mattered most, that has made it possible for evil to triumph." No matter the consequences, I wanted to stand up for what I knew to be right, because bad things happen when good people fail to speak up.

That day I would be putting my job, and possibly my life, on the line.

Forty-Nine

"Where the corpse lies is where the vultures congregate."

ON TUESDAY, FEBRUARY 2, 2010, mere minutes before the start of the Nigeria Federal Executive Council (FEC) meeting, I was feeling hopeful and also conscious of the weight and implications of the hours ahead. I had about four dozen copies of the five-page memo, titled "If we fail to act now, history will not forgive us," printed out to be circulated.

At the appointed time, with white sheets handed around for review, I stood to the side of the large hall, watching eyes dart across the pages. I wondered what part of the memo would attract their attention. The part assuring the other members of the cabinet of my loyalty to the president and to the country? Or my detailed opinion on the critical vacuum created by the president's now seventy-day absence, insisting that the president was not infallible, and neither was the country? Or how it was up to us to act in the best interest of the president and of the nation?

As a way forward, I proposed that it was imperative that Yar'Adua present a letter of vacation to the senate as required

by section 145 of Nigeria's 1999 constitution, effectively allowing for the transfer of executive powers to his vice-president,
Goodluck Jonathan.

"If we fail to act now," I shared in my concluding words,
"history will not forgive us."

Within minutes of members reading the memo, Yar'Adua's
loyalists began shouting it down. The minister of agriculture
was very vocal in insisting that the memo had not been properly presented to the body through the office of the secretary to
the federal government. Not easily bullied, I stood my ground,
insisting that the memo be discussed.

My courage didn't inspire other ministers. No voices joined
mine, as none wanted to be perceived as disloyal, especially
should the president make a full recovery. The repercussions
were too expensive — inaction was the wisest course for
self-preservation.

Sensing that the memo wouldn't make headway, I eventually agreed to withdraw it to be officially resubmitted for
discussion at the next FEC meeting.

The next day, a draft version of the memo was leaked via
unknown channels — not mine — to the media. The memo-
randum became known simply as the "Doctrine of Necessity"
in reference to the article in the constitution that pertained
to transition. After its release to the public, low whispers
and then louder and bolder voices joined in support of my
proposal. Some did so publicly, while others reached out
privately. Others still, figures loyal to the president, publicly
called for me to step down.

In the coming days, I rode the momentum of love and
hate, appearing in various televised interviews, making bold

statements about the need for Nigerians to speak up on behalf of the country and defend what is right.

Many Nigerians celebrated the courage it took for me to break away from the rest of the cabinet. I personally felt that I was doing the only thing I knew to do. Others still called on fellow Nigerians to see the situation for what it was. Nobel Prize winner Wole Soyinka was one of the strong voices critical of the motives of the cabals who had been empowered by the president's prolonged absence, saying, with his signature clarity, "The issue is that certain elements within the ruling party love this hiatus; they love the headlessness of government because they can proceed to loot and create their own little empires while the president is away."

On Tuesday, February 9, thanks to pressure from the public backing the proposals of the memo, the National Assembly decided to empower Vice-President Goodluck Jonathan to assume presidential functions as acting president. In doing so, they effectively resolved the constitutional breach by President Yar'Adua in failing to transmit a letter to the National Assembly upon his departure.

Two weeks later, on February 24, in what seemed like a desperate measure by the cabals, the still-ailing president was flown back to Nigeria, the extent of his sickness masked by the cloak of night. In the days following the president's return, many asked what I would do. Unintimidated by the prospect of being labelled as disloyal to the president, I issued a clear and public message.

We needed the truth, I said, to normalize things, especially in a highly charged political situation. The problem was not that the president was sick, but the insistence on hiding the fact. The current chaos was further exacerbated by bringing back the president without informing the acting president, causing even more tension. As minister of information of the country, I had no information. "It's not just a slight on the acting president," I said. "It is also a slap to the faces of almost 160 million Nigerians." It wasn't too late, I implored, for the actors involved to explain the situation and assure the nation that everything would normalize with time.

In spite of the urgent call, Yar'Adua stayed silent in the coming weeks.

He died just a few months later on May 5, 2010. A day after his death, Goodluck Jonathan was sworn in as the substantive president of the Federal Republic of Nigeria.

Fifty

"Fire makes strong salt."

ONLY TWO FULL TERMS into Nigeria's reconciliation with democracy, the country was at a crossroads.

There was an unwritten "gentleman's agreement" with the ruling Peoples Democratic Party (PDP) that the presidency should alternate between North and South after every two four-year terms. As well, each presidency would be balanced by a vice-president from another region. While it might have seemed like a practical solution to those who shook on it, it did nothing to move the country towards unification.

As former president Obasanjo had been from the South, Yar'Adua's presidency was the North's turn at leadership. His vice-president, Goodluck Jonathan, who hailed from the South, had been chosen as a balance to his northern leadership.

Following Yar'Adua's death, Goodluck Jonathan succeeded him to become the interim president in what should have been the North's second term; it was a heavy blow to northern power brokers — even more so when in May 2011, after winning the election, Jonathan was sworn in a full-term president.

I knew Goodluck Jonathan from brief interactions at Aso Rock. He always struck me as quiet, a persona that may have been exaggerated given the expectation that he would provide unthreatening support of the then president. And now, this quiet man, appointed for his non-intimidating demeanour, had become the elected president of the Federal Republic of Nigeria.

Many feared the worst, recalling past history when one side felt cheated by the other.

Nigerians have a widely expressed view that each time we find ourselves, as a country, at the edge of the cliff, needing but a brief gust of the wind to blow us over, some divine intervention always enables us to regain our balance and step back, albeit temporarily, to safety. Luckily, nationwide violence did not erupt at the election of Goodluck, and life continued its steady wobble.

While many, especially Northerners, were frustrated by the prospect of a Goodluck Jonathan full-term presidency, many more were happy to see what they hoped would be an end to the ruling party's unsustainable agreement.

In his role as the president, Jonathan was poised to appoint members of his new cabinet. I held a renewed dream to serve as the minister of health, and this time, I was not shy, nor did I make any assumptions. In my newly launched book, *War Against Counterfeit Medicine: My Story*, I had made every effort to outline my leadership journey and contributions to the health sector, not only to share everything I had learned from my years at NAFDAC but also to show my readiness for the next mountain. Many voices assured me that my appointment was all but assured. The president himself was one of these voices guaranteeing his interest in offering me the position in the months I spent volunteering as a campaigner for his election. This I did both from a desire to dismantle the power-sharing status quo as well as in the belief he could bring peace to the embattled Niger Delta region, since he himself hailed from the Delta.

Then the news came — I was to remain the minister of information and communication.

I was not the only square peg in a round hole. The announcement of his cabinet of mismatched candidates and portfolios was one of the first signs of the woes that would cripple Goodluck Jonathan's government. The very talent for which he was chosen to be vice-president to Yar'Adua was marring his presidency. Nigeria needed a decisive leader who was willing to rock the boat as needed. Instead, we got a quiet, slow-moving man with a distaste for speed and a preference for neutrality to the point of inaction.

Through the veil of my renewed disappointment, I reminded myself of my deep trust in God. God of perfect timing, He had His reasons, and I would keep faith even though, once again, I found myself let down by politics.

Frustrated by President Jonathan's decision, and sensing that this in itself was a sign, in 2010, I stepped down as minister of information and communication. I cited my official reason as being ready to begin a new chapter of my life. Unofficially though, I wanted to have more authorship on the direction of my journey, free from the whims of a seated president. I felt very clear about my decision, especially as I recognized my own unmet desire to work closely supporting the needs of the people. Even more specifically, my people.

In 2009, I had been invited to support the ambition of

Peter Obi to once again serve as the governor of Anambra State. Peter and I knew each other from our university days in Nsukka. We had stayed friends since then, and when he asked for my support for his campaign, saying yes was a natural answer. Never one to do anything halfway, I threw myself into aiding him, accompanying him to several villages in the region. On these visits, I felt a deep connection to the many people I met, who reminded me of my roots. I started nursing the thought that if lending myself to the people was not to be found in a federal government cabinet position, then perhaps I would have more success in the senate.

The seeds of this idea had been germinating in my mind and now could sprout. Without much delay, I decided to run for a seat in the senate under the All Progressives Grand Alliance (APGA). Founded in 2003 by the former leader of the also former Republic of Biafra, Odumegwu Ojukwu, the APGA was the embodiment of a party for Igbos and by Igbos. Joining them, my first party affiliation at fifty-seven years old, was like coming home.

Anambra, the heartland of the APGA, with a population of about four million, was represented by three senatorial districts. I planned to run to represent the Anambra Central district.

Before diving in, I asked my immediate family, my six children, my husband and my brother Anny, to join me for a meeting. We were gathered in our upstairs living room in Enugu. On the low square table in the centre were mounds of foods, including roasted suya meat, spicy Congo meat, and freshly cut pineapple and pawpaw. Clad in a loose housedress, I watched as my daughters Somto and Njideka, who had come home to support me and do their youth service, dug happily into roasted snails. I had enjoyed having them with me in the last months. It had already been so many years since the children left home.

Once every plate was filled, I dialled the rest of the children on three of my phones and on Chike's. "*Kedụ,* Juku, Donkwe, Chikin, Bummy," I greeted them all fondly with a smile in my voice. I was enjoying the growing excitement around the room. Once the excited chatter of niceties had died down, without beating around the bush, I started.

"The reason I asked for a meeting *bu maka* our people are suffering. *Ogbenye na-ata afụfụ,*" I repeated in Igbo for emphasis. "I want to do something about it. I want to run for senate," I said emphatically. I paused long enough to take in the renewed excited chatter before continuing. "Look at even just the salary of senators, let alone their allocations. Just this money could change the lives of so many of our people. I want to make sure that money will reach the people, and that we can watch lives change across Anambra."

They all listened patiently and at the end each offered their support with words of caution to be safe, knowing the roughness of the past years and of running for an elected position. Had they known the hardships that would follow, I wonder if they would have supported me with the same excitement.

Fifty-One

"When you wrestle with a pig, you both get dirty,
but the pig enjoys it."

THERE IS ALWAYS a large step between desire and action. My yes felt like a great leap towards what had been a desire of mine for many years.

There was something about potentially being elected by the people that felt so much more gratifying than an appointed position. Once I released an official public statement of my intent to run, opinions abounded. Some were critical, calling me disloyal for breaking with the ruling Peoples Democratic Party (PDP) to join the APGA. I rebuffed this criticism easily, reminding all that I had never been a member of any political party but merely an appointed government representative. Other critics feared that I would be tainted by the politics of running for an elected position, a notoriously dirty game. I reassured them of the staunchness of my values, my tough skin, and my commitment to the people.

What I had not realized was just how hard it would be to fight clean in a dirty fight.

In early 2011, I began my campaign in earnest. I thought

I knew what to expect from a lifetime of hard work, but this was to be my greatest trial yet.

There were several layers to the campaign to win the Anambra Central senate seat. The first and most critical one was to be nominated as the APGA's candidate for the Anambra Central senatorial district. This involved delicate politicking to secure the support of the heavy hitters of the APGA, including the seated governor, Peter Obi.

With the support of Peter Obi, this hurdle was overcome and I was selected as the APGA candidate for the senatorial race. Soon after this endorsement, Dr. Chris Nwabueze Ngige entered the race. This significantly raised the stakes. A former governor of Anambra State, Ngige was the very embodiment of a political godfather.

His entry into the race was in itself a surprise. Given his critical role in the political landscape of the state, and our acquaintance of many years, I had paid him a personal visit in the weeks leading up to my announcement. It was in this meeting that he assured me, of his own initiative, that he wasn't running and gave his blessing and goodwill for the road ahead.

When he presented himself a few short days after my own announcement on the Action Congress of Nigeria platform, my victory went from being relatively easy to being deeply contentious.

I had a formidable opponent in Ngige. He was notorious for not playing by any rules and was even on occasion known to lean on the support of supernatural forces — cut from a different cloth — to aid his chances of victory. He had made local and international news in 2003 for his visit to the Okija shrine, also known as the death shrine. By Ngige's admission, he visited the shrine to perform oath-taking rituals in order to be installed governor of Anambra State as well as to pledge his allegiance to the political godfathers supporting his campaign. In a 2004 raid of the same shrine, Nigerian police discovered over seventy dead bodies, human skulls, hundreds and possibly thousands of human parts openly displayed, some still fresh and headless, others still in their coffins.

This was the man I was up against, and given his recent losses in two pre-gubernatorial elections since his 2003 win, the stakes for him had never been higher.

The race had just started and we, my camp and I, were already at full speed.

The next hurdle after the primaries was to raise campaign money, which very quickly ran into a bill of millions of naira. Between Peter Obi and me, we had access to a long roster of donors. However, there were a few challenges.

The first was that Peter Obi had built a reputation as a tight-fisted governor who did not believe in the common practice of "sharing money." It was one of the reasons I believed in him and campaigned for him. But in his bid to end the practice of distributing money from the state coffers to buy the goodwill of his constituents, he made a lot of enemies. While everyone bemoans corruption, it seemed no one wanted a governor who didn't share money in what was seen by many as part of an informal economy, albeit an ineffective channel for government funds to trickle down to the people.

Second, I was intent on running the race as true to my values as possible, so I had to make daily decisions about whose money my conscience was willing to accept without compromising myself.

The most important piece of the campaigning puzzle was to earn the votes of the people. This meant many hours on the road moving from one village and one local government to another, speaking to women, men, youth, church groups, and various communities, speaking at the top of my voice at open-air rallies, in stuffy halls, schoolyards, and churches, and under hot tents. It also meant reconciling with the lingering anger of market traders, especially those whose livelihood importing fake drugs I had tampered with and even destroyed.

"Vote for me," I said, "and I will ensure every village in Anambra Central has a school, a medical clinic, running water, and roads, even if it means using my salary to get the job done."

Many villages felt so familiar: dirt roads and small houses surrounded by farms and large trees. In each community, the first stop was always at the home of the traditional ruler and titled men, whose blessing I solicited. I knew the importance of having their support, and together, shoulder to shoulder, we addressed the expectant crowds.

"This election," I said, my voice booming on speakers that were loud and scratchy, "this election will be different, because you will not be quiet!

"Some of you," I continued in Igbo, varying my accent to suit the ears and dialect of the people before me, a gift and legacy of years in the village, moving through the years of the war, and then living in Enugu. "Some of you don't even understand what the senate is, and I don't blame you, because for too long they have done nothing for you. But I promise that I will stand up for you at every opportunity, that you might understand what it means to have a representative working for your rights at this highest office in the nation's government structure." At this the applause was always deafening, followed by a chorus of *adadiọramma* — "the daughter of the people."

After five hard months of campaigning and garnering money and support from voters and well-wishers, the April 9, 2011, senatorial election day was at hand.

Fifty-Two

"The millipede says that one who steps on it cries out,
but it itself who was stepped on does not cry out."

I WOKE UP EARLY, as I always did. I had slept even less than usual, if at all. I would have been surprised had the opposite occurred. When I got up and kneeled by the bed, my rosary at hand, I felt the last of the superhuman strength that had fuelled me seep out of my body. I knew I was running on reserves. There would be time for rest after the election, at least for some days until I assumed my responsibilities. With the optimistic thought of pending victory, my prayers were thanks for God's miracles in my life and the fulfillment of His wish to use me in the service of the people.

My mind drifted to the offer that had come the week before: actual thugs offered up for my use. I hadn't known what to be more shocked by: the offer itself, or the normalcy of it all. I wondered about my opponents. If I had been offered the chance to hire thugs, surely they had too. Would they have been as quick to deny such an offer?

I knew they would try to buy votes; I had even warned voters about the tactic, reminding them that while they might accept the money and gifts offered, there was no obligation to cast their vote in favour of their benefactor. But thugs would be harder to ignore.

I chose my outfit for the day with great care, nothing too flashy but not too demure. I went for a blue and yellow pattern sewn into a long skirt and short-sleeve fitted top. I took my time to line my eyebrows, pulling my soft curls back before covering my hair with a matching headscarf. I complemented the outfit with a simple drop pendant jewellery set. Satisfied, I made my way out the door, slipping my sandals on for the walk from our village home to the town hall where I would cast my vote.

At the hall, I could feel eyes watching my every move, yet I was used to it.

After voting, I awaited the news of the day in the privacy of the upstairs parlour, surrounded by a small group of close family friends and aides. My phone buzzed ceaselessly. Text messages were pouring in by the dozen per minute. Many were prayers and well wishes, many more were stories from the day, and too many of them were in warning.

The situation was even messier than I had expected. For one, there was an unprecedented voter turnout, which should be celebrated, but the electoral commission was unprepared and overwhelmed. This had been exacerbated by the late arrival of voting materials and of election officials. By all accounts, it didn't stop there, as there were several reports, some with photo-graphed evidence, of compromised conduct by Independent National Electoral Commission (INEC) officials.

After hours of voting, the ballots had been cast and the sun was setting. My team and I were trying our best to follow the official results of the tight race, but the chaotic tallying process made it hard to get accurate information.

In a bizarre sequence of events, an INEC official by the name of Dr. Alex Anene independently, and from his hotel bedroom for that matter, announced to the press a victory for Ngige. Though his announcement, we would all soon learn, didn't hold, the false information caused a lot of confusion, especially since it came from an official.

When an official announcement did come through, it was inconclusive. As a result, the INEC declared a rerun in a handful of polling zones.

It would seem that the night would not offer me the rest I was desperately seeking.

When the INEC made that announcement, amid controversies and smears for and from both sides, I was leading with 66,273 votes against Ngige's 65,576 votes. If the results held from that day, the interim figures signalled victory for our camp.

The rerun was to be held in about two weeks on April 26 in the local governments where the results were cancelled due to discrepancies or where no results at all were received. We accepted this, and my team and I injected the remainder of our sparse energy into campaigning once again, this time in a more concentrated region. Given the small margin between Ngige and myself, we knew that every vote was critical.

If there was discreet rigging on the first election day, on the second, there was a full-blown affront to democracy. Ngige spared no antics and offloaded truckloads of hired thugs — "area boys" — whose job was to intimidate voters into voting for him.

Ngige came out victorious, with 69,725 votes, against 69,236 votes for me. A difference of 489 votes. The official result was called. I had lost.

Deeply disturbed and disappointed by the actions of Ngige and his cronies, I called foul for all the malpractices of the second election day, and those of April 9, and vowed to contest the result of the elections. I felt a deep sense of outrage about the manipulation and intimidation tactics used by my opponent. But with the results of the runoff showing him as the winner, Ngige was not shy about loudly claiming his victory. It would be our word against his. It was in no one's interest to testify against the elected senatorial candidate, and as such many chose to remain silent instead of denouncing what had transpired, including the INEC, whose job it was to do just that. I was in no way shocked by the turn of events, as time and again I had seen how the easiest choice is often the silence of self-preservation.

Loss has such a bitter taste. And even more so when there is injustice.

I was frustrated by the broken system, and knew that the vote of the people had not been counted. It was a time of deep self-reflection. I couldn't shake the feeling of having been sullied by the entire process.

I wondered many times if there was anything I could have done differently. I looked back on the choices and sometimes compromises that I'd had to make. In the heat of campaigning, obscene amounts of money were changing hands, and I constantly struggled to stay on course and true to my values. In the grey area where what is right is muddied by so many shades of what could be acceptable or pass unnoticed, where did I find my truth?

Had I compromised myself?

The one immovable piece was that I was not willing to cheat my way into office. But what did cheating mean in a country where money is so often procured in dubious ways? I would never take that which did not belong to me, but if those who supported my campaign hadn't shared the same beliefs, what did it mean to accept their suitcases full of money in a world where no suitcase full of money is untainted? How many questions can you ask of those wanting to fund your campaign because they believe in it, even if you might not believe in the source of their wealth?

The entire experience left me weary of our nascent democracy and concerned for its future. As staunch as my commitment to zero compromise was, there was no denying that the grey areas in politics would not have withstood my strictest scrutiny. And it pained me to see that at the end of the day, there was no repercussion for straying far beyond the edges of decency.

Chike shared with me words of consolation, saying, "When you wrestle with a pig, you both get dirty, but the pig enjoys it." I felt the weight of the last months like a cake of mud that I wanted to wash off.

Fifty-Three

"Injustice anywhere is a threat to justice everywhere."

THE INJUSTICE OF THE ELECTION all but broke me. With my time-chiselled skills born of difficulty, I pushed aside the pain. As this point in my life, pain was a companion I knew not only too well but also how to deal with.

True to my promise to myself and to my supporters, I contended the loss in court. For months my lawyers and I demanded acknowledgement of the fraudulent activities of the election and the irregularities that surrounded my supposed loss to Ngige. With each passing day, as Ngige further entrenched himself as the victor, it felt increasingly like a one-woman fight against a system of disenfranchisement. The battle was to clear my name of all the smears of campaign wrongdoing that Ngige had mounted against me in his defence — a classic reverse psychology tactic — and claim my victory.

It was however all for naught as our submission to the court was stalled for exactly 180 days, with Ngige's lawyers continually asking for adjournments until just enough time passed to surpass the statute of limitations stipulated in a new electoral law. By November 2011, my petition had been dismissed.

As Helen Nkumeh famously sang, *"Hichaa m anyammiri dị m nʼanya"* — "Father, wipe the tears from my eyes." I played the song on repeat.

For the first time since I could remember, perhaps since before I was in the village with Nne, I had time on my hands. I struggled with idleness. The worst symptom of my predicament was the feeling of not being useful. I felt rudderless.

Without my title and the powers that came with it, I soon ceased to receive the steady stream of visits from friends and acquaintances at both my homes in Abuja and Lagos. My multiple cellphones, a signature part of my life, stopped ringing with such insistence. I no longer needed two people working around the clock to copy out books full of text messages for my review and response. Everything, including time, slowed to the rhythm of palm wine trickling into a waiting gourd.

I did my best to keep busy. I woke up every morning intent on maintaining normalcy, a routine complemented by the vibrant colours of my signature matching ankara, sewn into various versions of three-quarter-sleeve tops and long skirts. I spent more time than usual choosing matching jewellery to go with each outfit, nothing too noisy but without the tone of defeat.

I took up positions on boards that sought my counsel, and I paid visits to old allies to stoke the embers of a potential political comeback. I resumed going to Mass every day, praying for guidance because, for the first time in my entire life, I didn't feel the fire of purpose.

An unexpected gift of this time was reconnecting to being

a mother and now a grandmother to Ijeoma's two children
and Dozie's newborn. I made a point of reaching out to all
six children in calls I made one after the other. I could sense
sometimes the awkwardness of such calls, asking questions
to catch up with their lives and the women and men they had
become.

So much had happened in the last decade, during which I
had been consumed with public service. My two eldest children, Ijeoma and Dozie, were medical doctors working in the
ER, and the third, Somto, was soon to become a doctor as
well — a radiologist. The fourth, Njideka, was intent on pursuing art, which I had initially resisted out of fear of the many
stories of starving artists, but I was now pleasantly surprised
to see her successful and wasn't too proud to admit as much.
My two youngest were still finding their feet, with Chidiogo
completing her master's and Obum his undergraduate studies,
in what exactly I wasn't quite sure.

Three of them were now married, including two of my
daughters, Ije and Nji, and my first son, Dozie. It still struck
me that the girls were both married to foreigners, Ijeoma to
an Ivorian man she had met in her years at Harvard, and Nji
to a white man from Texas whom she had met at Swarthmore.
Initially, I had been disturbed when Ijeoma, the first to be
married, had expressed her interest in marrying a foreigner.
Not only was he not Igbo, he was not even Nigerian. I consoled
myself with him being African, and his family was very
respected, which gave me a lot of confidence in the kind of
man he was.

When Nji announced her interest in marrying a white man,
I found solace in knowing that his family was Catholic. I was

particularly touched by the story that his parents had asked for money in lieu of gifts at their own wedding decades in the past, all of which they donated to the Missionaries of Charity founded by Mother Teresa. To know that my daughter would connect to such a family filled me with joy and inspired me to question my own prejudices.

Seeing them both so happy in their marriages, for years to come I repeated to my unmarried son and daughters my evolved philosophy that they should not concern themselves with the tribe, nationality, or race of the person they married. The key to a happy marriage, I shared, is not being from the same hamlet, but love and devotion to each other and to God, which transcends all else. It was my greatest wish that they each found this for themselves, for I knew, from the past experience of a sometimes different reality, that no matter one's success in life, a loving and stable partnership was key — it was the palm oil with which life can be savoured.

I spent this unforeseen rest phase catching up on things I had deprioritized over the years, my health included. However, in spite of my extended rest, my energy did not recover from its depleted state. In the spring of 2012, a weakening body and the time to attend to such things forced me to go for a medical checkup.

Part V

2012–2014

Fifty-Four

"A good thing for a house to lack is sickness."

SOMETHING I LEARNED over the years — especially in the pockets of my life that allowed me access to sometimes thousands of people in any one single day — is the human desire to care for a beloved. In a country like Nigeria, I also learned that once people opened their hearts to you, they would go the distance with you and for you.

Such people were our family friends — the Egbujiobis. Dr. Leo and his wife, Beatrice, lived in Beloit, Wisconsin, not far from Chicago. For my medical visit, they insisted that I come stay at their home to be checked at Dr. Leo's hospital.

During the checkup they found abnormally large fibroids in my uterus and a mass in my ovary. The doctors could not rule out cancer. I shook off the worst of my fear, assuring myself that it would turn out just like it had almost two decades prior — that this too would be no cause for concern.

As a pre-emptive measure, pending test results, my attending doctor, Dr. Vogel, prescribed that I undergo a hysterectomy to remove my uterus and with it the offending fibrosis. It was of some significance to know that the part that had conceived all nine of my children, six of whom it carried and birthed, would be cut out. The only bright side was that I would no longer have my menses to worry about. I was well into my fifties and still receiving this monthly visitor, years after I felt it had lost its value.

On the day of the surgery, though I had a smile on my face as I changed into a blue hospital gown, and in spite of all my attempts at positivity, I was nervous. I recognized the nurse who wheeled me into the operating room, a familiarity that allowed a break from the dread of what was to come.

Once in the OR, I greeted the main surgeon, two supporting doctors, and the nurses, all while my lips continued to whisper the words of the rosary, which I still held. Perhaps noting my attachment, the surgeon made an exception to allow me to hold on to it. This meant so much to me because, while I trusted the doctors to do their best, I knew God's work on me was what I needed.

I woke up to a throbbing pain in my lower abdomen, and pads soaked with blood, which a kind nurse, a different one this time, changed three times in the space of one hour, all the while closely monitoring my blood pressure and pain levels. Once the anesthesia had worn off, the doctors came by to confirm that the procedure had been a smooth one, with minimal bleeding; they were optimistic for my recovery. Should there have been any cancer cells, the hope was that they would have been removed in tandem with my uterus.

When the tests did come back, however, they were positive for cancer cells. Not wanting to take any risks, the doctors recommended chemotherapy. My quick trip to the United States was becoming an extended one.

Dr. Leo's home in Beloit was tucked on a quiet street at the curve of a roundabout. It was one of many similar houses in a row, each lined with manicured shrubs. Theirs was a big house and an empty nest since their children had left home. I stayed in a room on the second floor overlooking the silent street.

Three weeks following surgery, it was time for my treatment. Between surgery, recovery, and chemotherapy, my visit to Beloit was to become a three-month stay. I often marvelled at the perfection of God's timing: should my checkup have fallen at any other time, I would surely have had a lot more difficulty making the space to prioritize my own health and recovery.

My third daughter, Somto, had been with me for my operation and stayed on during my recovery. She arranged to spend her fourth-year medical school rotation in Beloit to make this arrangement work.

The treatment itself was administered via a peripherally inserted central catheter line — a PICC line — that was introduced through my arm into my veins and up into a larger vein above my heart. During treatment, the PICC was attached to a drip containing my chemotherapy.

I wore a smile against the onslaught of the chemo, dispelling the worried voices of my children with a sing-song promise of my good health. When I was not being a model patient, together with Somto and Beatrice, Dr. Leo's wife, whom I called B, we spent long days chatting and cooking. I realized, to my chagrin, that I had failed to teach my children, specifically my daughters, how to cook. I had been so busy all these years either raising them or raising funds for their upkeep. Once they had all gone off to boarding school, I focused on nurturing my career, so much so that I had completely missed that they couldn't cook. The first sign of my failings was when Somto asked me innocently how to cook jollof rice! She might as well have asked me how to fry an egg. So, I made it a point to spend as many hours with her as possible in the kitchen.

When we were not cooking, a messy and joyous affair, or spending quiet afternoons in the house, or calling friends who had sons of marrying age, I was out walking, which became a therapeutic highlight of my day. I walked daily to and from a nearby church, where I spent the remainder of my time either in silent prayer or in Mass.

I found the time and energy to visit my other children scattered around the country, where they mostly remained after their undergraduate and graduate degrees — even my youngest daughter, who constantly moved from one country to another, was living in America. In her years on the move, I had sometimes worried that she was running away from something.

Unable to fully detach from Nigeria, I also kept abreast of politics in the country, making strategic calls to journalists and political allies to stay up to date and relevant. On one occasion I even managed to attend a conference in Chicago where Baba — former president Olusegun Obasanjo — was speaking.

When my hair started to fall out, I made light of the situation; it was either that or despair over the inevitable. Instead of waiting for it all to fall out, I shaved my whole head. I didn't even mind that I ended up looking like a kiwi.

The very next day, Somto and I went to shop for wigs. I wanted something understated and as natural-looking as possible. Something I could wear on its own or under my head-tie so that just the ends of the hair peeked out below the fabric. My decision was less about vanity than to avoid the uncomfortable stares of strange eyes and, perhaps more importantly, to hide the evidence of my cancer treatment from Nigerians when I did return home.

I had made the decision to keep the details of my illness from everyone except for a few intimate friends and family whom I trusted to keep my secret. Ours was a country that shunned sickness as weakness; not only were the afflicted condemned, but so too were their children, given the potential hereditary nature of the affliction, and with them their marriage prospects. I was loath to give anyone a reason to question my capacity in the future or to impose any judgement on my children.

Somto registered us in a makeup class so I could learn to draw in my eyebrows, which had also thinned; it reminded me of the early 1990s, when it had been in vogue to shave off the eyebrows and pencil them in with thin dark lines.

The first time I saw myself reflected in the mirror, my eyebrows and scalp bare of hair, I thought I would be more depressed. Instead, I nearly laughed at the absurdity of realizing the things I had put so much value on all these years were no more. The perfect coif and arch of my eyebrows, even the weight I had sought to shed over the years, were all departing of their own free will.

Fifty-Five

*"Two events are in the sky: if rain does not fall,
the sun will shine."*

WHILE MY PHONE STILL BEEPED intermittently, my schedule
was a far cry from what it had been in the past decade. Try
as I might, I couldn't run away from the thoughts of my own
mortality that creeped up in moments of stillness. In those
days, I was keenly aware that the one thing we all get is a
lifetime. I wondered what I had done with mine. Was there
more that I could have done? Did I have any regrets? What
did I want to be remembered for?

I wondered about my legacies: as a daughter, mother,
wife, sister, and in service of the people. I wondered about
my relationship with my family, specifically my children, and
if anything or anyone needed my attention.

There was still so much for me to do in life, not least of all
with my children. My thoughts went from one child to the
next, my anxiety focusing on those I saw as not settled, either
professionally or in marriage.

Somto had just turned thirty and had yet to find a suitable
husband. I wanted only the best for her; she was so sweet in

an innocent way, reminding me of myself without the tough skin that life had cloaked me with.

Chidiogo was also not married, but she was still young enough. She was graduating soon from her master's program at Johns Hopkins — I was disappointed that I could not attend, as travelling to Washington, DC, was now impossible with my ongoing treatment — and I wondered about her next steps with sadness about my past actions.

I had been critical of her abandoning a dream we had for her to pursue a law degree in favour of international relations and economics. I could still hear my own voice telling her she was making a grave mistake.

"ChiChi," I had said, "look at all the presidents in America — Clinton, Bush, Obama — Hillary, all of them studied law. Look at Condoleezza Rice, she also studied law. Which one is in international relations? You will end up being Condoleezza Rice's secretary. That's the kind of job for these types of degrees."

I could tell my words had struck a painful chord. But she refused to reconsider, sharing with me data on the lucrative careers, including in politics, that former students of her program had gone on to pursue. It was the first time she had ever pushed back against my advice. While I had experienced dissent with Nji — who went against my advice to study medicine, only to prove us all very wrong with her global success as an artist — I still felt like I was right this time. Upset by Chidiogo's unwillingness to heed my warning, I said things I regretted even as I spoke them.

"Who will pay for this?" I had asked scornfully, knowing she needed my financial support. It was unfair on my end, an outlet for my frustration at not getting my way. Over the years, the pressure of my work and my tendency to bulldoze through obstacles meant that I had to be careful not to be a bully. Not heeding my own wisdom, I continued.

"Mark my words," I added, "you will regret it." And with that, I hung up. I am not too proud to say that I was wrong, for here she was, two years later, selected as the speaker to represent her graduating class.

Although I was not able to make it to her graduation in person, I was happy that Chike was there on our behalf. Also, Somto set it up for me to watch online, placing the screen on the table of Dr. Leo's bright dining room. As I watched the ceremony, it occurred to me that the moment was a reversal of roles; in the past, my children watched my key moments online and from afar, and now it was I who was watching.

Listening to the keynote speaker and to Chidiogo's speech, I realized that I'd resented that she hadn't trusted and followed my guidance without question, as I had my father's. But in that moment, I understood that simple continuity did not exist. She was her own woman, and I had the chance to give her something I'd never had — the freedom to live her own life and find her own way, unburdened by expectations imposed either by others or by herself.

I felt so much joy watching her that I forgot all about my present predicament. I called her after the ceremony was over.

"Chickin Chickin baby," I crooned in my usual greeting. "*Ubuntu* — I am because you are, you are because we are," I said, repeating the phrase from her speech that had stayed with me. It was also my way of saying "I see you, and I am proud of you."

ChiChi came up to Beloit a few days after her graduation. I held her in a lingering embrace, hoping that she might feel my pride and joy.

Njideka had also come up to Beloit. With three of my children, it felt like a scene from decades earlier, before boarding schools, before NAFDAC, before the ministry, before the senate run, when they were still children, content with being close to their mother. In that moment, I could just be their mother, without the distraction of caring so much for the needs of others. While the thought of the many years apart saddened me, I felt content. I didn't regret the path I had chosen; it was a sacrifice I'd made with eyes wide open.

Those days together in Beloit were happy: Nji playing old-school Nigerian tunes, me and Auntie B singing in the background with nostalgic abandon, chuckling at my children's surprise that I knew who Fela was!

With all the time available to me, I was even able to focus on Obum's weight. As my youngest, he was the one I worried the most about. While all the other children had left home at a young age, during their secondary school days, they still came back every holiday. This was not the case for Obum. With him being so far away in the United States and with me being so busy, we had less and less time together. He had put on a lot of weight and had become more withdrawn, both of which concerned me. Since he had stopped playing American football, at our counsel, he had ballooned to four hundred pounds in a few short months. This was not just about vanity, this was a matter of health and life expectancy. I knew something had to be done, and we were far beyond urging him to eat less and drink less of the sugary drinks he was so fond of. Once I had some space to think about the approach, within a few hours of having the idea, we got him enrolled in a boot camp.

At the end of a twenty-four-week program, he had lost 131 pounds. I started to call him Denzel, to his mortified joy. He was a new man, and I thanked God daily for his life and for mine that I could live to see this day and many more.

My mood at the time was further lightened when Bishop Hilary Okeke visited from Chicago to spend time with me and pray for my recovery.

Soon my chemo treatment came to an end. My doctors, including Dr. Leo, had made it clear that all we could do was wait and see if all the cancer cells had been eliminated. Only time would tell. For now, I could return home to Nigeria. I was amused by their lack of faith. God was in control, and time would reveal what I felt to be true: that I was well on my path of healing.

Between eye pencils, a wig, and head-ties, no one needed to be aware of my struggles; the last thing I needed was pity or others worrying about me. All I would share was that my absence had been a much-needed break and time spent with my family. In many ways, this was very much the truth.

Fifty-Six

"The axe forgets, the tree remembers."

SIX MONTHS IN NIGERIA went by both slowly and quickly—soon it was time to return to Beloit. I returned to Beloit for my scheduled checkup. The American summer heat in 2013 was as suffocating as ever, but I didn't let it deflate me, as I was sure this trip would be short. The Egbujiobis welcomed me back with so much grace.

Days after my return, I was once again in the familiar building of the hospital. A doctor I did not know came into the waiting room where I was seated. His body language gave away the message before he opened his mouth.

After a minimum of niceties, he dove right in. "You have a very rare cancer called uterine leiomyosarcoma. It is not hereditary, and frankly, we have little understanding of definite causes." He paused, watching for signs that I understood, then continued. "The cancer has metastasized from the uterus to your ovaries and is already in other parts of your body. This means it is now stage IV cancer." He paused again. his eyes softening and searching mine. "There is a tumour in your lungs."

311

All I could think was how this explained the pressure I had been feeling in my chest.

"The tumour is so big that it's right against your heart." He gestured to his heart as he spoke, and I fought irritation that he thought he had to show me where my heart was.

Gaining some composure, I asked, "Do I need to do another round of chemo?" My voice betrayed my horror at the thought.

"No," he answered, "the chances of success with chemo are so slim, there is truly little more we can do."

Such simple words with devastating implications. It was as if my spirit had been punctured like a balloon and all that was left was a crumpled shell.

"This is a particularly aggressive cancer," he continued. "It kills by squeezing things. You might already be feeling some pressure. This will continue to your internal organs, squeezing your bowels, causing obstruction. There will be nowhere for food to go, which will cause a loss of appetite and impact your overall health."

I could tell he wanted to be very clear about the situation. I didn't mind his bluntness and urged him to continue by nodding my understanding.

"Your muscles, including your heart muscles, will weaken, impacting your heart's ability to pump blood efficiently, and that could lead to cardiac arrest. This is basically a cancer that sucks the life out of you to feed its own growth until it kills you."

I let this sink in before I found my voice and said, "Listen, there has to be something else you can do. What about chemo? Is not the whole point to attack and reduce the cancer? Why would it not work in this situation?"

Together, like students working on a project, we weighed

the various options, with him restating that there were no more treatment plans. As I was not interested in doing nothing at all, we agreed that I would undergo another round of chemotherapy, this time oral.

Without a doubt, it was a sad day, but the potential of a successful therapy gave me faith.

I was to spend another month in Beloit to complete my treatment, after which they could determine a way forward. Somto once again came up to be with me.

In the days after I received the news of the fight within my body, my mood changed considerably; a dark cloud hung over me and I seemed helpless to dispel it. I would get very irritated or angry for no reason, perhaps to distract myself from reality.

It was a struggle for me to connect my behaviour with the woman I had been. The woman before me was a meaner version of myself, snapping at everyone and making a scapegoat of anyone who crossed my path.

Once, my mood translated into words that hurt Somto. I was truly grateful to her for the care she had shown me, and I hated that I'd caused her pain, especially as it hadn't been my intention. Afterwards I called her into my room and opened up about my state of mind. I was sad, simple and true, and in a rare moment I let someone in behind my walls.

"Sommy," I said, tears beginning to fall. "*Cancer a dịrọ na family anyị,* cancer is not in our family. What kind of diagnosis is this! I am depressed about this and I want to let my daughter know how I'm really feeling. I am sorry I hurt you."

"It's going to be okay, Mummy," she said. "God is on the throne. He will keep you safe."

We sat together for a while like this, sharing and praying.

Somto told me later that it was only the second time she had ever seen me cry. Somto later explained to me that my mood change could be a manifestation of depression, which she said was to be expected with my diagnosis.

Everyone despaired for me and the diagnosis and what it signalled, which meant that I had to stay strong. My faith had always been firm, but now it needed to move mountains.

I had to believe I would be healed; in fact, I was certain of it. My conviction was supported by some strong rationales. The first was that, in the Bible, God promised man seventy years; I wasn't yet even sixty. The second was based on my deep trust that God had saved me from the clutches of death on multiple occasions, most notably in the attempt on my life. The same God surely would want those responsible for the assassination attempt, notably the accused pharmaceutical drug baron, to be brought to justice. The case was still in court, and I knew that the only chance of justice was if I stayed alive. And lastly, three of my children were still to marry, and I saw it as my duty as well as my joy to support this critical phase of their lives. Surely, I would live. To seal this deal, I reminded God of Isaiah 43:26 — "State your case, that you may be acquitted." My case was stated as above: the desire to live a long life, for justice and to see my children settled.

I committed myself to the oral chemo treatment as my way of fulfilling my part of the bargain that "heaven helps those who help themselves."

Unfortunately, between the treatments and accompanying medications, my health took a turn for the worse, and I lost my last facade of good humour. This was made worse when, after a month of treatment in Beloit, the doctors concluded that the cancer was still growing. There was truly nothing more they could do.

At Dozie's recommendation, as a physician himself, I didn't give up on Western medicine and instead went for a second opinion at a cancer specialist hospital in Houston, where he lived. Chike and our dear friend Father Muoneke accompanied me. I stayed with Dozie and his wife and young son, Chike, named after his grandfather. At the Anderson Cancer Center, once again, I was put on chemo: Adriamycin, a stronger chemo than before, delivered via a venous access port placed under the skin in my upper chest.

As much as I didn't want to admit it, my body and spirit were getting weaker by the day. My irritability continued and spared no one, and on more than one occasion I lost my temper with Dozie's wife, about whom I complained to anyone who would listen. It was as if I was borrowing a page from my own lived experiences with Chike's family. Luckily, said daughter-in-law wasn't foolish enough to take the bait, which acted to both pacify and exasperate my temper at various intervals.

I knew that idleness worked against my desire to regain my positive disposition, so in spite of the advanced state of my illness, I continued to work, serving on boards, as an adviser and consultant. I kept going as if by sheer will, though I was quite frail and my soft brown curls, which had started to grow back after my last treatments, had once again fallen out, and my face was beginning to take on the hollow look of a skull.

Later that year, with my second round of chemo treatment completed, the cancer was still growing and spreading. The oncologist in Houston too had come to the end of the road — there was no other curative treatment they had to offer. I was to await my death. They gave me but a few months.

I assured them politely that they were wrong and thanked them for their best efforts. Now it was up to God to heal me with a perfect miracle, just like the miracle in Cana of Jesus turning water into wine. It would be my greatest testimony to date, of this I had no doubt: we would beat death.

Homesick after months of being away, I booked my ticket back to Nigeria. There was no longer any reason to be in America.

Fifty-Seven

"No matter how the rain beats the guinea fowl,
its colour remains the same."

I HAD ALWAYS BEEN prayerful, and over the years it had become a critical part of my life. In the days and weeks that followed, I took it to another level. Having no full-time job, my full-time occupation became praying and seeking divine solutions for my illness.

For support, I recruited an army of priests. Hundreds of Masses were said for me in those months. Having expanded my religious viewpoint over the years, I also called upon various pastors to join in saying prayers, inviting them to my home to lay their hands on me. Some prayed loudly, others spoke in tongues, others still engaged in curious practices, like the one who threw salt around the compound of my home in Abuja to ward off the evil spirits responsible for my sickness.

While prayer had its place, I still had to take concrete actions to help myself, and with Western medicine unable to assist, I researched alternative remedies. Fortunately or unfortunately for me, the internet was teeming with various miracle pills, healing practices, herbs, and foods.

On this quest, I heard of a woman in Lagos who had cured her own cancer. She saw patients out of her home on the outskirts of the city. I made the trip late at night with a good friend, Kate Isa, and my daughter Chidiogo. The woman was for me a living miracle. I was inspired to hear that she had beaten cancer by changing her diet and drinking only raw fresh juices. Juicing, she said, was the key. I started to make connections between the food I ate and the growth of my cancer.

"ChiChi," I lamented to my daughter, who was now living in Lagos and on one of her visits to see me in Abuja, where I was spending the majority of my time. "Do you know that pounded yam feeds my cancer? And all these months I have been eating *swallow*," I said, upset that my doctors had failed to caution me about my diet.

Juicing met prayers, and they were a formidable force. Overnight, the soups and rice, meats and chicken in the fridge were replaced by beets, celery, broccoli, carrots, bitter leaf, and spinach. For weeks I ate no solid food, depending on the juices.

The first time I threw up was after a glass of beet juice. I hadn't even known we had beets in Nigeria. It was an eerie feeling to see the red liquid, which looked like thick blood, projected from my body onto the carpet. It was to be the first time of many. I continued to throw up for many weeks after. I reasoned that it was a temporary setback in my body's recovery. As I knew that the sky was blue, I knew that I would be healed.

Over time, I learned the tricks to keeping the juice down. When I finally reintroduced solids, it was chunks of apple, pawpaw, pineapple, soursop, banana, and grapes washed down with two freshly squeezed oranges. For the next months, I focused on nothing but my healing, each day soaking my increasingly frail body in a salt bath, another tool to fight the enemy within; drinking vegetables and fruits; and praying.

Every morning, I monitored the growing swell of my belly in the mirror for signs of a reduction that would signal that the cancer was being killed by either the juice or the holy spirit.

When I went for a checkup in Houston, and to have the port removed, the doctor remarked that I looked good, even going as far as to say that my skin was glowing. I brightened up, wondering if I had been right and my juicing had defeated the tumour.

Test results showed that the tumour was not gone, but never once did I allow myself to acknowledge the possibility of death.

Instead of growing smaller, every day the cancer grew visibly bigger, inversely proportional to my strength. It was as if the mass was feeding on my energy, but still I refused to let it have the upper hand. Instead of slowing down and allowing death to run its wicked course, I decided that I could accelerate my healing by showing God the proof of my faith.

I once again threw myself into work, accepting an appointment as a delegate to represent Anambra at the National Conference (CONFAB), which was intended to address various causes of unrest in the country. In spite of my poor health, I was ready to give my all in service. Not only would I join the conference, but I also came prepared to present a speech. It was my first public appearance since the previous year, before my second and third rounds of chemo.

On the day of the first meeting, I spent a long time getting ready, carefully applying my makeup, putting on my wig, and choosing a bulky outfit to hide just how thin I had become and how swollen my stomach was. Try as I might, I could not conceal the evidence that my once-round face was hollowed out, my neck seeming too frail to support my head, its skin wrinkled as if drained of its juice.

I walked into the hall, my head held high, ignoring the alarmed looks and concern of colleagues and the press.

When it came time for me to deliver my prepared address, the chairman, unconvinced by my insistence that I was well, invited me to stay seated. I respectfully declined and, with as much effort as I could muster, I got up, only slightly visibly shaky under close scrutiny, my body holding me up by sheer willpower.

I proceeded with my speech, calling for our national unity. Halfway through, standing tall and proud and trying to hide the tremors of my weak body, I spoke directly to the hearts of the people about the importance and the power of our unity.

"The founding fathers of Nigeria had a dream of building a united, prosperous, and developed nation-state where social justice reigns." In sharing this, I reminded everyone of the responsibility we had to each other founded on the strength of our unity. In calling for us to reclaim the dream of a unified Nigeria, I invited Nigerians to continue to dream because, as I shared, "once we stop dreaming, then life is gone." I allowed myself to pause to ensure my words found their mark, willing my body not to shake. In closing I said, "Mr. Chairman, distinguished delegates, I leave you with the words of this Greek proverb: 'A society grows great when old men plant trees whose shade they know they shall never sit in.'"

Content, I thanked the committee and sat back down to resounding applause and a standing ovation, but the real reactions of the day were still to be felt. After the conference, several news agencies carried the news of my health, sharing front-page pictures and images of me that even I could see looked like a dead woman walking. Nigerians were surprised and alarmed to see me in this way, and the news and pictures went viral.

Still stubbornly insistent upon keeping my illness private, I denied all accusations of being sick. In addition to avoiding the stigma, perceived or otherwise, I wanted to believe that I wasn't sick, perhaps as a way of keeping my faith alive and the negativity of others at bay.

Desperate to curb the prevailing rumours of my terminal illness, I even went as far as to issue a public statement on March 4, 2014, rejecting any truth of my illness: "This story is baseless, unfounded, and the handiwork of mischief makers. It should be ignored and discarded in its entirety.

"While it is true that I recently came out of a major sickness, for which I thank Almighty God for delivering me, I have since been declared fit by my doctors and returned to my normal activities. I shed much weight in the course of the sickness — which is normal — but I am well now and only need time to regrow some flesh."

For someone who had always prided herself on honesty, I justified my words with the belief that my healing was only a matter of time. I was merely stating a future truth.

Fifty-Eight

"A fully grown-up tree cannot be bent into a walking stick."

DESPERATE TO FIND my healing, and listening intently for God's guidance, I was overjoyed when Somto, the most devout of my children, mentioned the option of drinking holy water from Lourdes, France, where our Lady had appeared to Saint Bernadette of Lourdes and the site of numerous miracles. Why hadn't I thought of that? It made sense to fight the disease from within in this manner!

We immediately ordered the healing water from the apparition site. I took to drinking the water daily, still looking for evidence of the defeated cancer each day. After a few weeks, when no change was forthcoming, I decided I needed to improve the effectiveness of the miracle. Perhaps given the advanced stage of my illness, and how far the cancer had spread, I needed to immerse my body fully in the holy water.

As my health declined, my faith rose to counter the failings of my physical body. Lourdes was to be the site of my miracle; it had to be. I shared this thought with Somto, who volunteered to travel to Nigeria to accompany me on the trip to Lourdes.

On the afternoon of our planned departure, even though I was in great discomfort and relying only on acetaminophen to relieve my pain, I was happy to welcome General Yakubu Gowon, the former military ruler of Nigeria and notably the head of state during the Biafra war, for a visit with his wife. He had become an unlikely ally during my years at NAFDAC and with time had become a friend. I sometimes looked upon him and tried to see the monster we had cast him as in those years of the war, but try as I may, I could only see and hear his soft-spoken demeanour and kind heart. I wondered if he had always been that way or if he had found his calm and peace at the other end of a costly war.

On April 14, 2014, Somto and I travelled to Paris, where I was joined by four of my children. Dozie came in from Houston and met us at Charles de Gaulle Airport. With one look at me, weak, in pain, and surely looking very frail in a wheelchair, I saw his face take on shock and alarm. Njideka and Chidiogo would join us at the hotel from New York and Geneva respectively.

Once at the hotel, a round structure with a view of a busy Parisian roundabout, Dozie dropped his bag and promptly left for the pharmacy at Montparnasse to buy me much-needed pain relief. He was grateful to the pharmacist, who kindly accepted his American medical licence to get prescription-grade relief in fentanyl patches.

Upon his return, Dozie pasted two patches at a time on my skin. I had been in excruciating pain for days with nothing but over-the-counter painkillers as my solace, desperate for a pain-free moment. Now, as if by magic, there was instant relief. I felt like a freshly watered tree.

I felt vaguely irritated that I had been unnecessarily managing the pain these last weeks when relief was just a patch away. I was also now able to speak freely, as well as drink, downing water to relieve my parched cells. I even managed to eat some food, which a Nigerian couple who had heard I was in Paris had brought for me and my children.

The next day, Somto, Njideka, and I were on a flight to Lourdes. Dozie and Chidiogo could not join us and returned home. We were met and welcomed in Lourdes — a quaint mountain village with a beautiful cathedral — by a gentle priest who spoke slow English. A kind nun showed us to our quarters at the Accueil Notre-Dame. Though I was in considerably less pain, I was still feeling quite fragile, and as such we opted to get a wheelchair. My daughters took turns wheeling me around. We had just enough time to drop our bags in a simple dorm room with single beds and a wheelchair-accessible bathroom before going straight to the cathedral to join the procession of the stations of the cross.

I felt so much peace in the simple and very familiar acts of being wheeled from one station to the other, whispering prayers before the impressive statues and caves that told the struggles of Jesus on his journey to the cross, His death, and His resurrection.

Afterwards, we visited the grotto where it is said that Mary, the mother of Jesus, appeared to Saint Bernadette in 1858. There I prayed before the statue of the Blessed Virgin.

"*Nne anyị dị asọ ekwekwana ka m gbalụ aka naa. Ekwekwana ka m gbalụ aka naa,*" I pleaded, asking that I not go home empty-handed. "Please do not let my enemies laugh at me."

I did not allow myself to dwell too much on my disappointment when I came out of the grotto and, contrary to my hopes, felt no outright change. I stayed optimistic. I just had to be patient. I couldn't have come all the way for nothing.

The main miracle was still up ahead, and it was with excitement that we went to the healing waters of the baths. It didn't matter to me that the water was cold. Without hesitation, I got off the wheelchair, supported into the private stone tub by my daughters, and plunged in, naked but for my wedding and engagement rings. Soaked to my chest, I willed the water to seep into my body and fight off the invader.

Over the days, we found there was no lack of things to do to cater to the millions of pilgrims like myself who had sought out Lourdes and its healing waters. I only took a break when I was tired and needed to sleep, which was relatively often. Otherwise we were at Mass, where I would wheel myself up front to face the impressive altars; at stations of the cross; at the bath; or at the cathedral saying my rosary. I always felt an inexplicable joy whenever I was praying, reminding God of His promise to me, that it wasn't my time, and that I was ready for His miracle in my life.

Luckily in those days, with my pain controlled, I enjoyed a newfound appetite, which allowed me to eat and even taste the delicious food, which I washed down with copious amounts of the juice of sweet oranges they had in the town. I enjoyed the nostalgia of peeling off the orange skin with a small knife until the fruit was a round white ball, at which point I would cut it in half, squeezing its juice directly into my waiting mouth with the simultaneous action of hands and lips. I had spent a lifetime consuming bags of oranges brought in fresh from trees of nearby villages, many of which I got to know by their fruit.

Every night, before we went to sleep, I asked my daughters to pray with me: *ka Mummy bịa mee m operation n'abanị —* that mother Mary would come and operate on me at night. I woke up each morning excited to see if the tumour in my stomach was reduced or even gone, and with it my pain. Day after day, night after night, we prayed, and every morning I woke up expectant of my miracle, observing my stomach for signs of healing. My faith was unshakable; it was just a question of when.

We had been making daily trips to the sacred waters. The morning before our departure from Lourdes was my third and last visit to the bath. I was feeling especially excited, as I'd woken up at 4 a.m. from a dream and premonition of an impending miracle.

Once there, frail as I was, not waiting for my daughters to support me, I got up from my wheelchair and ran into the water, submerging my entire body in spite of the freezing temperature. "God, please," I prayed, "if you are alive, and I know you are, please just do this for me."

When I came out and didn't feel or see a visible difference, and when I drank from the pitcher with fresh water from the source, and still nothing. I concluded once again that perhaps my healing would come at a later hour of the day.

We spent a total of four days at Lourdes, which, thanks to the patches, were the most comfortable I had been in a long time. It truly was a happy trip.

Fifty-Nine

"The young bird does not crow until it hears the old ones."

BACK IN NIGERIA, even as my condition continued to deteriorate after Lourdes, I maintained hope that the healing was simply delayed. I held this truth to be sacred, knowing that I had never been let down before by God, and there was no reason why now should be different. I continued to hold on to the Biblical story of Job: this was my trial, and all I had to do was stay true to my faith.

By the end of April, I was in so much discomfort I had to be checked into a hospital in Abuja. Nizamiye Hospital was run by Turks and smelled of cleaning detergents — that unique hospital smell I knew all too well from years working at the university hospital. I felt so depleted; even breathing had become hard. But I remained ever hopeful. It took two people now to get me out of bed, supporting my head, back, and armpits and dodging wires protruding from my body.

In the early days of May 2014, my hospital room was like a bazaar, with a steady flow of family, including Chike, my brother Anayo, my sister Ngozi, my daughter Chidiogo, visiting from Geneva, and my son Obum, who had moved back to work in Nigeria, as well as friends, my priest, and even political allies who knew the truth of my illness. I could tell from the looks on their faces, especially those who hadn't seen me for a while, that they were genuinely alarmed.

The hospital couldn't do much more than manage my pain, which had become once again unbearable after I ran out of the patches from Dozie. It was on a Friday evening, and in the height of my desperation, when only family members were left in the room, that my attending doctor told us about a hospital in India famed for healing cancer, even at stage IV.

"They have this new technology, it's a Gamma Knife," he said. "They can use it to target and cut the tumour. They can heal cancer."

"Even metastasized?" Chike asked, his eyes filled with care, fear, and concern.

"Yes, they can heal her!"

Magic words to my ears.

By 8 p.m. the next day the decision to go to India had been made among my doctor, Chike, Anayo, and me. Anayo was the most vocal in his support, since he had always been of the opinion that my treatment been mismanaged in America. I could barely speak anymore, as it cost too much energy and breath, but I was very vocal with grunts of approval for this journey. Once again, I had something to keep my hopes alive. I simply had to do my part and God would do the rest. The feeling was like light piercing through dark clouds, renewing my spirits.

I had an urgent call made to Ijeoma, who was to arrive in the coming days, to ask that she cancel her flight to Nigeria.

I was going to India to meet God's miracle. Soon, various members of the family were out on frantic missions that involved waking up the Indian ambassador to Nigeria to issue a visa and confirming details of a private jet that had been offered for my use. I thought with gratitude about how this was the goodwill I had.

In their absence it was just me and my youngest, ChiChi, in the room. I was propped up on the bed, my breathing laboured over my hunched body, while she sat beside me, gently supporting my frame while simultaneously rubbing me lightly and comfortingly. I moaned my gratitude, for words had become too difficult. Mustering some strength, I angled my body to face her, straightened up slightly, and said "I love you" in a faint yet strong whisper.

It was the first time I had said those words to her, not because I didn't feel it, for she knew of my love, but because it just wasn't part of our shared culture and I hadn't felt an urgent need to let her know. Now I did, especially after a vicious quarrel we'd had the previous year about her boyfriend, of whom I'd disapproved.

I saw her freeze, unsure of how to respond. She smiled widely and weakly at the same time, her confusion apparent. I saw her relief when a nurse came into the room. I didn't mind; the words were for her to always remember over my other ones.

I didn't question that she wasn't coming with us to India — I had too little energy to think much of it. I had to trust that I would see her again soon, and we'd have time to heal.

Sixty

*"Ụkwa ruo oge ya ọ daa — the breadfruit will fall
when it is ready."*

IT WAS CHIKE WHO shook me awake. He wanted to personally share the good news that it was time to go. I smiled my
thanks and drifted back to sleep. The few personal items I
had were already packed up by unknown hands. Asleep, I
was wheeled into the car that would drive me to the airport
and then wheeled again into the waiting jet. Extra measures,
I was assured later, were taken so that as few people as possible saw me in this state. Heavily sedated, I moved in and
out of consciousness.

Once in Bangalore we had a car waiting to take us to the
hospital. I only fully woke up a day later to the prick of a needle.
My treatment had begun, and once again it was chemotherapy.

At the hospital, in addition to my small entourage —
consisting of Chike, Anayo, my doctor, and my aide, a young
woman named Ijeoma — Dr. Leo had joined from the States.
Even Peter Obi, the former governor of Anambra, would come
all the way to pay a visit. While their presence was important, I
had a strong urge to be with my children. The doctors departed

shortly after we settled in, leaving only Chike, Anny, and Ijeoma with me. With the little energy I had, as my renewed chemotherapy treatment was now taking the last of my health, I asked again and again for my children.

Chike let me know that Nji was on her way, while the rest of them were working on getting their visas to India. It was a most unfortunate coincidence that there was a strike happening in India that was impacting embassies and slowing the visa process.

A small voice in my mind was beginning to whisper, "What if?"

"What if I am not healed? What if I die?"

I didn't want to die so far from home in such a strange place and without my children.

The voice was gaining even more traction because the hospital where I was supposed to find my healing was in truth a horrible place. I regretted the trip the moment I woke up. Everything was old and dirty; one wouldn't have been surprised to see a mouse scurrying around. Even the hospital gowns were dirty and unwashed, with yellow and orange stains on them. Nothing felt or looked sterile.

I had quickly surmised that the doctor who had been so insistent that I come to this world-class hospital had deceived me. I didn't know what he had to gain, but he surely had not acted for my benefit. That belief rang even more true when I heard that he had departed shortly after arrival. Every movement hurt, and neither the infrastructure nor the doctors seemed to prioritize my comfort or well-being.

The chemo, which I had to receive in another building accessible only though a hot and unshaded walkway, further weakened my very compromised immune system and organs. In addition, it caused obstructions in my bowels, which meant that I couldn't relieve myself. Worse still, the hospital had no protocol to support me through my painful predicament — a challenge I discovered is quite common during chemo treatment for a person with stage IV cancer. At some point, Chike had to intervene. He remembered a procedure he had learned as a young doctor, which he was happy to teach and guide the care team through. It involved me going on all fours, at which point a sigmoidoscope was inserted from behind and a tube passed through to untwist my intestine. I was finally able to pass stool, but this was not the end of my problems.

It was impossible for me to stand up on my own, and now coupled with heightened pain levels and a restroom that was far from me and the bed, I had to relieve myself in a bedpan, with Chike telling me that all would be well and not to concern myself with the indignity of it all. My pain got worse by the hour, and the most curious part of the cruel experience was that my doctors refused to increase my dosage of pain medication.

Just when all seemed bleak, I got news that Njideka had arrived and was on her way from the airport. I must have asked for her every five minutes since I heard she was on her way. I was not expecting to cry the moment I saw her at the door.

It was in Nji's eyes that I saw the undeniable truth that I was dying. I realized then that I was no longer fighting for my life. All I wanted was at least one of my children to be with me.

"Thank you," I said. I repeated, "Thank you," my tears flowing freely. It was all I could really muster, and I repeated it again to convey the extent of my appreciation.

She sat by my bed and held my hand, simply saying, "Of course, Mummy," her eyes also wet with tears.

While her visit greatly raised my spirits, the pain soon got the better of me, causing me to go in and out of consciousness. When I was awake, I felt incoherent until Nji had the idea to try writing on a piece of paper. But even this was for naught, as I didn't have the strength to hold the pen steady enough to manage a single word. It was the oddest feeling, as my mind was sometimes fully alert, but I had no control over my bodily functions.

Njideka had brought over a special basin to facilitate me relieving myself with some respectability. It did not help matters, as its weak metal frame broke, its contents spilling across the floor. I didn't even blink. I was at the point of my sickness where nothing fazed me anymore. Just about everything was going wrong with my body and I had reached a forced acceptance of this. I didn't even wipe away the stains from the spill, as every move took precious energy. I simply got back into bed as if nothing had happened, and inside I died a little more.

The pain after each chemo treatment was the most unbearable. Sometimes I would be screaming without cease, but the doctors remained resolutely unhelpful. I heard on more than one occasion Nji's pleading voice or Chike's angrier one, begging and demanding that the doctors give me another shot of pain relief, even getting my other children, the doctors among them, to call and attempt to persuade them. They did not budge.

Nji had tears in her eyes when she told me that the doctors were saying no because the pain medicine could burden my respiration. Even though it was now apparent that the burden to my respiration was the least of my problems, they still wouldn't give me medication that would reduce my pain. Why not? Because of its possible fatal side effects!

We soon understood that the philosophy of the doctors was to keep treating me until I died; they had no intention of doing anything that could alleviate the pain of the journey or exacerbate the speed of its eventuality.

It was Anayo who, with his sharp mind for sly business practices, explained the unfortunate nightmare we found ourselves in: they needed me alive to make money, and extra pain medication could reduce my billable days left on earth. All arguments for giving me relief fell on deaf ears. They left me to bear the pain.

Nji took advantage of my rare moments of lucidity to ring her brothers and sisters, who talked to me on speaker-phone. I was excited to hear that Dozie's visa was finally being processed; that brought me great relief.

Knowing it was no longer possible for me to hold a conversation, Somto and ChiChi sent messages for me through Nji. Somto's was a letter and Chidiogo's an email. Listening to Njideka read them made me emotional to the point of tears. I feel like I cried more in those days than I did all my life.

I asked Nji to read each letter and email to me twice, relishing hearing from my children. In other moments of lucidity, Nji told me stories — I could tell she was sharing whatever came to her mind just to distract me from my pain. Through it all, I kept asking for Dozie.

"Is Dozie coming? *Dozie a na abia nu?* Is he coming?" Potentially running out of time before he arrived aggravated my impatience.

Nji kept replying with the only thing she could: "He's coming, he's on his way. He is just now waiting for his visa."

When the pain was too much, Nji would sit with me in silence until late in the evening, at which time she would return to her hotel, only to come back again the next morning.

Soon my appetite disappeared. Just a few days before, after we arrived in India, I had been craving a Maltina drink and had everyone in India scouting for a bottle. But now I couldn't so much as think of drinking anything.

With every sign now pointing to the likelihood of death, I wanted to go back home to Nigeria. But no matter how often I asked, speaking in Igbo to conserve words, "*Ka anyị naa,*" I was told that it was impossible. I could no longer be moved. This truth didn't stop me from insisting, "*Ka anyị naa. Ka anyị naa. Ka anyị naa,*" my voice a desperate plea.

My daughter soon gave up telling me the futility of the request and instead answered, "Okay, Mummy," sensing the power of hope her words gave me.

Things took a darker turn. Not having eaten anything for two days, I was surprised when a brown substance started to come out of my mouth. It smelled foul, and it took me only a few seconds to realize that it was my own feces. Alarmed, Nji called for the doctors, who, when they finally arrived, did nothing. Chike had gone out on an errand, perhaps to find me a bottle of malt in the hope that my appetite would return. Nji called Ijeoma, an ER doctor. Crying, Ijeoma explained that my bowels were so obstructed because of the chemo that my body was eliminating waste in this manner.

My mind was alert as I lay there, in pain, my body having fully betrayed me, while my daughter wiped the brown liquid away. I felt her continuously cleaning the offending liquid as it came up. There was nothing more that could be done.

The next days would show that these were some of the better days.

At this point, even the doctors must have known that it was all over, as I was not digesting food and nothing in my body seemed to be working, but still they wouldn't give me adequate painkillers. The only action they took, beyond pumping me with chemo long after it made sense, was to move me to the ICU. My other organs had started to fail, and I was less and less often conscious, but each time I did come to, without fail, I asked if Dozie had arrived.

First to go were my lungs. Ijeoma and Dozie had already predicted this, so I was ready. The same lungs for which I was bearing the pain were now relieving me of their service. I never thought I would celebrate the failure of my respiration. For now, surely, the doctors would give me the pain meds I sorely needed!

The doctors, not ready to let me go, against the counsel and wishes of my children and husband — four of them doctors, who knew how excruciating intubation would be — went ahead and intubated me.

I thought I had already felt the worst pain any human would ever have to endure, but nothing could have prepared me for the agony of the intubation. I suspect the doctors had a sense, for they did not allow my family anywhere near the room. Njideka was crying as she left the ICU, telling me again and again that she loved me as she walked backwards to the door, her eyes never leaving mine. I couldn't even answer for the tears streaming down my own face. We held eyes as she backed out of the room and until the doctors closed the door. Somehow, we both knew it was the last time we would see each other.

My screams of pain from my failing body, the lack of pain medication, and the intubation could be heard through the halls of the hospital. Even I, who had fought death with such a furious dedication to life, wanted it to end. All I wanted now was to die in peace and with dignity. They denied me both.

I lost consciousness soon after the process was completed, but they still didn't stop. They were intent on keeping what was left of me alive as long as they could, even against the will of my family.

I lay there on the hospital bed, but in many ways I was no longer there to feel the chemo they continued to drip into my body. Beeping machines were keeping my body alive, and though I couldn't respond, I heard the music Njideka played to me and all the stories she shared of her life.

The next morning, on June 7, 2014, my body gave up to join me. I was fifty-nine.

Part VI

Chidiogo — My Mother And I

2014–2021

Sixty-One

"No one shows a child the sky."

I WAS ON A FERRY en route from Geneva to Yvoire, a medieval town famed for inspiring awe and nostalgia for the past. It was a beautiful late-spring Saturday, the type that made staying indoors unappealing.

I had just broken the silence between me and a young woman with blond hair and light eyes who had smiled sweetly at me when I sat beside her on the crowded ferry. I had only learned her name, Julia, and that she was Austrian, when the call came. It was from my sister Nji. I promptly excused myself, standing up from our low bench behind a railing to move away from the chatter and closer to the quieter stairwell.

"ChiChi, Mummy *anwugo*, Mummy is dead," she said in a hurried voice, from which I deduced she had others still to call. "She just died a few minutes ago. It's not public yet, so that you know, please don't tell anyone else." She spoke quickly in one breath, her tone matter-of-fact.

"Okay," I mumbled and hung up. This was not the time for questions or emotions.

Time didn't slow down; instead it took on the texture of a farce. The sun continued to shine against the still, blue lake. The boat maintained its steady glide and Julia waited patiently for my return to resume our conversation. I turned back to her, and in a signature move to conceal my feelings — a turmoil of acceptance and rejection — I pasted a soft smile on my face, narrowing my eyes to achieve the desired effect. Not knowing what else to do, I continued the conversation.

"You live here in Geneva?" she asked.

I nodded my response, my smile not reaching my eyes.

"How long have you lived here?"

"Just a few months. I moved here in January of this year," I answered. Surprised by my calmness, I mumbled a few more responses until I couldn't hold up any longer. I went silent, staring blankly at the lake, a forlorn look replacing my softer gaze. "My mother just died" was all I could say.

The expressions on her face were predictable — shock and disbelief and compassion. What was missing, though, was pity, and perhaps that allowed me to soften into the moment.

"It's okay. She has been sick for so long," I said. "For well over two years! She was so sick," I repeated, finding peace in this recollection.

My companion was listening intently, her body language encouraging me to share.

"She was already dead yesterday, but they kept her alive with machines!" I said, my voice pained and beginning to shake. My anger was directed towards the mysterious doctors and an equally mysterious hospital in Bangalore.

"Everything was at a cost, including the illusion of life they offered — hundreds of dollars charged for one last night of life! The 'miracle treatment' they were promising was chemo! They continued to give her chemo even after intubation!

"Why?" I asked, half to myself and half to these forces that worked cruelly against her. I didn't have to be a doctor to know the strength one needed to withstand chemotherapy. Strength that she didn't have. I had witnessed my once strong mother struggle through years of failed treatments at great costs to her body and spirit. How could she tolerate it in her incredibly frail state, let alone already dead? My anger rose.

"My sister called it a deathtrap! The hospital was awful, a scam. Her one doctor promised her that they had a cure in India, but he was just in it for the money. He probably earned a commission for sending her there in the first place. Imagine luring someone with terminal cancer with the false promise of a cure!"

"Oh my God, I am so sorry" came the quiet voice of my patient audience of one, her eyes encouraging me to go on.

"There had been no time to think, no time to question, just the relief of action. In a matter of hours, my mother had a visa and a private jet. Even from her hospital room in Nigeria, she could move mountains." I smiled at the bitter irony of this contrasted with her helplessness in India.

As I continued my rant, grateful for the opportunity to share my frustration, I tasted my pain, questioning if it should be as it was. There were no tears, no shattering of my heart to a million pieces. It had a deadened quality, a numb core that begged not to be disturbed.

"The worst part is that I never got to say goodbye. She didn't believe she would die, and anything other than also believing in a miracle would have seemed like a betrayal of her faith. But I think a part of me knew that it would be the last time."

IT HAD BEEN FIVE MONTHS since I'd moved to Geneva in the middle of the winter. A shocking change from the dry heat of Lagos, my most recent of many homes. I had made the move to take on a senior role at the World Economic Forum, focusing on supporting the reach and impact of a community of young leaders called Global Shapers.

I poured all of myself into becoming the best community manager to the thousands of Shapers I was tasked with supporting. The last weeks had been the culmination of a lot of hard work, which peaked at the World Economic Forum meeting in Africa. In that year, 2014, it was held in my home country of Nigeria and specifically in Abuja.

The serendipitous coincidence meant that I got to see my mother.

I stole a few hours in the lead-up to the meeting and afterwards to be with her. Nothing could have prepared me for what five months had done to her already weakened body. She looked like a ghost of her old self. The slit of her blue hospital gown revealed that the former plump rolls of fat on her back were reduced to deflated folds of skin. Her body had become frail and deformed, her belly protruding, pregnant with a disease that was eating her from inside and vomiting its excrements within her body, her figure reminiscent of old posters of hungry African children, bellies swollen from kwashiorkor.

I knew then that, as much as she still denied this truth, it was over. Even more so, I knew that this might be the last time we saw one another. But I still didn't board the flight to India when we heard of a miracle cure that awaited her in Bangalore.

I muttered excuses about work and the million emails and things waiting for me to deal with them. An unplanned trip to India for an untold period of time simply was not in the books, I reasoned, allowing my mind to tell my heart it knew best. A day after her departure to India, I was on a flight back to Geneva.

It had been three weeks since my return. Finally able to unwind after the whirlwind of a global meeting, I had boarded a ferry to visit the picturesque Yvoire, which everyone said was a must-see. It was aboard that ferry that I poured my heart out to Julia, a stranger who soon felt like an old friend and an angel in one.

IN YVOIRE, JULIA AND I sat outside on a restaurant patio for lunch, spring flowers already in bloom and tourists walking in a colourful stream up the narrow cobbled streets, potted plants hanging from windows. We were shaded from the sun and the human traffic by an umbrella.

We discussed banal topics that allowed us to get to know one another as we waited for our lunch to arrive. With the food laid out on the table, Julia guided the conversation back to my mother, encouraging me with gentle cues to share.

I allowed words to flow from me like molten lava, cooling once it hit the surface. I found in my looped stories deep sadness and guilt that I hadn't been there with her in her final days.

"I feel awful that I am not with her now, that I was not with her."

I paused after each sentence to weigh my emotions and my words. There it was again — guilt mixed with pain, whirling in a jumble within me. There were so many reasons to feel guilty: for not saying "I love you" back to her when we said goodbye — not because I didn't but because it was the first time she had said it out loud and I froze. Then there was the guilt for not having had more faith, for not liking to be around her in her last months, when her energy was so volatile, and — my greatest guilt of all — for not being with her in India.

"I had been given the choice that night when visas were being stamped. There was space in the private jet, but I made polite excuses. 'Work,' I said. 'I have to get back to Geneva.' While this was true to some extent, the whole truth was that I didn't know how to be around her anymore. She had become so different since the diagnosis. It felt like her frustration had no direction or easy target and so made a target of anyone close to her. I couldn't understand it fully, how scary it must have been to be staring at death, and how easily fear can turn into aggression — especially for a woman who was brave to the point of knowing no fear.

"It didn't help that we didn't have closure," I told Julia. "We'd never spoken about an awful incident that involved her and this guy I was seeing."

Julia watched me go through so many emotions. "I am so sorry" was all she said, her body language still encouraging me to go on.

"She never apologized. I don't think Nigerian parents know how to apologize to their children."

I had tears in my eyes, though I wasn't sure if I was crying for my mother, for the pain she had inflicted that still lingered,

for my guilt, or all of the above. I was thoroughly confused
by my state of mind. I was in an internal conflict about how
I should be mourning, and all the ways I was falling short.

"We left so much unsaid."

The afternoon spent with Julia deepened. The sun was high
in the sky, the air cool from the lake breeze. We had finished
our lunch specials of wiener schnitzel. Julia ordered some
coffee, and I went for hot water, a habit from my years living
in China, and a moelleux au chocolat, enjoying the hot, soft
chocolate centre and spongy chocolate coating.

The foot traffic across Yvoire had slowed to a trickle.
Between bites of sweet, which I had always relied on to lift
my spirits, I continued to erupt in little bursts.

"I wrote her an email, just a few days ago," I said, feeling my
heart lighten at this thought. "I am so happy I did. It feels like
in some ways it brought closure. Can I read it to you?" I asked a
nodding Julia. I smiled weakly and reached for my phone, which
I had tucked away, not wanting to face the chatter of the world.

Dear Mummy,

*Maya Angelou just died. Did you know her? She was one
of the few women in history with your same breed of strength,
a strength that has inspired and will continue to inspire a
generation.*

*I hear you are in pain, and I am so sorry. I hear also your
mind is alert but it's your body that is betraying you. I hope I
never know what it feels like to be so strong yet feel so weak,
but I am sure the lifetime of prayers you have said for each and
every one of us, your children, will protect us from ever knowing
such pain. And for this, I am eternally grateful.*

Your life is a prayer, one that is a rare manifestation of God in man. Does this mean you are perfect? Of course not. Imperfection is the very first definition of our humanity by virtue of the original sin.

Most of my young life, I was afraid I could never be as great as Ije, or Somto, or Nji. Then your career and your personality exploded into the limelight, and suddenly everyone knew you as this great woman, who for us had just been Mom. You were suddenly added to the list of people who I could never be as good as.

Over the years, I have grown more confident, and I no longer fear not being great. Why? Because I am your daughter and you are my mother. You also raised me, and you are Mummy and that is the strength that is now mine and the rest of your children's. It is also the strength of a whole nation, which is right now praying for your speedy recovery. You touched so many lives, and that is a blessing that must not be taken lightly.

I realize I should have thought of writing to you earlier; writing after all is the only way I really know how to express myself.

I hope that by writing to you daily and introducing you to the woman you formed, it will be my single act of standing up to the past and welcoming the future with my mother.

I love you,

Chidiogo

Julia had tears in her eyes, as did I; her presence allowed my tears to become a steadier stream.

"When was this written?" Julia asked.

"Just a few days ago. I wrote her a second one, and a third

was only in draft form; since she was getting worse I wasn't sure how heavy or light to be, and eventually I gave up writing it."

"Did you hear back from her?" she asked, with curiosity and care.

"Yes and no. She couldn't really speak anymore, but Nji, my sister, said she listened intently and cried after hearing the first message. It was why I wrote her an even longer second one and on a topic I know she was passionate about: religion and God." At this I laughed, a low, throaty sound that surprised me, and Julia smiled in response.

"My mother loved God. He was what Nigerians call her personal person. For me, God feels more feminine and She is an inner voice, found as well in the guidance of nature, in voices and all the spaces between. That's how different we both are, and how similar — as the moon is to the sun." At this my mind drifted to the wide-toothed gap between my mother's left incisors, which reflected mine on my right, her name Ugogbe — "mirror" — for the first time taking on a new meaning for me.

THE SUN HAD LOST its intensity and was beginning to sink west. The last ferry from Yvoire was departing shortly and I couldn't linger any longer. We had long left our post at the restaurant patio for a short stroll around the small town. Its beauty was not lost on me, allowing me momentary respite from the reality of what had happened.

Julie was continuing on to another town and didn't need to take the ferry back. It was only when I was alone, sitting in almost the exact same spot to the right of the rails, overlooking the now dark waters, that I was fully with my thoughts for the first time since the call. I enjoyed the respite from churning emotions and the peace the water always provides.

Once back in Geneva, with the sun gone and the air fresh, I quickened my pace walking from the dock towards my apartment. I decided to take the five flights of steps, perhaps to tire myself, and opened my door half expecting to see everything as out of sorts as I felt. But everything was exactly as it had been when I left in the morning.

My living room had always been my sanctuary, something about the large orange-hued paintings of a scene of Lagos traffic, the earth-toned Moroccan rug, and pillows of every colour highlighting a grey couch on which I spent most of my time. It was on this couch that I curled, staring at the blank wall above an empty fireplace. I didn't find the solace I was seeking, just a sadness at being alone with my thoughts.

I had been avoiding my phone all day, not sure if the news had become public and not ready for the barrage of messages that would follow if it had. Unable to avoid it anymore, I turned it on with a single mission to check on my siblings. It was the middle of the night for Njideka in India, who had since been joined by my brother Dozie, so speaking to them was out of the question.

I called each one as I always did, in order of their birth. Ijeoma had been awake when Nji called, as she had fully expected the news. She was taking it pretty hard, and I listened to her talk, her sadness and the flow of her words reminding me of my afternoon. Being the oldest meant that she'd had the most years with our mother, something that I had never before considered.

I reached out to my next eldest sister, Somto, who was

calm and insistent on finding out if I was okay, then my little brother, Obum, the only one of the six who was junior to me.

Each conversation was an acknowledgement of how we had all seen it coming and that death was an escape from her pain. Each call also provided pieces of updates.

Exhausted from the day and my own emotions, I went to bed, hoping that tomorrow might allow me to feel something other than numb.

Sixty-Two

"If you want to know the end, look at the beginning."

BY MONDAY, FOLLOWING a press conference by the former governor of Anambra, Peter Obi, who himself had been informed by my father, the news of my mother's death had spread across Nigeria and was carried by every major news outlet. There was shock and disbelief, especially since many hadn't even known that she was terminally ill.

Back at the office, I felt empty still. Overwhelmed by everything, I focused on the logistics of moving her corpse.

First, as per Nigerian and specifically Igbo customs, her body had to be flown back home from Bangalore, and that was organized in a matter of hours. Many came to the airport to receive her, tears in their eyes, still in shock to learn that their suspicions had indeed been true and that, contrary to her public denials, their beloved Dora had been sick and was now dead. I felt sorry for them; at least we had had some time to grieve, albeit secretly.

Once her body arrived from India, she had to be embalmed, her body frozen until the appropriate date for the burial could be set. Setting this date was a dance between not clashing with any major political or social event, avoiding the rainy season, and allowing enough time for preparations and invitations.

I wondered how she would have felt about being kept in this manner. She was always a woman who never sat still, now frozen in time.

Nothing could have prepared me for the number of messages I received in the coming days from friends, acquaintances, and even strangers, some of whose grief dwarfed mine.

I wasn't surprised, as she was beloved in a way that everyone felt like they knew her personally. Over the years I had seen her pay attention not just to her work but also to people. From her staff to drivers, maids, gatemen, assistants, technicians, mechanics, and well-wishers, she paid attention to everyone. At every meal she ate, she checked in that all had eaten as well. Every place she went, she confirmed that those with her also received attention, which would be disproportionately lavished on her. Every person she met, she looked in the eye. She remembered details of people's personal stories, the names of their children, their likes, favourite foods, you name it. Her attention to detail was matched only by her generosity. At some point I avoided complimenting anything she owned because it would result in her automatically giving it to me.

Now she was gone, and without warning, so many were reeling and seeking pieces of her to cling to.

IN THE WEEKS FOLLOWING my mother's death, I would close my eyes and try to see her face behind my lids. Some memories stuck out more than others. Like sitting around her bed in Enugu, Mummy wearing nothing but her classic full-cover white underwear, with no sense of shame or even awareness of her own nakedness, asking questions about our lives while going from one arm or leg to another on each of the children, picking at scabs left from mosquito bites. As much as she hated mosquitoes, she loved to pick at the evidence of their feast. Other memories were of her blowing air with exaggerated force into our bared belly buttons, to our embarrassment and delight, long after we were too old for such games, and of pulling sharply at our noses at unexpected moments, an action she was convinced would make them pointier.

Memories of moments over the years spent holding either her legs or shoulders down as she did her sit-ups and leg-ups in times when she was inspired to prioritize her physical fitness. Other memories were of her driving in her grey Peugeot 505, all six children crowded into every corner. It wouldn't matter where we were headed; most roads in Enugu led to one short stretch of road, known then as Bisala Road, which was the closest we had to a highway. Here we would shriek her cue: "Mummy, run fire." At this, she would exaggerate her readiness, shift gears, and proceed to drive recklessly, swerving right and left, causing us to squeal with joy and fear all at once at her exaggerated mania. It had been our version of Disney World, and we couldn't get enough.

I smiled thinking of my mother's fun side — when she was silly and unhinged — and in tandem felt sadness at how little time we had together. And though now she was gone, my mind was still piecing our life together so that I might grieve the loss of a shared future.

I couldn't help but wish we'd had more time, a feeling I

suspect I'd had since birth. Research speaks to the importance of the bond between mother and child in the first hours,
weeks, initial years of a child's life. Our first challenge, given
the circumstances of my birth, began in the months spent
apart, followed by a brief reunion before she was once again
gone. How does one explain to a three-year-old that her
mother is getting a Ph.D. in a foreign land and will return
in a year? And only to come back with a newborn that took
the rest of her attention. I wondered about the little girl and
her confusion. Did she feel her mother's abandonment in the
womb, at birth, and in those first years of her life until she
closed her heart to feeling too close to her mother?

It didn't help matters that at age nine, I left home, never to
come back. While I knew that leaving home at such a young
age to go to boarding school all the way in Lagos paved the way
for so much for me, it didn't erase the pain of the many years
spent crying over missing my mother. One day, when I must
have been about thirteen, I cried so much that something shut
down in me. I never again missed, or cried for, my mother. In
truth, I still carry the emotions of the girl who was and still is a
part of me. The pain lingers and reappears in moments when I
am aware of my own loneliness, when I am afraid of once again
being abandoned and unseen. Unloved and unwanted — of not
being chosen. In those moments I have to remind myself of
all the ways I am held by a greater force, which now includes
the very spirit and essence of my mother. It brings me a smile
to know that our bond could be formed after her death. It was
like we got it backwards, and that's okay.

For a long time I regretted the many years apart. My jour-
neys had taken me farther and farther from home: from Lagos

to Philadelphia, Paris to Berlin, Beijing to Bologna, Washington to Geneva and back to Lagos. So many years of catching
up with my mother via headlines. But no matter where I lived,
no matter how far I went in search of pieces of myself, with
the now-famous Akunyili name as my own, she followed me.
Whenever I'd meet a Nigerian, they would do a double-take
and excitedly ask, "Are you Dora's daughter?"

It seemed just like yesterday when in 2004, at the height of
her NAFDAC years, she was invited to speak at the Wharton
Africa Business Forum. I was at Penn and excited to have
her visit me in my world, so far and different from Nigeria
and NAFDAC.

She arrived the morning of her talk. We had agreed that I
would meet her directly at the conference, which started late in
the afternoon. I rushed back from dance practice to my dorm
room for a quick shower and change of clothes before heading
to the meeting hall. I felt a mixture of excitement and awe to
see my mother, and in such a unique setting.

I watched with pride as she spoke with fire, holding the
attention of the room in her undeniable magnetic embrace.
She communicated effortlessly and with so much passion in
her voice and an intense gaze in her eyes. On stage, she stood
bold, every bit the fierce woman in her signature colourful
African wax fabric skirt and blouse — the reds, yellows, and
oranges as vibrant as a volcanic eruption — sharing the story
of the war against fake drugs.

We clung to her every word. There were brimming eyes
when she recounted the pain of losing Nwogo to fake insulin.
She spoke of the millions just like her who had lost loved ones
or who themselves had died preventable deaths. She spoke

of the spoils of NAFDAC's war: the mountains of confiscated fake drugs and substandard foods to be destroyed, showing pictures of the heaps ablaze and belching black smoke. And of the pressures of shutting down markets, including the largest of the subregion. The talk peaked with her detailing the attempts on her life, culminating in the assassination attempt in which a bullet grazed her head.

She spoke without notes and without pause, and we drank her words in like parched wanderers. Seated up front, I couldn't take my eyes off her. I was still getting acquainted with this side of her, as this was the first time I had seen her speak live publicly since the beginning of her ascent. I was in pure awe of the woman I called Mother.

After her speech came to an end to a thunderous ovation, a crowd began to swarm her. From my seat up front, beside her personal assistant, I got to her just in time for a quiet moment before the throng descended.

"Mummy, that was amazing," I said, hugging her, my pride evident in my wide smile and bright eyes.

"Chickin Chickin baby," she crooned, hugging me briefly then holding me at arm's length to look me up and down. As we hadn't seen each other for months, I stood dutifully for the appraisal.

"I dikwa happy, are you happy?" she asked in her usual manner.

I smiled and nodded at her question, totally out of context but fully on brand. "Yes, Mummy," I replied.

"How was it?" she asked, surprising me with the vulnerability of the question.

"How was it?" I repeated. "You were amazing, Mummy, that

was amazing" came my response, injecting ample excitement and optimism into my voice that she might understand just how powerful her talk was.

"*Daalụ nwa m*, thank you, my daughter," she said, before the gathering crowd overwhelmed any further chance of a conversation. I smiled again and moved to the periphery of the growing circle surrounding her.

Sixty-Three

"Peace is costly, but it is worth the expense."

OVER TWO MONTHS after she died, I was at the airport in Geneva on my way to my mother's funeral. Looking around, it dawned on me that for all my own flights, and for all my mother's travels, only once had we travelled together internationally, and that was almost two decades ago, when we went to the United States for the first time.

I felt a twinge of pain to recall how we had plans to all take one more trip together — a repeat of the cruise of 2002. The joyful memories of the cruise came flooding back. We had all thought we'd have more time. I felt the weight of how hard it must have been on her to know that she had no time left. No wonder she had fought so hard.

On the flight, I started to think of other significant trips I had made back to my home country. The most recent one had been just a few years ago, after graduation from my master's, when I got a job offer to work out of Lagos. I moved in the late summer of 2012, ten years after I had left for college in America. My mother had just returned to Abuja from Beloit, hopeful that the cancer had been caught in time. I too was confident and hopeful.

I remember calling her for advice on everything from which bank to open an account with to which phone provider was the best. I saw how much she loved that I needed her and the joy it brought her, and I, in turn, enjoyed the feeling of being my mother's child.

She went out of her way to make my return home comfortable. She gave me my first car, a black Volkswagen Polo, and my very own apartment, a small two-bedroom bungalow that she had built on land she owned in Lagos. We spoke more in those months than we had in years. It felt good to be home and to connect with my country, my friends, and my mother. I even met a boy.

My mother, through a driver, got the notion that said boy turned boyfriend was married, and this triggered her like nothing I could have ever imagined. I had never seen or heard her lose it the way she did when she found out. It was like the pain she was hurling at me was her own — a reminder of her own unhappy story on the receiving end of such a betrayal.

My mother had a temper and she could raise the roof, but it had always been controlled. But this time was different. It was like her demons had been let loose and I could see and hear them.

I held on to the cellphone that had been shoved into my hand to hear my mother, calling from Abuja, screaming, "Useless whore, anụmanụ, animal, good for nothing, obsessed prostitute!" It was so strange for me to hear such unbridled insults about me, and from my mother. Even more so as it was

the first time in my twenty-seven years I had heard her insult
me or anyone, for that matter, with such venomous language.
The pain of her words numbed me as tears streamed from my
eyes; I could hardly believe this was actually happening and
was not a scene from a colourful Nollywood movie.

Beside me, as I held onto the phone, was my father, his
heavy frame heaving with anger. He was the one who had
taken it upon himself to get on a flight from Enugu to Lagos
to beat sense into me, if he had to.

"Don't you know who you are?" he barked at me, choking
with anger, punctuating his words with hands raised as if to
hit me — a gesture that brought back buried memories of those
same hands finding their mark. It was not lost on me that
the main memory was of a four-year-old version of myself,
in my blue-and-white lace-trimmed dress, with a pillow on
my stomach, announcing with a wide smile to my father that
our driver had impregnated me. My statement was met with
heavy lashes from a branch broken off a nearby plant for the
crime that I can only suppose was unseemliness. I was now
cowering in a corner, my hands thrown over my face as if to
protect myself from the onslaught of memories of the past and
the nightmare of the present reality. And still he continued.
"Don't you know you are a brand?" he demanded, referring
to the household Akunyili name. "How can you bring such
shame to yourself, to your family?"

He wasn't done.

"A married man," he spat, "how could you?"

It didn't matter that they were wrong, that he was not
married; it didn't matter that my father's stance felt on the
heavy side of hypocritical. It didn't matter that all my life I

had tried to be their model child. I saw then, as I do now, the fallacy of living one's life for another.

A few days later, my mother came to Lagos for a visit. We sat across from each other in her hotel room. She was not remorseful, that much I could tell. We spoke, but mostly she talked at me, telling me all the things I did wrong, the crux of which, given that she now knew the truth that he wasn't married, was allowing him to drive her car. "Imagine what people will say" was her preferred sentence. It alarmed me how so much of her anger, like my father's, was about the perception of others. She argued, reprimanded, and counselled, and in the true fashion of a Nigerian child, I listened, only able to insert a clarifying word or two. It felt like an out-of-body experience. Like she was speaking and advising a version of me who wasn't real, and in that moment I understood just how distant my mother and I were. Once she was done, I said my goodbyes and left the hotel. A week later, I had found an apartment in another part of the city and moved out.

My pain stayed with me for many weeks and over time morphed into other shapes, before finally settling into disappointment. The way I saw things, everything could have been avoided had we had a relationship that allowed for us to talk before resorting to attacks. Afterwards, especially as we never again spoke of it, I sometimes wondered if my mother even remembered the incident. She was quick to anger, but just as quick to cool her temper. She could be spitting fire one minute and smiling the next, like when the gas is on a moment too long and the fire catches in a burst of flame, only to settle a few seconds later.

I sometimes wished I had her gift of letting go with such

ease. Instead, my heartbreak lay dormant but alive. My plan was to keep my distance from her until time healed the wound she had inflicted. I even skipped an American Thanksgiving celebration later that year with the entire family, hosted by my sister Ijeoma in Houston.

I couldn't have known that it would be the last time we had to all be together as a family.

I DIDN'T CRY at her funeral. For one, so much of the event was spent greeting various dignitaries and well-wishers. For another, it was an exhaustive multiday affair from Abuja to Enugu and Anambra, with satellite events happening in Lagos and other cities across Nigeria, attracting thousands of mourners.

The first of the planned activities was a night of tribute, which took place in a beautifully decorated hall of the International Conference Center in Abuja. Colourfully clad bodies with sad faces sat in rows across the vast hall, singing happy songs in celebration of the life of Professor Dora Akunyili. The night might have been more emotional but for a loud sound system and overexuberant band.

The next morning, my siblings, our father, and I dressed up once again in our finest, this time for Mass in Abuja, which took place in our mother's preferred church, where she had spent many mornings and Sundays. The Mass was attended by President Goodluck Jonathan along with the first lady, former presidents such as Yakubu Gowon, as well as state governors, senators, ministers, and even Nollywood celebrities. It was a humbling show of respect, their eyes seeking out her family, observing us closely, as if to find traces of the famed Dora.

The next days involved a series of vigils and Masses, culminating in her actual burial. Every day and every step of the elaborate journey was lovingly and intentionally curated by my father, sparing no cost. It felt in many ways like his love letter to his wife.

On the burial day of August 28, 2014, her darkened, aged corpse lay dressed in the uniform of a certain women's league, which she wouldn't have chosen herself, but such were the limitations of being dead. Her funeral Mass rites were attended by two cardinals, thirty-two bishops, and 192 priests. At her wake keeping, her body was in an open casket in the centre of the large visitors' room of the house in the village that she had built in the days of her senatorial ambitions. The room had been stripped of its usual furnishings and on the walls hung her over eight hundred plaques and awards, including *Time*'s "Eighteen Heroes of Our Time" and her Transparency International Integrity Award. For hours, thousands of grievers walked by her open casket to see for themselves the truth of life that had been and was no more.

Even when they finally lowered her body into the ground, I didn't cry. Our father howled, but this was expected of a grieving husband. As we watched, solemn and reverent as the priests said prayers, I said my goodbye to my mother, perhaps for the first time.

It would take two more years for me to fully cry. This was the time it took for me to reconcile all my emotions. I cried tears for the distance, for our bond, for the memories, and for the gaps. Tears for the woman I was becoming that she would never meet and for the woman she was that I never met.

* * *

A LITTLE OVER A YEAR after her funeral, on a cold January night, I was sitting on my L-shaped couch in my apartment in Geneva, journaling, when I heard a familiar yet unexpected voice. It whispered to me a new idea, fully formed — to write the story of my mother.

I contemplated the four walls of my living room, as if in search of the source of the inspiration that had fluttered my way with such ease. With the experience of trusting in the guidance of my inner voice, I quieted to listen. My writing frantic, almost afraid to lose the inspiration of the moment, I captured disjointed words and fleeting details of what would become the first outlines of this book.

I went to bed that night with a lightness in my heart at the guidance and an acceptance of the task, accompanied by a heaviness at the amount of work that lay ahead.

I spent weeks agonizing about everything as relates to writing my mother's story: where I was to find the time, what would be the voice of the book, the tone of the story, the purpose of writing. Each step was met with fear and insecurities. The journey was to be an exercise in trust, in myself and in the guidance of intuition.

A few months later, days away from my last day at work — having made the decision to focus my energy for the foreseeable future on writing her story and following a desire to find more freedom for myself — I was seated in quiet meditation by the lakeshore of Geneva, soaking up the June sun. Behind the hooded semidarkness of my closed lids, I felt my mother's presence. It was the same whisper of January, and I was surprised by how quickly she filled my consciousness. Her voice within me sounded like mine, but I felt and experienced it as hers. I quieted any lingering disbelief within myself to tune into what I was hearing.

"Mummy, *kedụ*, how are you?" She was well, I could feel this, and I felt so much joy to know this.

I asked about the book, requesting that she guide me.

"Write in my voice" was the first answer, leading me to wonder how I could possibly capture a voice that was so different from mine, spoken and written. She added, "Speak with all voices."

The word *healing* came up as a repeated whisper. "The book is about healing." She didn't elaborate, her silence suggesting I knew what she meant without fully comprehending it. I opened my eyes and allowed my tears to fall.

Andrew, my then boyfriend and now my husband, was looking at me curiously.

"Mummy came," I said. "She said she is well, and that she is proud of us all. She likes you! She said the book is to be centred on healing." I spoke in one breath, wanting to get the words out lest I forget anything. "I am not sure what she means, though. Maybe it's healing for our family? For her? Perhaps for the country? Or for me? I don't know."

"Ask her" came Andrew's response, and I smiled and closed my eyes again, sinking into the quiet space in which she could reach me.

The word that stayed with me that day was *healing*. A seed had been planted, and I desperately wanted a tree to sprout, but it would take time.

Slowly I started to unravel what healing meant. My own healing? My mother's healing? Her journey's? The struggles she endured? I had more questions than answers. To fill in the blanks, I interviewed dozens of people — family, colleagues, friends, and allies who were with her at various stages of her life from childhood to her last breath.

Thus began the journey of gathering the threads of her life, weaving the unruly strands into a coherent story. With time, I started to see her everywhere, feeling how pieces of her linger in me and in the people whose lives she touched, and all around.

The last years of filling blank pages with her story have been a journey of leaning even more deeply on the broad shoulders of trust in the guidance of intuition. It would take many years of writing her story for me to fully understand what she meant by the invitation to centre her story on healing.

Epilogue: Chidiogo and Dora

"The best time to plant a tree is twenty years ago.
The second best time is now."

IGBO TRADITION HAS a deep reverence for the lives that came before ours. It starts with the importance of being buried in one's ancestral land, that the departed might easily find their way home, and continues with the ways the living honour the dead — libations of gin and palm wine poured into ant holes, that the spirit of the dead might drink and know that they are remembered. Such efforts are rewarded when the spirits return to the land of the living as masquerades, dressed in colourful garbs of raffia and thick swaths of cloth, their faces covered by intimidating masks designed to evoke their essence. These masquerades, accompanied by keepers of the secret of their incarnation, roam the streets, going from home to home, speaking in the language of spirits, sharing praise, condemnation, and wisdom with the living.

I reflect on how writing this book is my own unique ritual of connecting not only with the spirit of my mother but all those who came before, that they too might share their wisdom.

This wisdom is captured by Ubuntu.

"I am because we are" or, in its full rendition, "I am because you are, you are because we are" — Ubuntu speaks to the potential of the human experience in harmony with one another and the world around us.

The first time I took the stage to speak in public, my mother was there to hear me. I spoke about the concept of Ubuntu, of an interconnected web of humanity that binds us all — something I had learned from my mother. In writing her story, I saw how pieces of her were moulded by the people and the world around her, each experience soaked into the soil from which she bloomed.

Years after her passing, the guidance of my mother has led me on a journey of embracing a global campaign on this very philosophy, in a time when the forces of disunity are stronger than ever.

I conclude my writing as many people, on a larger scale than ever before, are starting to realize the need to reject notions of otherness that separate us from one another. Ubuntu has gone from an idea to an urgency.

As I write the last words of this book, I am once again pregnant. Today I felt the baby kick and smiled to know that my mother too had felt this, as has every mother since the beginning of time. This is further truth of the experiences that connect us all.

As disparate as our lives can be, as deep as the inequalities are, and as blatant as the injustices that plague society continue to be, undeniable connections exist. These bonds illuminate the universality of human experience and invite us to reclaim the ties that bind us as stronger than the forces that would divide us.

I am going to step aside now and allow my mother to speak.

MY STORY IS ONE, *but in many ways it is shared. We are not separate. That you, the reader, can feel and hear me is testament to this. As another's joys can be shared, the suffering of another demands our attention.*

There is no secret to my success. I followed a true and tested recipe—I believed; I trusted, in God and in myself. I worked hard, and I always acted from a desire to help others, especially those who needed it the most. The more I did so, the greater my success. Never giving up, always asking for guidance knowing that onye ajụjụ anaghị efu ụzọ—one who asks never gets lost—and trusting in the messages I received in response. I learned that when you truly care, and act in accordance, forces rally behind you, excitement builds, and hearts are engaged.

The phrase for love in the Igbo language is A hụrụ m gi n'anya, which translates as "I see you in the eye." To practise love is to first know thyself—to see yourself in the eye, which allows in turn for you to see and love another.

Much damage can be done through stories that distort this sequence. Stories others tell of us that lead to the belief of being less, denying both self and other of seeing what is true. And so the distortion propagates itself. Much healing lies in the power of stories that allow us to see the possibilities that abound in ourselves and in each other.

Because Ubuntu reminds us that we are stronger together, it is important that we seize the power of working in brotherhood and sisterhood, believing in our individual and collective power, and remembering that society grows great when old men and women plant trees whose shade they know they shall never sit in.

To my fellow Nigerians, we are a good people and a great nation, if only we would believe this as our truth and act in response — for only then can we heal.

I hope and I trust that my story can be one of your guides.

Afterword

"A bird on an iroko tree cannot be shot down
with a bow and arrow."

THIS TIME IT WAS my brother Dozie who called. I was
sitting at home, holding my newborn of just five weeks, when
I answered. Forgoing any pleasantries, he said, "We think
Daddy is dead. We think he was shot, but we're not sure." As I
had expected him to be calling to wish me a happy birthday,
my mind had to work overtime to understand the unrelated
words that swiftly spilled from him. "There is a picture of a
dead body that looks like Daddy, but we cannot be sure it's him.
Don't post anything in the family WhatsApp," he added as an
afterthought, signalling that some calls were still to be made.

With tears streaming down my face, I clung to hope instead
of giving in to despair. Seeking solace, I called my sister Nji. "You
sense things," she said. "Do you think he is alive?" I didn't know.

Needing air, needing something, anything, I headed to
the one place I knew I could find some peace. Seated at the
water's edge in Toronto, my husband beside me holding our
daughter, I went through various emotions, questioning the
sequence of events as I'd heard them. Andrew broke through

373

my thoughts, asking, "Do you think he is alive?" I closed my
eyes and breathed into the question. This time I answered
simply: "No. I don't think so. He is at peace now." As I said
this, I spotted a bushy-tailed red fox to the left of us, its eyes
locked onto mine. Slowly, it sauntered past our bench and
disappeared into the dense foliage. "Do you think that was
Daddy?" I asked my husband. Seconds later, the text came
through. It was official. He was dead.

Ever since our mother passed, I wondered how I would
react to the passing of my father. This time, there was no struggle. I allowed myself to feel everything, the tears, the disbelief,
the numbness, even the laughter — I felt it all.

My mind went back to the phone call I'd had with my
father the day before. We hadn't spoken in a while. His tone
was jovial, and our conversation was easy, flowing with
talk of Mummy (whom he called his patron saint, whose
intercession was evident in his continued blessings), of the
memorial lecture in her honour he was going to attend the
next day — "her birthday present to me," he called it. He asked
after his newest grandchild, to whom he had given the name
Mmesomma — "the one who does only beautiful things." He
commented on how he had prayed for a safe delivery and how
my pregnancy was reminiscent of our mother's: strong until
the end, he said, with deep admiration for her. He asked about
the progress of the book, reminding me how he had stayed up
all night reading a final draft, and requesting copies at his next
visit. "Of course, Daddy, you'll get copies." I thanked him for
his input, which he had sent via DHL, including a meticulous
list of the various places named after Mummy, and I assured
him that I received all his suggestions with immense gratitude.

That got us planning for Thanksgiving. He proposed that, in the coming year, we have it in Canada, laughing away my observation that my home was surely too small for a family of more than twenty and counting. He disagreed, reminding me of times we had all thrived in a one-bedroom apartment in Philadelphia, with him and my mother sharing a sofa — a "three-seater" as he called it.

He went on to bemoan the state of affairs in Nigeria. As a surgeon, always on the front line of the people's suffering, he shared just how rampant the current hardships were. Patients, he said, were no longer able to pay for care, and many more treatments were given for free. It didn't help, he added, that no one was safe. I asked him if he was being careful, and he assured me that he was, adding that he rarely went out anymore and, when he did, he made sure to be home by 6 p.m. I reminded him to be even more cautious, and to take care of himself.

We couldn't have known it would be our last conversation.

I continued to search my memories of him. How he would repeat to all who would listen that one of the happiest events of his life took place in a big basketball stadium, watching his daughter, a Black woman, "majestically stand up in a sea of white faces as the 2012 valedictorian at Johns Hopkins." It did not matter that I was class speaker, not valedictorian; the difference was a nuance he did not care to acknowledge. My heart swelled to think of how he had thrown my husband and me a wedding to remember, how he had beamed to know that he had gifted us the best party possible — his love made evident. None of the more difficult memories of him surfaced; instead I felt nostalgia for the relationship we had been building and, with it, the pain of having what could have been taken away from us all in such a brutal manner.

In the coming days, we would learn that he and the two men with him, a driver and an orderly, were killed by "unknown gunmen," a ubiquitous phrase in our country for the faceless, gun-wielding men who are often never identified. From several accounts, my father was simply in the wrong place at the wrong time, an explanation that makes his death all the more painful — collateral damage in the increasingly unsafe Southeast. The insecurity in the region had worsened in the lead-up to state governorship elections.

We would learn that, at the hour of his death, he was alone, asking for help as he bled to death. "Call my children," he begged, holding up his phone in one hand, the other holding together his face, which had been shot off — degloved from his skull — that he might slur the words though blood and the gaping hole where his mouth had been. "Call my children," he repeated, yet no one did anything. Worse still, once he lay dead, his corpse was robbed of everything, even his shoes, and his car was moved to a different location and stripped of all valuables.

My father's death shook Nigeria, not least because he was the husband of a beloved daughter of the country. Why, many asked, would the country repay her dedication in such a manner? Many others, myself included, asked how he could die in this way, killed for no reason by his fellow human, to whom he had dedicated his life as a surgeon to treat and heal.

Ubuntu — "I am because we are." If this holds true, then the man who pulled the trigger *is* because we are — the senselessness and injustice of his action, his anger, and his violence *are* because they are mirrored in the world around him. If "I am because we are," then my father's pain, gasping for breath in his last moments, *is* because we as a nation are in pain.

If Ubuntu holds true, that Chike Akunyili — a son, a beloved father, a loving grandfather, a healer, a friend, a brother, and so much more — *is* because we are, then this is an invitation for us to find the good in all of us.

The current path, marked by injustices, atrocities, exploitation, and frustrations, only leads to more senseless death and pain. We can choose a different path.

The colonial past of Nigeria is no different from that of many other colonized countries, in that various groups and communities have been pitted against each other using the tried-and-tested tactic of divide and conquer, which lies on the opposite end of the spectrum from Ubuntu. We were told that taking from others would make us better off, and for decades we have continued to take from one another. This has led us to become a society lacking the very ingredients needed to thrive: honesty, integrity, and compassion. Instead, the goodness of our people and the greatness of our nation remain a dream.

We need peace, not violence; we need unity, not division; we need change! It starts with acknowledging what is broken, and what values have contributed to the breakdown. The path forward is to not only dream the future we desire but also to identify our various roles in achieving it.

Ubuntu reminds us of the critical role each individual plays to make up the whole. Ubuntu underpins the value placed on human life and its potential. Not only does everyone matter, but we are also responsible for one another. And when we realize the power we each have, we also acknowledge the responsibility to ourselves, to each other, and to society at large.

That we all have a role to play invites us to challenge our apathy and the belief that there is nothing we can do. To give up is to accept that the system has already failed. Real change will require everyone to not only believe that it can be different but also to live up to this dream.

My mother's story has taught me that one person living with integrity, courage, and compassion, not deceit and self-ishness, can shift relationships, a village, and a nation. My father's death teaches me that our pain is at the surface; we cannot continue to hide it like "dust under a dark stairwell," hoping it will disappear. This pain must be acknowledged. Only then can we begin to heal.

"A society grows great when old men plant trees whose shade they know they shall never sit in."

Ọ ga-adị mma — "It is well." But only if we will it.

Appreciation

THIS BOOK WOULD NOT be possible without those whose story it tells. For them, and the lives they lived that inspire mine and so many others, I am deeply grateful.

I want to thank my family, especially my siblings, Dr. Ije Akunyili, Dr. Edozie Akunyili, Dr. Somto Asuzu, Njideka Akunyili Crosby, and Obumneme Akunyili, for all the ways they encouraged and supported this journey. It has been beautiful to see how each of their support is amplified by that of their partners, and for my in-laws, and their help, I give thanks.

Sincere thanks to my father, Dr. John Chike Akunyili, who also happens to be a Knight of Saint John, where he rose to the highest rank of the order, and was made a Papal Knight of Saint Sylvester, a title that brought much joy to him. This book enjoys his blessing, and I am thankful for the grace of his support.

The power of going far by going together weaves throughout the book. Hours and hours of interviews, the many eyes and ears I sought out, the many questions I had about details of my mother's life. I come from a culture that honours names, that others might know who to thank for me. It is a long list, and for this I feel immensely blessed. Deep gratitude to my mother's siblings Rose Okpala, Elizabeth Nwankwo, Ngozi Ezenwankwo, and Dr. Anayo Edemobi, and to her cousins Jane-Frances Umeokolo, Cosmos Okoli, and Uchenne Okoli.

Particular thanks to my mother's friends, mentors, co-workers, staff, and extended family, in no particular order: Adeline Idike; Dr. Ijeoma Mbadiwe; Sister Helen Ndiche; His Royal Highness Igwe Dr. Innocent Elochukwu Obodo-akor (Igwe II Agulu); Donald Duke; Dere Awosika; Suresh Chellaram; Father Muoneke; Adaobi Ndibe-Okoye; Lady Christiana Onumazi Etolue; Peter Houghton; Mrs. Odabi; Tope Ojeme; Elizabeth Awagu; Peter Etalong Otogo; Lillian Uche Anyanwu; Dr. Barbara O. Chukwurah; Dr Jimoh Abuba-kar; Chinyere Nwankwo; Kalu Ugwumba; Uchechukwu Peace Ude; Michael Alurame Eruaga; Linus Okorie; Chinwe Helga Echebiri; Ifeanyi Emmanuella Obiorah; Ijeoma Nweze; Dozie Edemobi; John Ezenwankwo; Nonye Soludo. Thank you for your time and stories.

Special thanks to Bruce Geddes, Hima Batavia, Gary Le Blanc, Daniel Browde, Nonso Asuzu, Fatima Kamenge, Maxine Shifrin, Ijeoma Theresa Opurum, and Chinaku Onye-melukwe for reading the book even at its most nascent stages and supporting me to find its voice and message.

Thank you to Joop Berkhout of Safari Books for loving my mother and constantly checking in on the progress of the book. Thank you for inspiring the title of this book by remind-ing me of its core message.

To House of Anansi Press for seeing the book and saying yes to a story like Dora's. What an excellent journey it has been with you as a whole and the many individuals that make up the great team. Immense gratitude that you are and that we are.

Continued thanks to my publisher, Bruce Walsh, editor, Jane Warren, in-house project editor, Michelle MacAleese, and the entire Anansi team for being the ones I prayed for.

Sincere thanks to some people whose support runs deep: Mark Wallace, Mel Rogers, Angie Aristone, Jennifer Spencer, Omayra Issa, Enuma Okoro, Anna Stancer, and Peter Baillie.

To my beloved, Andrew Parr, you are torch bearer of this healing journey of ours, and every single day, I feel such joy that I know you and call you my life partner.

And to my parents-in-law, Debbie Parr-Nash and Robert Nash, and the entire Parr-Nash clan, thank you for all the ways you love and support me.

To Nigerians, for loving my mother as you did, I thank you. She truly was because of every one of us, and I am so proud to be a Nigerian and cut from this shared cloth of strength and resilience. My prayer for us as a country is that we might know who we are — as individuals — healing the parts of us that feel separate from the strength we carry — and as a community.

To the people, institutions, and communities that have honoured my mother by naming the following places after her: the Dora Akunyili College of Pharmacy at Igbinedion University; the largest hostel at Nnamdi Azikiwe University; the Dora Akunyili Women's Development Centre in Awka; streets in Awka, Umuahia (Umudike), and Anaocha local government areas; the hall of the Drug Mark at Yenagoa (Bayelsa); a building in the National Council of Women's Societies in Abuja;

and the post office in Nanka. This is in addition to the many awards that bear her name. Thank you.

To everyone who picked up a copy of this book, I am so happy to share with you like this. I hope and trust that this book came your way for a reason that is made manifest.

For my mother — Ugogbe — I am in awe of you and all the ways you showed up in this life. I am grateful to you for how you've guided me in life and in death. Thank you for the invitation to write your story. Saying yes was the best and easiest thing I could have done, and for this I am so glad. Years ago, when the book wasn't finished, I was without a publisher, and I had doubts about the way forward, you showed me this book in a message, holding it up that I might know it was already written. All I had to do was trust and write. Years later, here we are; it is not only written but being read by so many. Thank you for the guidance and encouragement every step of the way.

Gratitude to all my ancestors. Know we rejoice together for this and for everything that will be because we are.

© Darius Basher

CHIDIOGO AKUNYILI-PARR is a Nigerian Canadian author, speaker, and consultant with a passion for human development and connection. She is the founder of She ROARs, an organization committed to coaching women of colour around the world to connect to their intuition and purpose. Her work is focused on harnessing the power of our interdependence with a foundation in the humanist African philosophy of Ubuntu, which celebrates our shared humanity. Chidiogo has lived and worked across four continents and speaks seven languages, including Mandarin, German, Spanish, and French, allowing for an even deeper connection with people. She led the growth and impact of the Global Shapers Community across Africa and the Middle East.